करावलम्बनम्

Functional Saṃskṛta : Concepts and Applications

Sridhar Subbanna

V Srinidhi

Published by Vidyasvam Adhyayanam, Bengaluru

VIDYASVAM

VIDYASVAM

https://www.vidyasvam.in

For permission to reproduce any part of this book, write to info@vidyasvam.in.

2023, FirstEdition

Cover design: *K M Sheshagiri*

Dedication

To the Bhāratīya Jñāna Paraṃpārā

that has kept the traditional knowledge systems alive and thriving even today, navigating through enormous challenges that came their way over the last thousands of years.

A word of appreciation

Dear Sridhar and Srinidhi,

Thank you for sharing the pre-publication version of your book with me. I am glad to see the amount of effort and dedication you've put into bringing out the essence of Saṃskṛta language in such a scientific and organized manner.

While there have been numerous efforts to introduce Saṃskṛta language to the world, each with its own objective, the current book is unique for its clear and concise presentation of the logical structure of the language. Starting with varṇamālā you've tried to explain subtle grammatical categories in a way that's easy for anyone to understand.

Saṃskṛta has a scientific structure. It is engineered with basic concepts like varṇas, prakṛti, pratyaya, etc. The very idea of introducing Saṃskṛta to modern students with technical backgrounds has made this book unique. Being students of Science, engineering, and medicine, you've been able to execute this novel experiment successfully. I also appreciate that you have added the essence of your teaching experience to create this book.

I once again appreciate both of you from the bottom of my heart for this unique attempt. I wish you all success in your future endeavours.

Dr Shrinivasa Varakhedi
Vice-Chancellor, Central Sanskrit University
New Delhi

Foreword

It gives me pleasure to write a few words by way of a Foreword to the work Karāvalambanam authored by Dr Sridhar Subbanna and Dr V Srinidhi.

The high level of sophistication embedded in most of the traditional Saṃskṛta texts can be appreciated by a modern student only when it is presented in such formats as he is usually accustomed to. Karāvalambanam is a simple proof of the truth of the above statement in respect of Saṃskṛta grammar. Saṃskṛta grammar is a field of unmatched cultivation and sophistication in the entire linguistic world, and especially as presented by Pāṇini, whose work has been famously deemed as "a monument of human intelligence". The two authors here (the former with an engineering background, and the latter with a medical background) form a commendable pair in making a novel presentation of a rather complex and difficult theme, not easy to master even after years of pursuit.

The book rightly begins at the beginning, treating the varṇamālā (Chapter 1), ostensibly an elementary lesson, after all, but which already presents samples of sophistication that Saṃskṛta initiated time immemorial (and which permeates the alphabetical system of all the Indian languages).

Kāraka, the Crux

The introduction of the Kāraka Theory in its essential outline at the outset (immediately after the treatment of varṇa-mālā) (Chapter 3) is indeed quite significant. All the key sūtra-s pertaining to the same are also presented intelligibly.

Speaking of sakarmaka and akarmaka (approximately, transitive and intransitive respectively) aspects of verbs in the context of the karma-kāraka is only befitting.

While Pāṇini takes up first apādāna and sampradāna, the rather peripheral and exterior kāraka-s, and then marches majestically towards the core and central kāraka, viz. the kartṛ-kāraka, an exact opposite direction is pursued here, reserving the exterior kāraka-s to the end (and even reverting the pair: (sampradāna first and apādāna next) which can be said to be useful to a beginner; after all, Pāṇini did not set out to teach novices.

The kāraka forms, in fact, the crux of Pāṇini, constituting Aṣṭādhyāyī's essential semantic hinge upon which all else revolves (and even though it does get invariably intertwined with the vibhakti component): Pāṇini did not propose to write a Universal Grammar, even though his work betrays all factors that such a grammar should take into account.

Pada (Word)

It is only after this that the authors introduce the concept of pada (not just a 'word') and its constituents (Chapter 4). It may be noted here in passing that the very notions of the root and the stem (invoking a botanical metaphor), are ultimate to be traced to their neat divisions and ramifications in Saṃskṛta grammar. After all, a great many linguistic concepts current in the West are traceable to their ultimate origin in India, even though the typical Westerner's overbearing Eurocentrism and brazen plagiarism dissuade him from acknowledging the same, as it did with numerous mathematical discoveries and applications.

That the basic unit of speech is the sentence and not the word, maybe a relatively recent discovery of the West, but it was an elementary idea to us (as evidenced by the primacy attached to the sentence in even the very title of the celebrated work Vākyapadīya of Bhartṛhari (5th c. CE)). Were it not for that realisation, Pāṇini could not have conceived of the Kāraka theory. Our small book deals with the sentence similarly in an early chapter.

Metadata

The classification of pratyaya-s and the various ways they go to form a word (indicating even the recursions involved therein) is well-presented with a compact flowchart (Chapter 4). The extraordinary technique of it-s introduced by Pāṇini, and their role as tags/markers/metadata (well-indicated by the apt label 'anubandha') are all well-elucidated.

Succinct presentation is also an important hallmark of this book, as is clear from the treatment of the brief yet clear statement of it-s.

Rules and Paradigms

The four factors that settle a finite verbal form (Chapter 6) - viz. the gaṇa and lakāra (which absorbs the parasmai/ātmane aspect as well as the tense/mood), and the it-scheme of the root, plus the final and/or the penultimate varṇa - have been neatly shown here. Many books miss the full-scale presentation of the verbal paradigms in all the 10 lakāra-s of the representative roots of all the 10 gaṇa-s, in both parasmai and ātmane formations, all in a single stretch; but this book provides the same, which is visually very effective.

The high semantic content of the tiṅ-suffixes (as too, the non-semantic content of the vikaraṇa-pratyaya) is well-indicated; else than being specific to puruṣa and vacana, these suffixes carry the burden of expressing the tense/mood and the voice (karmaṇi/bhāve) also (with certain modifications, though); and for which too the 10 lakāra forms for the representative roots of the 10 gaṇa-s are made available here. While indicating the anvartha nature of the nomenclature (as parasmai and ātmane), a mention that these are more or less frozen as mere features of the roots ought not to be missed.

Adjectival Roles and Primary Derivatives

In the chapter on sāmānādhikaraṇya (Chapter 9), the varied possible roles of the viśeṣaṇa-s as vidheya/vyāvartaka/hetugarbha are aptly pointed out. In the chapter on kṛdanta-s (Chapter 10), the issue of niyata-liṅgatva is well-taken into account. Drawing attention to tācchīlya and tāddharmya is important here, and has been done without fail.

Dealing with syaśatṛ and syaśānac alongside śatṛ and śānac helps economise explanation. An apt choice has been made in focussing on the most important kṛdanta-s. Relating the meanings of the kṛt/kṛtya suffixes to the kāraka-s is not treated conspicuously in many books on Saṃskṛta grammar, but is paid attention to here promptly. The roles that kta-pratyaya can play, upon affixing it to sakarmaka and akarmaka roots, have well been generalised. The gender-implication of certain kṛt affixes is well-organised. The final tabulated presentation of the kṛt suffixes under five columns gives a succinct picture of much information scattered through the chapter under various sub-headings, and is thus very useful - to the learner for a quick revision, and to the teacher to have a good perspective while teaching.

The Abhidhāna Criterion

The abhihita filter introduced at the outset in the subartha chapter (Chapter 11) is one of the key concepts in Pāṇini. In fact, this principle needs to be studied for relevance/implications with respect to expression in other languages too. The variation in focus in the kartari and karmaṇi usages is an important concept brought well into focus in this context, whereas with many teachers this comes about as a mechanical exercise, sans its semantic implication. The several applications of ṣaṣṭhī vibhakti under the kartṛ/karma/bhāva headings, as also their exceptions, have all been given together, which is very helpful. The non-kāraka senses of the vibhakti-s are naturally placed after the kāraka-senses. The subtle differences between (a) saṁvatsare adhīte, (b) saṁvatsaram adhīte, and (c) saṁvatsareṇa adhīte - have been set forth via presenting them side by side.

Non-Kāraka Vibhakti-s

The differences between hetu and karaṇa on the one hand, and hetu and phala on the other, are also similarly well-drawn: the factors of participation in action in the first case, and temporal sequence in the second one, are instrumental in marking out their specific roles. Similarly, nuances of nirdhāraṇa - as expressed by the pañcamī, ṣaṣṭhī, and saptamī vibhakti-s - are also contrastively presented effectively.

A well thought out example involving both adhikaraṇa-saptamī and sati-saptamī (within a single sentence) goes to pinpoint effectively where and how confusion can arise. The upapada-vibhakti-s find their natural place after the kāraka-vibhakti-s, in a concluding section in the chapter, and are presented as a useful table fit to be frequently referred to. In essence, the book follows the

Pāṇinian scheme of presenting the kāraka-s first and vibhakti-s later. The Genitive Absolute and the Locative Absolute have been briefly touched upon.

Secondary Derivatives

Secondary Derivatives or taddhitānta-s are dealt with next section (Chapter 12), with a choice of the most representative cases and illustrations; an exhaustive treatment of taddhita-suffixes can indeed need a whole volume by itself. The all-too-common senses of 'the descendant', 'possession', and 'abstraction', as also degrees of comparison, are key products of taddhita-application.

The bracketing of strī-pratyaya-s along with taddhita-s also makes good sense, as Pāṇini employs common anubandha-s between the two to indicate mutual affinities akin to slots and slot-fillers in NLP, or even the positive and negative charges of apposite valencies in chemistry.

Transformations

Transformations involving the prakṛti (dhātu/prātipadika) and pratyaya (Chapter 10 and 12) are next discussed along with their classifications. Bringing all types of transformations under one small section can facilitate the student's quick recapitulation. The indication that the ṇijanta-verbs are as a rule ubhayapadin-s, and that their function is kindred to curādi roots is a practically useful information for students. Indicating the alternative nomenclature of prayojya-kartṛ and prayojaka-kartṛ is also helpful while going through the grammatical literature in Saṃskṛta. The reallocation of kāraka-roles in the wake of the ṇijanta-verbs is an interesting phenomenon which has been briefly, yet ably, tackled. The different roles thereupon played by dvitīyā-vibhakti and tṛtīyā-vibhakti (the latter variously as prayojaka-kartṛ/prayojya-kartṛ/karaṇa is presented with contrastively presented examples and analyses. The interesting case of curādi verbs remaining unaltered in causative constructions is also noted without fail.

Key Grammatical Literature

In the chapter entitled Aṣṭādhyāyī (Chapter 14), a dozen key texts on Saṃskṛta grammar are introduced, though very concisely. The six types of sūtra-s are illustrated. Prescription of transformation, and extension and restriction of the same - are all set forth with clarity.

The general template of the vidhisūtra viz. "A sthānin undergoes a kārya in the presence of [certain] nimitta(s)" - has all the force of an aphorism of aphorisms; and the three technical terms here are exemplified while elaborating upon the yaṇ-sandhi rule. The triple actions viz. add/delete/replace (known since millennia in our grammatical tradition as āgama/lopa/ādeśa) are well-illustrated.

Sandhi

It has been indicated prefatorily to the chapter on sandhi (Chapter 15) that, rather than present a conceptual description, a sūtra-based explanation has been chosen in order to expound sandhi-s; this is indeed admirable, both by way of providing a taste of Aṣṭādhyāyī itself, as well as adhering to the precision in prescriptions and the authentic description of the processes involved.

Rightly has it been reminded here - that the word sandhi as such does not occur in Aṣṭādhyāyī (whereas "saṁhitā" occurs in lieu), nor are there the various labels to name the sandhi-s that beginners get commonly exposed to. There is a frequent overlap or coalescence of sthānin-based sandhi-s and ādeśa-based ones; treatment under the former heading has been preferred, with excursive notes on the latter.

The occasion is also utilised for elucidating the formation, structure and interpretation of sūtra-s. The notions of yathāsaṅkhya, anuvṛtti, pūrva-nimitta and para-nimitta, sāvarṇya and tapara-karaṇa, and the commonly required guṇa and vṛddhi - are all set forth with clarity with befitting examples and discussions. (The modern practice of using avagraha in the context of pūrvarūpa-sandhi is not lost sight of). The all-important utsargāpavāda-vyavasthā is explained in detail, where multiple "mutually conflicting" rules get reconciled logically.

The ṇatva/ṣatva phenomena have been taken into account, too. The long table, ably conceived, shows the sthānin as Conditions and the emerging ādeśa-s/āgama-s as Results. (In the midst of all this, the tripartite classification as ādeśa/āgama/lopa among hal-sandhi-s is not missed).

Asiddha

The ingenious Pāṇinian idea of asiddha is befittingly placed before visarga-sandhi. This meta-scheme par excellence handles concisely the otherwise elaborately necessitated statements of numerous nested ifs and thens, exceptions and blockages. The triple benefits of the asiddha mechanism are set forth here in a mathematical fashion, as it were.

Blocking substitutions, and making provision for the general rule - are accomplished by Pāṇini by attaching significance to the carefully rendered sequential presentation of rules – a veritable masterstroke that has impressed linguists all over the world by force of its sheer economic formulation. Pāṇini exploits an opacity of his own making, so as to render multitasking transparent.

Samāsa

Reserving the penultimate chapter for samāsa or compounding (Chapter 16) is a wise step as it necessarily involves a knowledge especially of subanta-s. The sandhi-rules operate almost ubiquitously, hence handled prior to samāsa. Pāṇini reserves the sandhi rules to the end of his work. The concept of the two types of sāmarthya has been laid bare, with very clear examples, (as also the notion of nitya-sāpekṣa-words which make for an exceptional situation).

The prescriptive rules (samāsa-vidhāyaka-sūtra-s) as also the ordering rules (paurvāparya-vidhāyaka-sūtra-s) are reckoned with at the outset. The latter is required in the formation of samāsa-s, while no such requirement is confronted in sentence construction as such, even though compounds could be conceived sometimes as veritable miniature sentences. The samāsa-table, graphically summarising and illustrating the various subtypes of tatpuruṣa is promptly followed by the Table of the Blockage Rules for ṣaṣṭhī-tatpuruṣa; which itself is followed by explanatory passages in fair detail. The droppage of the strī-pratyaya of the former component of Appositional Compounds (karmadhāraya) is explained via common examples.

Adding to the flavour of the book, the very word aṣṭādhyāyī is analysed as a dvigu (and dissolved as aṣṭānām adhyāyānāṁ samāhāraḥ). Throwing a hint that most cases of bahuvrīhi are in ṣaṣṭhī (along with appropriate examples), enables the student to pay greater attention to, and look for, which pattern he is more likely to encounter.

Dissolution

The vibhakti-s involved in the formation/dissolution of compounds invariably involve vibhakti-s serving kāraka roles as well as non-kāraka roles (which must also be why the samāsa section in Aṣṭādhyāyī succeeds, not precedes, the kāraka and the vibhakti sections).

While tatpuruṣa compounds mark independent entities and hence can have a gender of their own, bahuvrīhi compounds are all adjectival in nature, and invariably borrow the gender (and case and number) of the substantive they qualify. Dvandva-samāsa provides the context for the four senses of ca (in a footnote) and being a conjunctional compound, it needs rules for a preferential ordering of words; and as the multiple rules can clash, there is a need for requisite metarules, which have been promptly stated and explained in the book.

Conventions followed in the dissolution of compounds (as with a-svapada-vigraha compounds etc) are also neatly stated. In the formation of compounds, sometimes prior components undergo certain changes (as in aluk-samāsa), and again, certain changes are mandatory upon completion of compounding (respectively known as pūrvapadānta-prakriyā and samāsānta-vidhi) which have also been methodically covered.

Steps in Comprehension

The fitting finale of the book is in teaching comprehension of Saṃskṛta sentences which involve pada-ccheda and anvaya-jñāna, marking off word boundaries and exploring syntactical connections (Chapter 17, the last chapter). 'Syntax' is after all a poor semblance of the rich and rigorous kāraka circumscription; the versatility and vitality of the latter is hardly discernible in the former.

Other Merits

A brief note on vivakṣā could perhaps have enhanced the value of the book, as too, even a passing reference to the Pāṇini-Backus-Naur Form. The book is written in lucid and straightforward enough English, even though some lack sensitivity to certain corresponding English grammatical categories, as also standard usages, show up here and there, but in no way do they detract from the value of the work.

Beginners need Experts

The book serves as proof of the fact that it sometimes makes an excellent choice to have an expert teach the foundational lessons in a field of high sophistication. Pedagogy of grammar assumes a new shape and dimension when handled by men trained under the NLP rigour, precisely which the computing intellect of Pāṇini must have envisaged 2500 years ago as a sort of gedankenexperiment.

On more occasions than one, modern examples have been conceived, rather than the hackneyed ones repeated endlessly in numerous texts on grammar; the example of the wicketkeeper in a cricket match can be cited as an example.

On the whole, the work is an intellectual treat and does justice to what it seeks to present. Trained on lines espoused in this book, more students stand to gain, in terms of a thrilling introduction to grammar (always made out to be invariably boring), and they also gain a confident entry into Pāṇini, whose eminently algebraic mind the book holds a mirror to.

Saṃskṛta scholars and students keen on enriching their knowledge are bound to look forward to more writings from the pens of this pair of authors. Not least of all, Prof. Lalit Kumar Tripathi and Prof. Srinivasa Varakhedi and Sri Sri Vidyashrisha Swamiji – all mentors/inspirers of the authors, also deserve high credit and great praise.

ŚrīKṛṣṇa Jayantī
20-08-2022

- K S Kannan DLitt.
Sant Rajinder Singh Ji Maharaj Chair Professor,
Department of Humanities and Social Sciences,
IIT-Madras

Preface

In 2007, one of us (Sridhar Subbanna) started pursuing a Ph.D. in Pāṇini's Aṣṭādhyāyī. In that process, both of us and our friend Sreenivasa studied the Aṣṭādhyāyī under the guidance of Professor Lalit Kumar Tripathi. This study and many discussions that Sridhar held with his advisor Prof. Varakhedi Shrinivasa gave insights into the original ideas of Aṣṭādhyāyī and how one can understand them by drawing parallels with modern computing principles. We recognized that Aṣṭādhyāyī was not just a compendium of grammatical rules, but a linguistic tool that provides a method for encoding and decoding information communicated through the Sanskrit language. We thus realized the significance of learning the language through the approach provided by Aṣṭādhyāyī.

During this time, we also noticed an important gap in the contemporary approaches to learning Sanskrit. These approaches typically involve mapping Sanskrit with a known language, mainly English, and do not equip learners with ideas that are original and unique to Sanskrit. Although traditional pāṭhaśālās teach Aṣṭādhyāyī, it is mainly to learn vyākaraṇa as an independent field, with less emphasis on its exposition of language per se. We, therefore, found it important to emphasize how the Aṣṭādhyāyī can be, and arguably should be, used in teaching and learning the language, even for beginners.

These ideas resulted in a course that Sridhar designed and taught on various platforms, including Vidyāsvam and Pūrṇapramati. Classroom discussions refined the content and approach, while also calling for written material.

And thus, this book was born. Initially, Srinidhi had helped in shaping Sridhar's ideas in the form of a written dissertation, and continued to do so in the making of this book.

The book is aimed at beginners of Sanskrit, who have a good foundation in modern academics and basic English proficiency. Using the book as a guide, readers will be able to:

(1) Independently decipher and logically analyze Sanskrit shlokas, as well as interpret complex shlokas with the help of Sanskrit commentaries.
(2) Understand Pāṇinian Sūtras and identify parallels between Pāṇinian thinking and contemporary ideas.
(3) Appreciate the richness and rigor of Sanskrit works from ancient India.

We are grateful to Professor Varakhedi Shrinivasa for his words of appreciation. We also extend our thanks to Professor K. S. Kannan, who dedicated many hours of his busy schedule to carefully reading through the full draft of this book and providing us with a detailed foreword that highlights the book's significance. We feel truly humbled by the appreciation we have received from the two stalwarts, especially considering that they have taught us at various stages of our lives. Professor Kannan was Srinidhi's teacher during the 11th and 12th classes. Professor Varakhedi guided Sridhar through his PhD. Encouraging words from both Professors Varakhedi and Kannan serve as a great source of motivation for us to continue doing more.

We are grateful to our teacher, Prof. Lalit Kumar Tripathi, and friend, Sreenivasa Guttal, for their encouragement, support, and assistance at all stages of this effort. We also thank Sridhar's daughter, Kum. Medha, and son, Chi. Sudheera, for reviewing the book, helping to create tables/diagrams, and typesetting the initial draft. For Sūtras, commentaries, and declension tables, we referred to https://ashtadhyayi.com, and we would like to thank the team behind the creation of this useful and easy-to-access web repository of traditional texts.

We acknowledge the support provided by Sri Pasupati ji in shouldering the enormous responsibility of seeing this book through to publication. We would also like to thank our friend and talented artist, Sri K M Sheshagiri, for designing a fitting and beautiful cover page.

We also thank Clemens Lode, whose work "Even Better Books with LaTeX the Agile Way in 2023" provided us with a template used to prepare this book.

Sridhar Subbanna
V Srinidhi

Individual Acknowledgements

I am grateful to my mentor, Śrī Vidyāśrīśa Tīrtha Swāmījī (Prof. Prahladacharya in his pūrvāśrama, a renowned Sanskrit scholar and former vice chancellor of National Sanskrit University at Tirupati), who initiated and supported me on this path. I am also thankful to Prof. Varakhedi Shrinivasa, vice chancellor of Central Sanskrit University, New Delhi, my advisor, with whom I had memorable and productive discussions on innumerable concepts and methodologies.

I offer my praṇāmas to all my teachers who taught Vyākaraṇa and other streams of Indian traditional knowledge - Vidvān Ramachandracharya, Vidvān Venkateshacharya, Vidvān Yadunandanacharya, Prof. H Sathyanarayanacharya, Viduṣī Vijayalakshmi, Dr. Vedagarbha Sheshagiri Acharya and Prof. R.L.N Shastry.

I express my gratitude to the hundreds of Sanskrit enthusiasts who participated in the workshops I offered, and provided useful feedback, which played a key role in shaping this book. I also thank Pūrnapramati for providing a platform for some of these workshops and encouraging their teachers to participate and practice.

I also acknowledge the support of my wife, Smt. Lakshmi, who steadfastly stood with me in all these activities.

Sridhar Subbanna

I offer my praṇāmas to all my gurus – Śrī Vidyeśa Tīrtha Swāmījī, Śrī V.K. Rama Rao, Śrī Vyasanakere Prabhanjanacharya, Śrī Vedagarbha Sheshagiri Acharya, Śrī Gangura Hanumeshacharya, Śrī Umarji Srikaracharya and Śrī H Sathyanarayanacharya.

V Srinidhi

About Vidyāsvam

Vidyāsvam was established in 2019 as a platform for the traditional knowledge system to encourage learning of the Saṃskṛta language and enable understanding of Saṃskṛta literary texts in their original form. We believe that reading and interpreting original texts is always better than relying on someone else's prism of translation. It makes learning a joyous experience, a self-fulfilling journey, and reduces the bias and interpretation of the translator.

In modern approaches to learning Saṃskṛta, we notice an important gap. It typically involves mapping with a known language, mainly English, which fails to equip learners with ideas that are original and unique to Saṃskṛta. At Vidyāsvam, we believe that the best way to teach Saṃskṛta is to introduce learners to important components of Saṃskṛta grammar and then expose them to the marvel and richness of the ancient language. This is achieved through a structured approach that starts with Saṃskṛta grammar, with reference to the original Sūtra from Pāṇini's Aṣṭādhyāyī, where necessary. We have borrowed modern pedagogical tools such as graphics, mind maps, memorizing techniques, and references to online resources. To strengthen and internalize learning, we have devised a rich corpus of online practice exercises. To encourage continuous learning and sharing of knowledge, we use a collaborative platform that allows students and alums to discuss topics, raise queries, get answers, and showcase their progress in learning Saṃskṛta. The entire learning ecosystem is supported through mentorship programs.

We believe that the purpose of teaching any subject should be to encourage the students to fall in love with that field of knowledge and embark on a joyous journey of lifelong learning and a passion for exploring all of its dimensions. A strong foundation makes the entire learning edifice stand stronger and taller. Once the passion develops, it starts a virtuous cycle of learning and continuously discovering new concepts, keeping us moving forward.

Currently, Vidyāsvam is offering courses on foundational Saṃskṛta for modern-educated professionals and students in higher education. We have designed and delivered courses ranging from Saṃskṛta grammar and Kavya texts to Bhagavadgita. We intend to continue our journey by adding more programs and contributing to bringing Indian knowledge, in its fullness and rich glory, closer to keen learners.

Team Vidyāsvam
www.vidyasvam.in

Introduction

Saṃskṛta is one of the oldest surviving languages in the world. It has served as a vehicle for developing and transmitting knowledge traditions across multiple disciplines such as religion, philosophy, logic, theater, history, mathematics and linguistics for millennia in the Indian subcontinent. Understandably, many textbooks, compendiums, manuals, lectures, and courses are available to learn Saṃskṛta as a language, including its grammar, literature and richness. At one end of the spectrum are detailed analyses of the language, consisting of millions of word forms and their interpretations, which may be mechanical or purely grammatical exercises. At the other end are modern attempts to learn the language that bypass the linguistic concepts provided in traditional grammar.

Our experience has shown that learning the Saṃskṛta language without an appreciation for its original concepts can be inaccurate and sometimes even misleading. At the same time, a pure grammatical exercise may not benefit those who want to learn Saṃskṛta as a means to access the knowledge corpus. This book attempts to address this lacuna by equipping Saṃskṛta learners with tools that are not only intuitive, minimal and essential but also rigorous and traditional.

We believe that a conceptual understanding of Pāṇini's Aṣṭādhyāyī is possibly the best solution to this question. The traditional exposition of Saṃskṛta by its grammarians, starting from Pāṇini, is based on the premise that Saṃskṛta has a logical structure at its core. Therefore, we attempt to present the logical ideas embedded in Saṃskṛta, and encoded in Pāṇini's

Aṣṭādhyāyī in a way that is accessible to beginners and is yet an undiluted presentation of the tradition.

The book has three parts:

(Part-1) The basics and introduction to the foundations of Pāṇinian grammar.

(Part-2) Concepts of Sandhi and Samāsa, with an introduction to the Pāṇinian Sūtras, his approach to codifying the language and tools to deconstruct his Sūtras.

(Part-3) Illustrated methods of applying the concepts learned in the earlier two parts to logically analyze and interpret any classical composition in Saṃskṛta.

Summary

Chapter 1 introduces the concept of Varṇa, the basic phonetic unit of the Saṃskṛta language. It discusses the classification of Varṇas using multiple lenses and shows the application of these classifications in later grammatical uses.

In Chapter 2, the same varṇas are examined in Pāṇini's terminology, exploring how they are ordered differently for efficient usage, the creation of technicals labels using built-in tags, and the function of those labels in Aṣṭādhyāyī. Pāṇini invokes the idea of Māheśvara Sūtras to create this order and refers to the labels as Pratyāhāras.

Chapter 3 briefly explores semantics, examining what is communicated in any language. The chapter explains that the meaning of sentences is primarily anchored on actions and that other entities are connected to them. The chapter introduces the idea of Kāraka to define this relationship and different types of Kāraka to accurately depict the type of relationship between entity and action.

With that brief reference to semantics, we return to the structure of words in Saṃskṛta language in Chapter 4. Saṃskṛta is primarily an inflected language, meaning that all usable words are derived from two types of Prakṛtis (base words): Prātipadika (a nominal base) and Dhātu (a verbal base). The declensions that make the language inflected are carried out by suffixes called Pratyaya. This chapter provides an overview of Prātipadika, Dhātu and Pratyaya, and their classifications.

In chapter 5, we take a detour and introduce another concept of Pāṇini called "it". "It" is a label given to particular types of varṇas as used in Pāṇini's Aṣṭādhyāyī. These varṇas are part of the data but not part of the content. These are designed for effective and specific application of the content.

Continuing from Chapter 4, Chapters 6 and 7 give a detailed account of base words and words used in a sentence, dealing with both verbal and nominal bases and their usable forms. We also provide a detailed description of meanings, classifications, and declensions of verbal forms. In Chapter 11, we discuss the meanings of nominal words, which requires understanding a few more concepts to be discussed in the next three chapters.

All words used in a sentence by default have a declension described in previous chapters. However, certain defined words do not have declensions but can be used legitimately. Some of them act as prefixes too. Such words are labeled as Avyayas, Nipātas, Upasargas with some variations. Chapter 8 provides an introduction to these concepts.

After discussing the formation of legitimately usable words in previous chapters, in Chapter 9, we introduce a unique idea called Sāmānādhikaraṇya, a type of relationship between some words in a sentence. Identifying this relationship is central to making sense of a part or whole of a sentence.

In chapter 10, we introduce the concept of derived words. Saṃskṛta has two main types of derived base words: derived Prātipadikas and derived Dhātus. Derived Prātipadikas are again mainly of two kinds: Kṛdantas, derived from Dhātus, and Taddhitāntas, derived from Prātipadikas. The discussion on Kṛdanta revisits the ideas of Kārakas, introduces the meanings of kṛt-pratyayas, and equips readers to understand Subanta Padas (usable nominal words), which were left untouched in chapter 7.

Continuing from Chapter 6 and applying most of the concepts introduced until then in the book, we explain in Chapter 11 the meanings of usable nominal words. We introduce the concept of "anabhihita" to help readers understand the meaning of nominal words and comprehend the sentence accurately.

In chapter 12, we talk about Prātipadikas derived from other Prātipadikas. It provides a detailed account of the different meanings carried by different Taddhita Pratyayas.

Similar to the Prātipadikas, the Dhātus also have a category within them: derived from other Dhātus or Prātipadikas. Chapter 13 introduces them and the meanings in which they are formed.

Until the previous chapter, we would have dealt with ideas mentioned in Aṣṭādhyāyī, referring to the Sūtras, but without getting into the word-by-word meaning of any Sūtra. The following two concepts - Sandhi and Samāsa - are best learnt via a literal understanding of the Sūtras. It also provides us with an opportunity to explain the structure of Aṣṭādhyāyī, the types of Sūtras in it, and the methods to understand them. Chapter 14 is devoted to that.

Understanding the transformation of some varṇas that occurs when they are pronounced without a gap from certain other immediately adjacent varṇas, called Sandhi, (and conversely de-transform them to the original) is arguably the very first skill required in understanding a Saṃskṛta śloka. Chapter 15 deals with Aṣṭādhyāyī Sūtras that explain the rules of Sandhi.

Saṃskṛta is empowered with a unique tool called Samāsa that allows it to create innumerable new words by combining existing words. This process, called Samāsa, is explained in detail in Chapter 16.

In Chapter 17, we apply all of the previously discussed concepts to a text and illustrate a logical method for analyzing and comprehending classical compositions.

How to use the book?

The book linearly presents concepts beginning with the alphabets. Therefore, we suggest that readers use the book in the same order in which it is written. We have taken great care to ensure that no prior knowledge of anything in Saṃskṛta other than what is presented in the previous chapters is required. Some assumed concepts, like Sāmānādhikaranya, not explicitly stated in Pāninian grammar, are also discussed when appropriate.

Although the book emphasizes the conceptual aspects of grammar, it is not practical to refer back to the first principles of derivations every time we use a word. Therefore, memorizing some terms, usable forms, and sūtras is handy. We, therefore, recommend that learners remember at least the following wherever they are introduced in the book: the uccāraṇa-sthānas, declension or conjugation tables of prātipadikas and dhātus, any technical term and its definition, and the sūtras with their meanings.

We believe the book is self-contained for all essential concepts of Pāṇinian grammar, especially for comprehension. It is sufficient to break the language barrier in accessing original Saṃskṛta texts. Nevertheless, it's important to note that every Sanskrit text can use specific vocabulary, terminology, and methods that are exclusive to its particular subject matter. Training in that domain may still be required to understand the nuances accurately. We hope that the confidence gained from breaking the language barrier motivates serious learners to undertake higher studies and delve deeper into a domain of their interest under proper guidance.

Contents

1 वर्णमाला

1.1 Introduction

We use language to communicate an idea, an emotion or an event. We use many tools for this communication. It may be a sign like waving a hand, raising eyebrows, flashing some colours, or a sound

In addition to these preliminary ways of communication that are common to even animals, humans use a sophisticated tool of using some specific sounds, called वर्णs[1] that are used to form meaningful words.

These वर्णs form the basic building blocks of natural language. Scripts (लिपि) are symbols used for the written representation of those वर्णs.

[1]Some philosophers argue that these वर्णs are the sounds themselves, but independent ontological elements expressed by sound.

All Indian languages have the same set of वर्णs with minor variations accounting for local dialects. Some of those languages have their own scripts that have been changing over time.

Some languages, including संस्कृत, do not have a script of their own but can use any script to represent the वर्णs. The basic requirement is only a mapping between the वर्णs and letters in a script. Therefore संस्कृत-वर्णs can be represented in any script that provides such a mapping. However, for a few centuries, most संस्कृत-texts are written and printed in an Indian script called Devanagari. This script is also used for writing Hindi, one of the most popular languages in India. In this book, we will be using Devanagari to denote संस्कृत-वर्णs.

वर्णमाला is a specific arrangement of these वर्णs, accepted as a convention in all traditions. It starts with अ and ends with ह[2]. Table 1.1 gives the complete set of वर्णमाला in the defined order.

[2]This should not be confused with the order of वर्णs as per माहेश्वर-सूत्रs, which is a technical order for a specific purpose in अष्टाध्यायी. We shall deal with that later.

अ	आ	इ	ई	उ	ऊ	ऋ	ॠ	ऌ	ए	ऐ	ओ	औ
अं	अः											
क	ख	ग	घ	ङ								
च	छ	ज	झ	ञ								
ट	ठ	ड	ढ	ण								
त	थ	द	ध	न								
प	फ	ब	भ	म								
य	र	ल	व	श	ष	स	ह					

Table 1.1: वर्णमाला

1.2 Classification of वर्णs

The first and most common classification is to divide the वर्णs into स्वर, अयोगवाह, and व्यञ्जन.

The वर्णs from अ to औ are called स्वर. The following two are called अयोगवाह. The अयोगवाहs cannot be used or denoted independently but are always preceded by a स्वर. In the वर्णमाला, we conventionally use अं and अः for illustrative purposes. In reality, they can take other forms, such as इं इः, उं उः etc. The first one is called अनुस्वार and is denoted with a small dot on the top of the corresponding स्वर; the second one is called विसर्ग and is denoted with two small dots after the corresponding स्वर.

अ	आ	इ	ई	उ	ऊ	ऋ	ॠ	ऌ	ए	ऐ	ओ	औ
अं	अः											
क	ख	ग	घ	ङ								
च	छ	ज	झ	ञ								
ट	ठ	ड	ढ	ण								
त	थ	द	ध	न								
प	फ	ब	भ	म								
य	र	ल	व	श	ष	स	ह					

Table 1.2: स्वरs and व्यञ्जनs

The remaining वर्णs from क to ह are called व्यञ्जन. Here a clarification is warranted. The ones depicted in the वर्णमाला are technically a combination of two वर्णs - the व्यञ्जन combined with the स्वर "अ". This is done so for easier pronunciation. The actual व्यञ्जन is the first half of it (i.e., excluding the स्वर part) and is denoted with a stroke at the bottom of the Devanagari script such as - क् ख् ग्, etc. Different combinations of these वर्णs are possible.

When a व्यञ्जन is combined with a स्वर, it is called a स्वरयुक्ताक्षर. For example,

(i) क् + अ = क
(ii) क् + आ = का
(iii) क् + इ = कि
(iv) क् + ई = की
(v) ग् + उ = गु
(vi) त् + ऋ = तृ
(vii) भ् + ओ = भो

When two व्यञ्जनs are combined, it is called a संयुक्ताक्षर. For example,

(i) क् + त् = क्त्
(ii) ङ् + ख् = ङ्ख्
(iii) त् + स् = त्स्
(iv) म् + य् = म्य्
(v) क् + ष् = क्ष्
(vi) त् + र् = त्र्
(vii) ज् + ञ् = ज्ञ्

For easier pronunciation, we usually append it with a स्वर as described earlier. Then the forms will be as follows:

(i) क् + त् + अ = क्त or simply, क्त् + अ = क्त
(ii) ङ् + ख् + अ = ङ्ख or simply, ङ्ख्+ अ = ङ्ख

1.3 Classification of व्यञ्जनs

1.3.1 Based on grouping

The first twenty-five व्यञ्जनs, from क to म, are grouped into five categories of five वर्णs each; and the remaining eight are left ungrouped. This method has led to a classification of वर्णs as वर्गीयव्यञ्जनs (व्यञ्जनs that are grouped) and अवर्गीयव्यञ्जन (व्यञ्जनs that are not grouped).

The groups are called कवर्ग, चवर्ग, टवर्ग, तवर्ग and पवर्ग, each having five व्यञ्जनs in them. Those groups are represented with short forms कुँ, चुँ, टुँ, तुँ, and पुँ respectively. The same is depicted in Table 1.3

क्	ख्	ग्	घ्	ङ्			-	कवर्गः	-	कुँ
च्	छ्	ज्	झ्	ञ्			-	चवर्गः	-	चुँ
ट्	ठ्	ड्	ढ्	ण्			-	टवर्गः	-	टुँ
त्	थ्	द्	ध्	न्			-	तवर्गः	-	तुँ
प्	फ्	ब्	भ्	म्			-	पवर्गः	-	पुँ
य्	र्	ल्	व्	श्	ष्	स्	ह्	-	अवर्गीयव्यञ्जनs	

Table 1.3: वर्गीय-व्यञ्जनs and अवर्गीय-व्यञ्जनs

1.3.2 Based on pronunciations

व्यञ्जनs are also classified based on the kind of effort applied in pronouncing those वर्णs.

1.3.2.1 Classification 1: अल्पप्राणव्यञ्जनs and महाप्राणव्यजञ्जनs

The first, third and fifth वर्णs of each वर्ग and the first four वर्णs of the अवर्गीयव्यञ्जनs (i.e., य्, र्, ल् and व्) are अल्पप्राणव्यञ्जनs. The remaining व्यञ्जनs are महाप्राणव्यजञ्जनs[3]. This is depicted in Table 1.4.

क्	ख्	ग्	घ्	ङ्
च्	छ्	ज्	झ्	ञ्
ट्	ठ्	ड्	ढ्	ण्
त्	थ्	द्	ध्	न्
प्	फ्	ब्	भ्	म्

य्	र्	ल्	व्	श्	ष्	स्	ह्

Table 1.4: अल्पप्राण-व्यञ्जनs and महाप्राण-व्यञ्जनs

[3]This classification is based on the external effort (बाह्यप्रयत्न) involved in pronouncing these वर्णs. As we can easily see, the effort required in pronouncing महाप्राणव्यजञ्जनs is more than that in अल्पप्राणव्यञ्जनs.

1.3.2.2 Classification 2: कर्कशव्यञ्जनs and मृदुव्यञ्जनs

The first two वर्णs of each वर्ग and the last four वर्णs of the अवर्गीयव्यञ्जनs except ह namely, श्,ष् and स् are कर्कशव्यञ्जनs. The remaining व्यञ्जनs are मृदुव्यञ्जनs[4]. The same is represented in Table 1.5

क्	ख्	ग्	घ्	ङ्
च्	छ्	ज्	झ्	ञ्
ट्	ठ्	ड्	ढ्	ण्
त्	थ्	द्	ध्	न्
प्	फ्	ब्	भ्	म्

य्	र्	ल्	व्	श्	ष्	स्	ह्

Table 1.5: कर्कश-व्यञ्जनs and मृदु-व्यञ्जनs

1.3.2.3 Classification 3: स्पर्शव्यञ्जनs, अन्तस्थव्यञ्जनs and ऊष्मव्यञ्जनs

All the 25 वर्गीयव्यञ्जनs, namely क् to म् are स्पर्शव्यञ्जनs. The first four वर्णs of the अवर्गीयव्यञ्जनs, namely, य् र् ल् and व् are अन्तस्थव्यञ्जनs. The last four, viz, श् ष् स् and ह् are ऊष्मव्यञ्जनs. This is illustrated in the Table 1.6

[4]मृदुव्यञ्जनs have three properties, नाद, घोष and संवार; while कर्कशव्यञ्जनs have श्वास, अघोष and विवार. These will be discussed later.

क्	ख्	ग्	घ्	ङ्
च्	छ्	ज्	झ्	ञ्
ट्	ठ्	ड्	ढ्	ण्
त्	थ्	द्	ध्	न्
प्	फ्	ब्	भ्	म्

य् र् ल् व् श् ष् स् ह्

Table 1.6: स्पर्श-व्यञ्जनs, अन्तस्थ-व्यञ्जनs and ऊष्म-व्यञ्जनs

1.3.2.4 Classification 4: अनुनासिकव्यञ्जनs

In addition to the above classifications, the usage of a nasal sound (नासिक-ध्वनि) is uniquely found in some of the वर्णs. They are the fifth वर्णs of each वर्ग, namely, ङ् ञ् ण् न् and म्. For this reason, they are called अनुनासिकव्यञ्जनs. The remaining व्यञ्जनs can technically be called अननुनासिकव्यञ्जनs. However, the term "अननुनासिकव्यञ्जन" is not used, probably because it is by default.

Additionally, य् व् and ल् have two forms: the default form and an अनुनासिक form. The अनुनासिक forms require an additional nasal effort in pronunciation. In Devanagari, they are represented with a चन्द्रबिन्दु - यँ्,लँ् and वँ्. (Table 1.7)

क्	ख्	ग्	घ्	ङ्
च्	छ्	ज्	झ्	ञ्
ट्	ठ्	ड्	ढ्	ण्
त्	थ्	द्	ध्	न्
प्	फ्	ब्	भ्	म्

य्/यँ्	र्	ल्/लँ्	व्/वँ्	श्	ष्	स्	ह्

Table 1.7: अनुनासिक-व्यञ्जनs and अननुनासिक-व्यञ्जनs

1.4 Classifications of स्वरs

Unlike the व्यञ्जनs, we have only one type of classification of स्वरs, and that is based on pronunciation. Before we discuss different types of स्वरs, we need to appreciate a fundamental difference in the way we talk about the classification of व्यञ्जनs and the classification of स्वरs. In the case of व्यञ्जनs, we had a complete set of व्यञ्जनs, and we were attempting to put them under different buckets using multiple ways[5]. However, in the case of स्वरs, we start with a basic set of स्वरs and talk about different forms/variations of each स्वर based on various attributes arriving at a large set of स्वरs.

[5]Except in यँ्,वँ् and लँ्, where we introduced new forms of व्यञ्जनs, that were not accounted for in the वर्णमाला by default.

1.4.1 मात्राकाल attribute

Now, let's take the first important attribute called "मात्राकाल" or simply "मात्रा" in this context. "मात्रा" is a unit of time used to measure the time required for pronouncing a वर्ण. By convention, the time needed for pronouncing "अ" is taken as one "मात्राकाल". It is observed that the time required for pronouncing "अ" and "आ" are in the ratio 1:2. In other words, some स्वरs such as "आ" are pronounced in two मात्राकालs.

In शिक्षाशास्त्र, there are terms given to the स्वरs based on the मात्राकालs of their pronunciations. Those स्वरs pronounced in one मात्राकाल are called ह्रस्व, those pronounced in two मात्राकालs are called दीर्घ and those pronounced in three or more मात्राकालs are called प्लुत. Sometimes, we do pronounce these स्वरs taking a much longer time, such as the last स्वर used in calling out someone loudly from a distance, for example, "हे रामा३"[6]

Before we proceed further, let us revisit the वर्णमाला from this perspective of ह्रस्व, दीर्घ and प्लुत . As we can easily see, अ इ उ ऋ and ऌ are ह्रस्व, while आ ई ऊ ॠ ए ऐ ओ औ are दीर्घ. More importantly, आ, ई, ऊ and ॠ are the दीर्घ variations of अ इ उ and ऋ with no other change. Therefore, for the discussion of this classification, we ignore the दीर्घ variations, namely आ, ई, ऊ and ॠ and take them as some variations

[6]३ is a symbol which denotes प्लुत.

of अ इ उ and ऋ. Thus it suffices if we focus on only nine स्वरs - अ इ उ ऋ ऌ ए ऐ ओ and औ, rather than the 13 listed in the वर्णमाला[7].

1.4.2 Pitch attribute

So, we have now understood that there are three variations (ह्रस्व, दीर्घ and प्लुत) based on one attribute, the मात्राकाल. The second attribute of स्वरs is the pitch at which they are pronounced[8].

Fundamentally there are two pitches: a high pitch and a low pitch. High pitch is pronounced when the space through which sound travels is narrow; low pitch is pronounced when the space is large. In शिक्षाशास्त्र, high pitch is called उदात्त; and low pitch अनुदात्त. There is a third variation which is a combination of the two, and it is called स्वरित. Technically स्वरित is to be pronounced in a way that the first half is in a higher pitch (उदात्त) and the second half is in a lower pitch (अनुदात्त.)

उदात्त, अनुदात्त and स्वरित are denoted by the following notations:

---

[7]Why did we then use them in the वर्णमाला? Possibly because we have a much higher utility of these स्वरs in regular usage, and hence it helps to have them in the basic वर्णमाला than deriving them from their basic element. On the other hand, as we see later, माहेश्वरसूत्रs do not consider these स्वरs since they are just variations of the basic स्वरs.

[8]These are technically called "स्वर"s, NOT to be confused with the स्वरs in the context of स्वर-व्यञ्जन. These are, in a sense स्वर of स्वर.

(1) An underscore below the वर्ण denotes that the स्वर should be pronounced in an अनुदात्त form. E.g., the अनुदात्त variation of अ is written as "अ॒"

(2) A vertical mark above the वर्ण indicates that the स्वर should be pronounced in a स्वरित form . E.g., the स्वरित variation of अ is written as "अ॑"

(3) When a वर्ण is written with neither of these notations, then it is उदात्त. E.g., "अ".

1.4.3 Attribute based on nasal sound

Now, we come to the third attribute of स्वर. It is the presence or absence of a nasal sound. By default, a स्वर is pronounced without a nasal sound and is called its अननुनासिक variation. When the same is pronounced with a nasal sound, it is called "अनुनासिक". It is denoted by a चन्द्रबिन्दु on the top. E.g., अँ, इँ etc.

1.4.4 Combinations of these attributes

We can now look back at all these three attributes - the मात्राकाल, the pitch and the nasal sound - and see how the nine basic स्वरs take different forms due to different combinations of these attributes.

As an illustration, let us start with अ.

It has three forms ह्रस्व, दीर्घ and प्लुत (Table 1.8)

ह्रस्व	अ
दीर्घ	आ
प्लुत	आ३

Table 1.8: ह्रस्व-दीर्घ-प्लुत

Each of these can take 3 variations, उदात्त, अनुदात्त and स्वरित. So we get nine variations. (Table 1.9)

Attributes	उदात्त	अनुदात्त	स्वरित
ह्रस्व	अ	अ॒	अ॑
दीर्घ	आ	आ॒	आ॑
प्लुत	आ३	आ॒३	आ॑३

Table 1.9: उदात्त-अनुदात्त-स्वरित

Each of these nine can take another two variations: अनुनासिक and अननुनासिक. Hence, we end up with eighteen variations. (Table : 1.10). The same is depicted in Figure 1.1.

Attributes	अननुनासिक			अनुनासिक		
	उदात्त	अनुदात्त	स्वरित	उदात्त	अनुदात्त	स्वरित
ह्रस्व	अ	अ॒	अ॑	अँ	अँ॒	अँ॑
दीर्घ	आ	आ॒	आ॑	आँ	आँ॒	आँ॑
प्लुत	आ३	आ॒३	आ॑३	आँ३	आँ॒३	आँ॑३

Table 1.10: All eighteen variations of अ

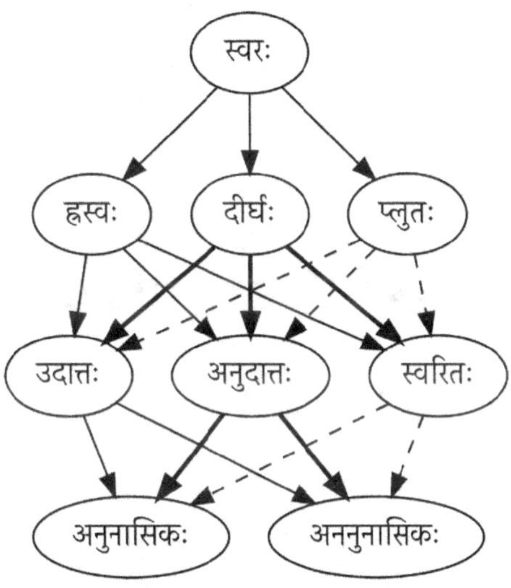

Figure 1.1: स्वर-विभाग

This calculation works for the four स्वरs - अ, इ, उ, ऋ. However,

(i) ऌ doesn't have a दीर्घ.

(ii) ए ऐ ओ and औ do not have a ह्रस्व.

Since ऌ doesn't have a दीर्घ, it does not have the six variations in which its मात्राकाल attribute is दीर्घ and hence has only eighteen minus six = twelve variations.

Similarly, since ए, ऐ, ओ and औ do not have a ह्रस्व, they have only twelve variations.

1.5 Other Classifications of वर्णs

1.5.1 Based on उच्चारणस्थान

As we have seen earlier, वर्णs are specific types of sounds. These sounds are produced only from a few parts of the vocal system. They are called उच्चारणस्थानs (anatomical parts of articulation), and are seven in number: कण्ठ, तालु, ओष्ठ, मूर्धन्, दन्त, नासिका, and जिह्वामूल. Their specific anatomical locations are mentioned in Figure 1.2

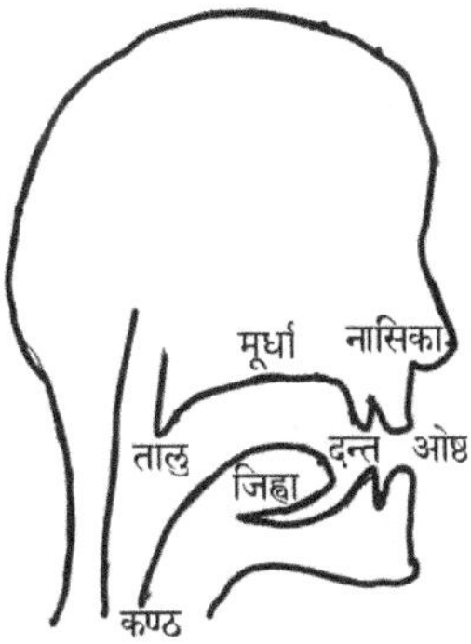

Figure 1.2: उच्चारणस्थान

Some वर्णs are produced at an individual उच्चारणस्थान, and some are produced when these स्थानs are used in combination. A list of वर्णs with their respective स्थानs is provided in these sentences[9].

(1) अकुँहविसर्जनीयानां कण्ठः ।

(2) इचुँयशानां तालु ।

(3) ऋटुँरषाणां मूर्धा ।

(4) लृतुँलसानां दन्तः ।

(5) उपूँपध्मानीयानां ओष्ठौ ।

(6) ञमङणनानां नासिका च ।

(7) एदैतोः कण्ठतालुः ।

(8) ओदौतोः कण्ठोष्ठम् ।

(9) वकारस्य दन्तोष्ठम् ।

(10) जिह्वामूलीयस्य जिह्वामूलम् ।

(11) नासिका अनुस्वारस्य ।

Here are a few definitions to understand these sentences:

कुँ, चुँ etc., refer to the respective वर्गs.

[9]These are taken from सिद्धान्तकौमुदी.

विसर्जनीय refers to the second अयोगवाह, that is विसर्ग (:)

एत्, ऐत्, ओत् and औत् refer to ए, ऐ, ओ and औ respectively.

उपध्मानीय and जिह्वामूलीय are labels for a special type of pronunciation applicable to विसर्ग in a few contexts. They are pronounced in a way that is similar to one half of a विसर्ग. When a विसर्ग is followed by प or फ and is pronounced similar to one half of a विसर्ग, then it is called "उपध्मानीय". Similarly, when a विसर्ग is followed by क or ख and is pronounced similar to one half of a विसर्ग, then it is called "जिह्वामूलीय". उपध्मानीय and जिह्वामूलीय are denoted as: ᳶप, ᳶफ, ᳵक, ᳵख. For example, काकᳵकाकᳶपिकᳶपिकः

It can be observed that 1 to 6 and 11 are referring to individual उच्चारणस्थान, while 7 to 10 are referring to two उच्चारणस्थानs. It means that those वर्णs listed in sentences 7 to 10 are produced by these parts together.

Since, कण्ठ, तालु etc., are उच्चारणस्थानs, the respective वर्णs are called कण्ठ्य, तालव्य etc., in शिक्षाशास्त्र. Using that terminology, the same statements can be re-written as mentioned in Table 1.11.

(1) अकुँहविसर्जनीयाः कण्ठ्याः ।

(2) इचुँयशास्तालव्याः ।

(3) ऋटुँरषा मूर्धन्याः ।

(4) ऌतुँलसा दन्त्याः ।

(5) उपूँपध्मानीया ओष्ठ्याः ।

(6) ञमङणनाः स्वस्थाना नासिकस्थानाश्च ।

(7) एदैतौ कण्ठतालव्यौ ।

(8) ओदौतौ कण्ठोष्ठ्यौ ।

(9) वकारो दन्तोष्ठ्यः ।

(10) जिह्वामूलीयो जिह्व्यः ।

(11) अनुस्वारो नासिक्यः ।

Classification based on उच्चारणस्थान	वर्णs
कण्ठ्य (Guttural)	अ (all 18 variations), कुँ (कवर्ग), ह् and विसर्ग (:)
तालव्य (Palatal)	इ (all 18 variations), चुँ (चवर्ग), य् and श्
मूर्धन्य (Cerebral)	ऋ(all 12 variations), टुँ (टवर्ग), र् and ष्
दन्त्य (Dental)	ऌ (all 12 variations), तुँ(तवर्ग), ल् and स्
ओष्ठ्य (Labial)	उ (all 18 variations), पुँ (पवर्ग), उपध्मानीय
नासिक्य (Nasal)	ञ्, म्, ङ्, ण् and न् in addition to the उच्चारणस्थान according to the वर्ग it belongs to, अनुस्वार
कण्ठतालव्य (Gutturo-palatal)	ए and ऐ (all 12 variations of each)
कण्ठोष्ठ्य (Gutturo-labial)	ओ and औ (all 12 variations of each)
दन्तोष्ठ्य (Gutturo-labial)	व्
जैह्व्य	जिह्वामूलीय

Table 1.11: Classification based on उच्चारणस्थान

1.5.2 Based on प्रयत्न (Effort)

वर्णs (which are specific types of sounds) are articulated through उच्चारणस्थान, and different वर्णs, despite having the same उच्चारणस्थान, require different efforts for pronunciation. This effort is called प्रयत्न, and is mainly of two types:

(1) आभ्यन्तरप्रयत्न (internal effort) which refers to the effort made at the beginning of pronunciation.
(2) बाह्यप्रयत्न (external effort) which refers to the effort made during the pronunciation

Let us now consider each of them separately.

1.5.2.1 आभ्यन्तरप्रयत्न

There are five types of आभ्यन्तरप्रयत्नs[10]:

(1) विवृत (Open)
(2) ईषद्विवृत (Slightly open)
(3) स्पृष्ट (Contacted)
(4) ईषत्स्पृष्ट (Slightly contacted)
(5) संवृत (Contracted)

[10] विवृतं स्वराणाम् । ईषद्विवृतमूष्मणाम् । स्पृष्टं स्पर्शानाम् । ईषत्स्पृष्टमन्तस्थानाम् । ह्रस्वस्य अकारस्य प्रयोगे संवृतम् ।

All स्वरs except the ह्रस्व अ require विवृत-प्रयत्न. At the beginning of pronunciation of these, the respective उच्चारणस्थानs are completely open. ईषद्विवृत type of प्रयत्न is used for pronouncing ऊष्म -व्यञ्जनs i.e., श्, ष्, स् and ह् . The corresponding उच्चारणस्थान is slightly open at the beginning of pronunciation of these वर्णs. The वर्गीय-व्यञ्जनs are pronounced with स्पृष्ट type of प्रयत्न, in which some parts of उच्चारणस्थान touch each other at the beginning of the pronunciation. In cases where the उच्चारणस्थानs are मूर्धन्, तालु or दन्त, some part of the tongue will be coming in contact with them. Hence वर्गीय-व्यञ्जनs are also known as स्पर्श-व्यञ्जनs. ईषत्स्पृष्ट प्रयत्न is used for अन्तस्थ-व्यञ्जनs, namely, य्, र्, ल् and व्. The उच्चारणस्थानs of these will be slightly touching at the beginning of their pronunciation. Pronunciation of ह्रस्व अवर्ण requires संवृत-प्रयत्न.

1.5.2.2 बाह्यप्रयत्न

बाह्यप्रयत्न is of eleven types:

(1) *संवार*

(2) विवार

(3) *नाद*

(4) श्वास

(5) *घोष*

(6) अघोष

(7) *अल्पप्राण*

(8) महाप्राण

(9) उदात्त

(10) अनुदात्त

(11) स्वरित

Out of these प्रयत्नs, संवार, नाद and घोष [11] are required for the pronunciation of मृदु-वर्णs while the प्रयत्नs विवार, श्वास and अघोष are required for the pronunciation of कर्कश-वर्णs. उदात्त, अनुदात्त and स्वरित प्रयत्नs are used to pronounce the स्वरs of their respective pitch attributes discussed earlier. Similarly, अल्पप्राण, महाप्राण प्रयत्नs are required to pronounce the respective types of व्यञ्जनs.

[11]More details can be found in शिक्षाशास्त्र.

2 माहेश्वरसूत्र and प्रत्याहार

2.1 Introduction

In the previous discussion, we have seen the nature of वर्णs, their conventional order, properties, pronunciations and consequent classifications. In this chapter, we look at the same वर्णs in Pāṇinian system - how they are ordered differently for efficient usage, how technical labels are created using some in-built tags, and what is the function of those labels in व्याकरणशास्त्र. पाणिनि invokes the idea of माहेश्वरसूत्रs to group the वर्णs in a specific order for efficient usage.

2.1.1 माहेश्वरसूत्र

It is believed that Lord Śiva appeared in front of पाणिनि in penance, and when Lord played his डमरु (a musical instrument), पाणिनि heard fourteen sets of वर्णs emanating from it in a specific order. These are named after Lord Śiva, and are called शिवसूत्रs or माहेश्वरसूत्रs. They are -

(1) अ इ उ ण् ।
(2) ऋ ऌ क् ।
(3) ए ओ ङ् ।
(4) ऐ औ च् ।
(5) ह य व र ट् ।
(6) ल ण् ।
(7) ञ म ङ ण न म् ।
(8) झ भ ञ् ।
(9) घ ढ ध ष् ।
(10) ज ब ग ड द श् ।
(11) ख फ छ ठ थ च ट त व् ।
(12) क प य् ।
(13) श ष स र् ।
(14) ह ल् ।

Here are some points to be borne in mind in interpreting these सूत्रs -

The स्वरs in these सूत्रs represent all of their variants, 18 or 12, as applicable.

"अ" that we hear as appended to each व्यञ्जन is only for ease of pronunciation. Hence, the स्वरयुक्ताक्षरs such as ह य व etc., refer only to their व्यञ्जन part, i.e., ह् य् व् etc.

Last व्यञ्जनवर्ण of each सूत्र is called "इत्"[1]

The main function of these माहेश्वरसूत्रs is to generate प्रत्याहारs, that we discuss in the next section.

[1]The concept of इत् is dealt in Chapter 5

2.1.2 प्रत्याहार

प्रत्याहार is a technical term equivalent to an acronym. It is similar to the idea of sets in modern mathematics. Specifically, it is a label formed using the माहेश्वरसूत्रs to denote some set of वर्णs. For example, अच्, हल्, इक् Here, अच् is a प्रत्याहार formed with "अ" as the first वर्ण and "च्" as the last वर्ण. Here, we should note that अ is non-इत्, and च्is one of the इत्-वर्णs coming later in the sequence. This प्रत्याहार "अच्" denotes the set of वर्णs starting from अ, upto च्, excluding ण्, क्, ङ् and च्. In other words, "अच्" is an acronym to represent the set of वर्णs अ इ उ ऋ ऌ ए ऐ ओ and औ. अच् is a प्रत्याहार that denotes the set of all स्वरs, including all their variants.

Similarly, "हल्", another प्रत्याहार, represents ह् य् व् र् ल् ञ् म् ङ् ण् न् झ् भ् घ् ढ् ध् ज् ब् ग् ड् द् ख् फ् छ् ठ् थ् च् ट् त् क् प् श् ष् स् and ह् and set of all व्यञ्जनs.[2]

One of the इत्-वर्णs "ण्" is used twice in the माहेश्वरसूत्रs once in the first सूत्र, अ इ उ ण्, and again in sixth सूत्र - ल ण्. This does pose a complication. Let's consider these प्रत्याहारs - अण्, इण् and उण्. Which इत्-वर्ण should one consider in these प्रत्याहारs?

[2]Here we can see that the वर्ण "ह्" is repeated. It is true that, in the concept of sets, repeating the same element doesn't increase the number of elements. However, why would anyone do that without reason? For more, please see the paper: A Mathematical Analysis of pāṇini's śivasūtras by Wiebke Petersen

उण् is a more straightforward problem. If one were to consider the first ण्, then उण् would refer to the set with only उ as its element. That would defeat the logic of brevity: when we can refer to "उ" directly with a single वर्ण, i.e., "उ" itself, what is the need to use a प्रत्याहार "उण्", that has two वर्णs?

Now, let's look at the other two: अण् and इण्. Here the discussion on why ण् is used twice is beyond the scope of this book. Advanced mathematical reasoning for this duplication is referenced in the footnote. For our discussions, it suffices to know that "ण्" in "अण्" when used in अष्टाध्यायी always refers to the second ण्, with only one exception in सूत्र 1.1.69: अणुदित् सवर्णस्य चाप्रत्ययः. इण् always refers to the second ण् without exception.

In summary, माहेश्वरसूत्रs are a set of वर्णs in a defined order, where in some of the वर्णs are called इत्-वर्णs. प्रत्याहारs are formed using the sequence of वर्णs and इत्-वर्णs in the माहेश्वरसूत्रs to generate labels that represent different sets of वर्णs. Because of the brevity of these labels, अष्टाध्यायीसूत्रs refer to these labels rather than enlisting the whole set of वर्णs. We shall see the actual applications of these प्रत्याहारs in the later chapters.

3 कारक

3.1 Introduction

In the previous chapters, we discussed the idea of वर्ण both as it is understood in widespread usage, and specifically in the Pāṇinian scheme. We have also claimed that वर्णs form the basic elements of communication. Before we delve further into this idea of how वर्णs are used in communication, let us first focus on understanding what exactly we communicate.

Communication is generally the transmission of information. As we can see in all our communications, this information is always about entities and how they are related to each other.

Let's examine a few common examples.

(1) Vishnu is constructing a house.
(2) Janaki went to school.
(3) Umesha will draw a diagram using a pencil.
(4) The children are laughing.
(5) You are at home.

(6) In the kitchen, Bhima is cooking rice in a pot.

Let's analyse the information conveyed in each of these sentences.

We can identify a common pivot point through which all the entities are connected in each piece of information. Let's take a closer look at each of them below:

(1) The act of "constructing" is connected to "Vishnu" and "house".
(2) "Janaki" and "school" are connected to the action of "going".
(3) The act of "drawing" combines "Umesha", "diagram" and "pencil".
(4) The act of "laughing" is associated with "children".
(5) The idea of "being", is associated with "you" and "home".
(6) The idea of "cooking" is connected with "Bhima", "pot", "kitchen" and "rice".

As we can see, each of these information bits centres around an action, with all the entities involved connected to that action. This is our experience universally, in all our communications, irrespective of language. This depiction of reality, which puts the action at the centre, is used in Saṃskṛta to develop the idea of कारक.

The "action" referred to in our previous paragraphs, is called क्रिया in Saṃskṛta, and we will be using the term क्रिया in the following discussions. कारकs are entities that are directly involved in accomplishing a क्रिया.

Returning to our examples:

(1) "Vishnu" and "house" are कारकs in the क्रिया of constructing.
(2) "Janaki and "school" are कारकs in the क्रिया of going.
(3) "Umesha", "diagram" and "pencil" are कारकs in the क्रिया of drawing.
(4) "Children" are कारकs in the क्रिया of laughing.
(5) "You" and "home" are कारकs in the क्रिया of being.
(6) "Bhima", "pot", "kitchen" and "rice" are कारकs in the क्रिया of cooking.

Not all कारकs have the same role. Some perform actions independently, some are used as instruments, some others function as locus etc. Considering the specific way in which these कारक entities are involved in accomplishing the क्रिया, they have been categorized into six types: कर्तृ, कर्म, अधिकरण, करण, सम्प्रदान and अपादान.

3.2 कर्तृ-कारक

Any क्रिया necessarily requires an entity in which the क्रिया occurs, and we can observe the said क्रिया in that entity. In other words, क्रिया needs a person or a thing that is considered primarily performing the क्रिया, and in which the क्रिया is observable. This कारक is called कर्तृ.

Technically, कर्तृ is defined by Pāṇini as "स्वतन्त्रः कर्ता"(1-4-54). It means that a कारक which we consider as having a primary role in a क्रिया is called कर्तृ. Later commentators have provided an alternative but interchangeable definition for कर्तृ: "क्रियाश्रयः कर्ता". This means that कर्तृ is the entity in which the क्रिया occurs.

In our earlier example, Vishnu is primarily performing the क्रिया of constructing; and in fact, we can observe the act of constructing in him. He is therefore considered कर्तृ in the क्रिया of constructing. Similarly, we can observe that Janaki, Umesha, Children and "you" are कर्तृs in the next four examples respectively.

3.3 कर्म-कारक

Let's look at other entities in the same examples. How is the house related to Vishnu and the act of construction? Or, how is the school associated with Janaki or with the act of going?

Any क्रिया is done to get a result. Vishnu, too, is involved in the act of "constructing" to get a result. In the end, he wants the house constructed. Similarly, Janaki's act of "going" will end when she achieves the result of reaching the school. In both these examples, the कर्तृ is performing an action to get a result. That result typically is not an entity, but a property of that entity. For example, "being constructed" is the house's property, and "having reached" is the school's property. So, that entity in which we want to get the result of this क्रिया is called कर्म. Thus, in our cases, house and school are कर्मs in those respective क्रियाs.

Usually, the property of a कर्म that we want to get as a result of क्रिया is of three types:

(1) निर्वर्त्य - to be created.
(2) विकार्य - to be transformed.
(3) प्राप्य - to be reached/understood.

By any क्रिया, we either want to create an entity, transform it or reach it. Such an entity is the कर्मकारक under discussion.

Technically, कर्म is defined as "कर्तुरीप्सिततमं कर्म" (1-4-49). It means that कर्म is an entity that is most desired by the कर्तृ as a result of the क्रिया that he is undertaking. As we saw, the result is typically a property, and hence an alternative definition says that कर्म is an entity in which resides the result of क्रिया - "क्रियाजन्यफलाश्रयं कर्म".

If we go back to the remaining examples, "diagram" is कर्म is the third activity. But which are the कर्मs in examples 4 and 5? There seem to be none. What is the entity in which children want to see get the result of the action of "laughing"? Or, what is the entity in which "you" want to see the result of "being"? There seem to be none other than themselves. That means, the क्रिया of laughing or being do not have any entity that can be called a कर्म. In व्याकरण, such actions are called "अकर्मक" = "without a कर्म".

3.3.1 सकर्मक-क्रियाs and अकर्मक-क्रियाs

Let's clarify this idea of अकर्मक-क्रिया, before moving to a discussion on the third कारक. By their very nature, some क्रियाs give the result of those क्रियाs in an entity, and some don't. For example, the "constructing" action resulted in a constructed house. But the action of "laughing" doesn't result in any such change. One may argue that it made the children happy, and therefore the act of laughing does have a result. However, that so-called result occurs in the same कर्तृ, and there is no other entity, that can be called कर्म, in which we can observe the result. In the Pāṇinian scheme, we can label an entity as only one of the कारकs, and thus the same entity cannot be called

कर्तृ and कर्म at the same time. Hence, we say that we have only कर्तृ and not कर्म in such क्रियाs, and call them 'अकर्मक-क्रिया's.

The acts of standing, sitting, sleeping, walking, being, liberating, hibernating, and originating are other examples of अकर्मक-क्रिया.

Other क्रियाs do need a कर्म, to accomplish the action, and are called सकर्मक-क्रियाs. Most of our daily activities fall into this category. The acts of eating, breaking, writing, thinking, saying and many more can be thought of as examples.

3.4 अधिकरण-कारक

Let's go back to our example, "You are at home". As we saw, the act of "being" is the क्रिया, and "you" is the कर्तृ. We also saw that this act is a अकर्मक-क्रिया and hence there is no कर्म. But, we know that "home" is also involved in accomplishing this क्रिया and is, therefore, a कारक. Which कारक is this?

Here "home" is an entity in which "you" reside. Such an entity, that acts as a substratum (आश्रय) for either the कर्तृ or the कर्म in a given क्रिया, is called अधिकरण-कारक in that क्रिया. Thus, "home" is अधिकरण-कारक.

Technically, पाणिनि defines this as "आधारोऽधिकरणम्"(1-4-45), "Substratum for कर्तृ or कर्म is called अधिकरण-कारक".

The other example was similar: "In the kitchen, Bhima is cooking rice in a vessel". However, there are two आश्रयs in this case. The kitchen is आश्रय for Bhima, while the vessel is आश्रय for rice. And, Bhima is कर्तृ while rice is कर्म. Hence, by definition, both are अधिकरण-कारकs.

Do we necessarily need an अधिकरण-कारक in accomplishing any क्रिया? There would always be a substratum, but we may not be intending to include that in the information communicated. In such cases, there may not be an explicit अधिकरण-कारक as a part of that information. However, two implicit अधिकरण-कारकs exist in any piece of information about any क्रिया, and they are'space' and 'time' - देश and काल. If we provide more details about the space and time, such as "He is doing this activity in the afternoon in Hanuman Ghat at Varanasi", then more specific coordinates of time and space such as "afternoon" and "Hanuman Ghat at Varanasi" would become an explicit mention of those अधिकरण-कारकs. In the absence of such information, a generic "some space" and "some time" would be the अधिकरण-कारकs.

अधिकरण is technically a broader term than what we generally understand by the word substratum. It can even be the locus of interest for our mental faculties or the subject matter of a text. This is technically called विषय. For example, consider this piece of information: “He has desire in Vyakarana”. Here, “desire” is a mental faculty which necessarily needs another relational term that explains “desire about what”. That entity is called विषय. Hence, Vyakarana is विषय. All those विषयs are also considered अधिकरण. Therefore, Vyakarana is अधिकरण-कारक in this example.

This is applicable in similar cases that deal with mental faculties or emotions (मनोवृत्तिs) like भक्ति (devotion), ज्ञान (knowledge), सुख (pleasure), इच्छा (desire), क्रोध (anger), राग (attachment), द्वेष (hatred) etc. Let’s consider another example: “The word कमल is used in the meaning of lotus”. Here “lotus” is the subject matter or वाच्य/प्रतिपाद्य of the word कमल. Therefore, lotus is विषय, and hence अधिकरण-कारक in this example.

3.5 करण-कारक

We have now seen कर्तृ, कर्म and अधिकरण. Let’s now consider the करण-कारक.

In our example, “Umesha will draw a diagram with a pencil”, the क्रिया is that of drawing. This क्रिया occurs in Umesha, and hence, Umesha is कर्तृ. The result of that drawing is the creation of the diagram. Hence, the property of “being created” is in “the diagram”, and therefore, "the diagram" is कर्म. What is the role of the pencil in this activity?

We do observe the क्रिया in both Umesha and pencil. However, Umesha has a primary role, and pencil's is secondary. That is, Umesha is making the pencil act. If we observe closely, the nature of the activity is a 'to and fro' movement. This movement is primarily in Umesha, and he is in turn transferring those movements to the pencil. In other words, he transfers the "activity" from himself to the pencil, and achieves the desired result of creating the diagram. Thus the pencil is an instrument in this क्रिया. Such an instrumental entity, is called करण-कारक. Hence, pencil is करण-कारक.

पाणिनि defines it as "साधकतमं करणम्" - "the most important causal entity in the क्रिया is करण". This phrase "most important causal entity" translates to "instrument".

3.6 सम्प्रदान-कारक and अपादान-कारक

We have discussed four कारकs so far, using broad definitions that helped us appreciate the concept of कर्तृ, कर्म, अधिकरण and करण. Also, these कारकs are usually present in most of the क्रियाs. However, the remaining two - सम्प्रदानकारक and अपादानकारक - are entities that take specific roles, lack a general definition, and are seen only in some types of क्रियाs.

The full list of cases, where entities are labelled सम्प्रदानकारकs, is mentioned in अष्टाध्यायी-सूत्रs. In Table 3.1, we refer to those सूत्रs and provide a list of only those that are seen commonly.

Similarly, the common अपादान-कारकs are listed in the Table 3.2

सूत्र	Meaning	Example
कर्मणा यमभिप्रैति स सम्प्रदानम् (1-4-32)	The person or thing, in the act of giving, to whom कर्तृ gives a कर्म is labelled as *सम्प्रदानकारक*	Kiran gives a pencil to **Himesh**.
स्पृहेरीप्सितः (1-4-36)	The person or thing, in the act of desiring, whom the कर्तृ desires is labelled as *सम्प्रदानकारक*	Mohan is longing for **mangoes.**
क्रुधद्रुहेर्ष्याऽसूयार्थानां यं प्रति कोपः (1-4-37)	The person or thing, against whom the कर्तृ is angry, in the acts of "getting angry at", "cheating", "grudging (not appreciating other's growth)", "feeling jealous (discovering fallacies in nobility)" is labelled as *सम्प्रदानकारक*	Gautam is angry at **Nishanth**.

Table 3.1: सम्प्रदान-कारक

सूत्र	Meaning	Example
ध्रुवमपायेऽपादानम् (1-4-24)	An entity, in the act of separating, from which the कर्तृ separates is labelled as *अपादानकारक*	Apple falls from the **tree**.
भीत्रार्थानां भयहेतुः (1-4-25)	An entity, which is the cause of fear, in the act of "fearing" or "protecting", is labelled as *अपादानकारक*	The boy is afraid of **lion** The king protects people from **thieves**
जनिकर्तुः प्रकृतिः (1-4-30)	In the act of taking birth, the entity from which a new person/thing takes birth is labelled as *अपादानकारक.*	A plant is born from a **seed.**
भुवः प्रभवः (1-4-31)	In the act of emerging, the entity from which a person/thing emerges is labelled as *अपादानकारक*	Ganga originates from **Himalayas**.

Table 3.2: अपादान-कारक

4 प्रकृति-प्रत्यय-व्यवस्था

4.1 Introduction

वाक्यs are the basic units of any form of text (कथा or काव्य or प्रकरण or ग्रन्थ etc.).

वाक्य is made of पदs. वाक्य is a set of related words (पदs) that communicate a complete meaning, comprising क्रिया, कारकs, and other associated components.

4.2 पद

A पद[1] has two building blocks प्रकृति (root) and प्रत्यय(suffix)[2].

प्रकृति is of two types based on the information that it carries: प्रातिपादिक and धातु. The प्रकृति that refers to an entity is called प्रातिपादिक. प्रातिपादिक can be thought of as a label given to an entity. प्रातिपादिक is equivalent to nominal stem. The प्रकृति that refers to action is

[1]पद is defined by Panini as सुप्तिङन्तं पदम् (1-4-14) i.e., पद is that which has a सुप् or a तिङ् ending.

[2]Some words may have a prefix called उपसर्ग (which is also a form of प्रकृति; more details follow).

called धातु. Again, धातु can be seen as a label given to action. धातु is equivalent to verbal root.

प्रत्यय provides additional information about the प्रकृति (such as number, tense, कारक, person, relations etc.). Some प्रत्ययs (such as सुँप् and तद्धित) are specific to प्रातिपदिकs whereas some (such as तिङ् and कृत्) are specific to धातुs.

It follows that neither प्रकृति nor प्रत्यय carries sufficient information to be used independently. Hence, any word that we use in the language is always a combination of प्रकृति and प्रत्यय.

This nature of पद (that embeds both basic and additional information together) makes Saṃskṛta an inflectional language. Because of this, the order of words in a sentence does not matter. We will revisit this topic with some examples after knowing the meanings of प्रकृतिs and प्रत्ययs.

4.3 प्रकृति

We had said that we use language to communicate action and all entities associated with that action.

How do we identify these two ideas - the action (क्रिया) and the associated entities (कारकs); or other connected entities or relations in that communication?

Any entity can be understood in two ways: its form and its label. The form is what we can perceive, experience, or imagine; the label we use to communicate it to others. For example, the form of an elephant is seen and we use the label "elephant" to communicate it. This label is called a प्रातिपदिक.

Similarly, we can see the action of an elephant moving, and we use the label "move" to refer to that action. Such labels are called धातुs.

4.4 प्रातिपदिक

पाणिनि defines प्रातिपदिक as "अर्थवदधातुरप्रत्ययः प्रातिपदिकम्" (1-2-45). It means that a प्रातिपदिक is a combination of वर्णs, that is used as a label of an entity; provided that label is not a धातु or a प्रत्यय[3].

The meaning (अर्थ) of a प्रातिपदिक is the entity to which it is a label. It follows that this couple/dual of प्रातिपदिक (label) and अर्थ (the entity/meaning) forms the fundamental mapping of a language. We

[3]Details on धातु and प्रत्यय follow in subsequent sections.

all can see that every entity in the world has a label. It means that any entity can be referred to by its प्रातिपदिक.

Now, how do we understand this mapping of प्रातिपदिक and its अर्थ? In other words, which entity is referred to by a given प्रातिपदिक?

प्रातिपदिक gets its meaning in two ways: one by usage and the other by its etymology. The former is called रूढि and the latter योग.

The रूढि meanings are obtained by convention or are given in dictionaries. We take them for granted without worrying about the meanings of their constituents. Examples: कूप, वृक्ष, घट, पट or names of each of us.

The योग meanings can be derived by understanding the meanings of the constituents. This concept can be understood better when we see how different प्रकृतिs and प्रत्ययs can form new प्रकृतिs. Examples: नर्तक, दाशरथि, पङ्कज, पादप, उरग

Mapping with a meaning is the first inherent attribute of the प्रातिपदिक.

The second inherent attribute is प्रातिपदिक's gender (लिङ्ग). Here we need to understand that gender is an attribute of प्रातिपदिक and not of the entity to which it is labelled.

Such gender of a प्रातिपदिक is of two types:

(1) नियत (fixed)

(2) विशेष्यनिघ्न (dependent on the प्रातिपदिक to which this acts as a qualifier)[4]

Some examples of प्रातिपदिक with नियतलिङ्ग are :

(i) दार, घट, योग - masculine

(ii) भार्या, कृति, लक्ष्मी - feminine

(iii) कलत्र, पुस्तक, ब्रह्मन् - neuter

The gender of these प्रातिपदिकs cannot be changed under any circumstance. However, there are some प्रातिपदिकs that can change their gender depending on the प्रातिपदिकs to which they act as qualifiers. Such प्रातिपदिकs are known as विशेष्यनिघ्नs. For example, let's consider the प्रातिपदिक सुलभ; it means simple. We can use it as a qualifier for another word, such as विषय, कृति or कार्य. The word विषय is masculine; hence the qualifier also takes a masculine form, and the resultant phrase would be: "सुलभः विषयः". Similarly, we get forms such as "सुलभा कृतिः" and "सुलभं कार्यम्"; since कृति has a fixed feminine gender and कार्य has a fixed neuter gender.

[4]The idea of विशेष्य will be clarified when we discuss विशेष्य-विशेषणभाव in chapter 9.

In summary, प्रातिपदिक is a type of प्रकृति, and it is a label of an entity. It has two inherent attributes: meaning and gender. Early dictionaries such as अमरकोश or modern dictionaries such as Apte's help us in identifying these two attributes. A learner's vocabulary is dependent on familiarity with प्रातिपदिकs and their associated meanings and genders.

4.5 धातु

As mentioned earlier, धातुs are labels of actions. While dictionaries help in identifying प्रातिपदिकs, धातुs are explicitly listed in पाणिनीय-धातुकोश (set of verbal roots)[5]; the set starts with "भू सत्तायाम्". पाणिनि, in fact, defines धातुs as "those listed in the set starting from भू" : "भूवादयो धातवः" (1-3-1)

धातुs can be classified on two grounds: meaning and transformations.

(1) Based on meaning, they can be classified into two kinds:
  (i) सकर्मक-धातु: that which refers to a सकर्मक-क्रिया (discussed under the topic of कारक).
  Example: गमॢ गतौ (to go).

[5]This is the popularly used कोश, many others are also available.

(ii) अकर्मक-धातु : that which refers to a अकर्मक-क्रिया.

Example: शीङ् स्वप्ने (to sleep)

(2) Based on the type of प्रत्ययs that a धातु can take, leading to different transformations, we can categorise धातुs into

(1) आत्मने-पदि-धातु

(2) परस्मै-पदि-धातु

(3) उभय-पदि-धातु

भ्वादि-गण-धातु, अदादि-गण-धातु etc., referring to धातुs belonging to one of the ten groups called गणs[6].

अनिट्-धातु, सेट्-धातु and वेट्-धातु. It is easier to understand these more when we discuss the transformations.

In summary, each धातु has five attributes:

(1) Meaning in the form of an action (क्रियात्मक-पदार्थः).
(2) Whether it denotes an action that requires a कर्मकारक or not (सकर्मक-अकर्मक).
(3) The kind of प्रत्ययs it takes (आत्मने-पदि-धातु, परस्मै-पदि-धातु or उभय-पदि-धातु).
(4) The गण to which it belongs.
(5) Whether it takes इट् or not (अनिट्-धातु, सेट्-धातु or वेट्-धातु).

[6]The ten गणs are भ्वादि, अदादि, जुहोत्यादि, दिवादि, स्वादि, तुदादि, रुधादि, तनादि, क्र्यादि, चुरादि.

4.6 प्रत्यय

We have seen earlier that a पद has two building blocks: प्रकृति and प्रत्यय. We have understood the two types of प्रकृतिs in detail. Now, let us understand प्रत्ययs in detail.

प्रत्ययs are those building blocks that provide additional information about प्रकृतिs. Such information is usually generic, and the specific meaning is always contextual. That is, the information provided by प्रत्यय is generally at an abstract level and can specifically be understood in the context of the sentence in which it is used[7].

Example: कर्मवाचक-प्रत्यय; but who that कर्म is and in what क्रिया can be understood when read in a context.

Even though प्रत्ययs are generally used to provide additional information with respect to the corresponding प्रकृति, some प्रत्ययs help in only transformation without any meaning associated. For example, समासान्त-प्रत्यय, विकरण-प्रत्यय, etc.

[7]This feature is also seen in प्रातिपदिकs / धातुs when they have multiple meanings.

4.7 Classification of प्रत्यय

प्रत्ययs can be classified on multiple axes. Some illustrative classifications are given below.

(1) Based on the nature of प्रकृति-
   (i) Those that are prescribed as suffixes to प्रातिपदिकs.
       e.g., सुप्, तद्धित, स्त्री
   (ii) Those that are prescribed as suffixes to धातुs.
       e.g., तिङ्, कृत्, सनादि

(2) Based on the function of प्रत्यय-
   (i) Those that have a meaning. e.g., सुप्, तिङ्
   (ii) Those that are used only for transformation without any specific meaning. e.g., समासान्त-प्रत्यय, विकरण-प्रत्यय.

Among all the प्रत्ययs, two sets of प्रत्ययs - सुप् and तिङ् - have an important role. As पाणिनि says, "सुप्तिङन्तं पदम्" (1-4-14); that is, a group of वर्णs can be called a पद (word) only when they end with a सुप्-प्रत्यय or a तिङ्-प्रत्यय. सुप्-प्रत्यय is a group of प्रत्ययs specified for प्रातिपदिकs, and तिङ् group of प्रत्ययs are for धातुs. Therefore, even though प्रातिपदिकs and धातुs have a meaning on their own, they can be used in a sentence only when combined with these प्रत्ययs. These प्रत्ययs act as delimiters in identifying where a पद ends in a sentence. They are, therefore, crucial in what is technically called पदच्छेद - parsing a sentence to identify its constituent पदs. The diagram 4.1 provides a summary of the combination of प्रकृति and प्रत्यय and the result of those combinations. Note the following in the given diagram (Figure 4.1)

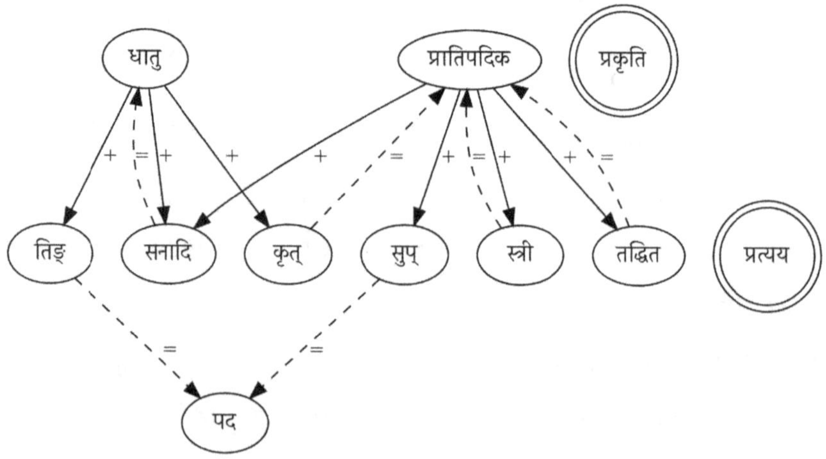

Figure 4.1: प्रकृतिप्रत्ययव्यवस्था

(i) These प्रत्ययs can be applied exclusively to either प्रातिपदिकs or only to धातुs.

(ii) तद्धित and स्त्री-प्रत्ययs combine with प्रातिपदिक and result in a new प्रातिपदिक.

(iii) Some सनादि-प्रत्ययs combine with धातु and some with प्रातिपदिक and result in a new धातु.

(iv) कृत्-प्रत्ययs combine with धातु and result in a new प्रातिपदिक.

There is a special significance of सुप् and तिङ् since a पद is formed only in their presence.

5 इत्

5.1 Introduction

In our earlier discussion on माहेश्वरसूत्र, we have briefly used the idea of इत्. We saw that these सूत्रs had two types of वर्णs - a non इत्-वर्ण and इत्-वर्ण. We also noticed that the set that प्रत्याहारs denoted did not contain इत्-वर्णs as their elements. In other words, इत्-वर्णs were not part of the actual content (i.e., the वर्णs in the set) but were providing information on which वर्णs are to be included in that set. This kind of a tool, which is not content by itself but provides some information about content that it associates with, is necessary in व्याकरण for multiple purposes, to be discussed later. इत्-वर्णs act as such tools.

We can thus formally define इत्-वर्णs as particular types of वर्णs mentioned in व्याकरण that are not part of the content but are designed for effective and specific application of the content.

This idea of इत् is very similar to the concepts of tag, marker, or metadata we commonly employ in modern usage. We see tags or markers in computational languages, identity cards, food labels, traffic signals, and other everyday activities. A synonym of इत् in Saṃskṛta is "अनुबन्ध" and means "something tagged onto a primary element".

Most data in व्याकरण that carry an इत् fall into these categories:

(1) माहेश्वर-सूत्र
(2) धातु
(3) प्रत्यय
(4) विधि (prescription of grammatical transformations)

For example, डुकृञ् is a धातु in which only कृ is the content, while डु and ञ् are इत्. Similarly, क्त्वा is a प्रत्यय, in which क् is इत्, while त्वा is the actual content. We shall discuss the idea of विधि and इत् in those विधिs later.

An obvious question would be: How does anyone identify these इत्s? How do we know which part of a धातु or a प्रत्यय or any other व्याकरण element is the content and which part of it is इत्?

5.2 Identification of इत्

पाणिनि has provided rules for identifying इत् in his and later works.

There are four sets of compilations by पाणिनि related to व्याकरण that have been handed down from one generation to the next as an oral tradition - माहेश्वर-सूत्रs, अष्टाध्यायी-सूत्रs, गणपाठ and धातुपाठ. Two more later व्याकरण compositions are considered central to the Pāṇinian school - वार्तिक of कात्यायन (also known as वररुचि) and भाष्य of पतञ्जलि. These works are referred as उपदेशs, in these उपदेशs the following are defined to be इत्-वर्णs:

(1) उपदेशेऽजनुनासिक इत् (1-3-2) : The अच्-वर्णs (i.e., the स्वरs) that are pronounced as अनुनासिक-वर्णs.

For example, in सुँ, ओँहाक्, वदिँ, युजिँर् , समानकर्तृकेषु तुमुँन् (3-3-158), the अनुनासिक-वर्णs उँ, ओँ, इँ, इँ, उँ respectively, are इत्.

(2) हलन्त्यम् (1-3-3) : All हल्-वर्णs (i.e., the व्यञ्जनs) that are the last वर्णs in उपदेश are इत्.

For example, सुप्, तिप् , ओँहाक्, युजिँर् have प्, प्, क् and र् respectively as इत्.

(3) न विभक्तौ तुस्माः (1-3-4) : However, there is an exception to rule 2, mentioned above. When the वर्णs of तवर्ग, स् or म् are the last वर्णs in विभक्ति (सुप् and तिङ्), then they are not considered as इत्.

For example, स् and म् are not इत् in जस् , भ्याम्, आम्, भिस् and तस्.

(4) आदिर्ञिटुडवः (1-3-5) : ञि, टु or डु at the beginning is इत्. Such usage is found only in धातुपाठ.

For example, ञिमिदाँ, टुनदिँ, डुकृञ् have ञि, टु and डु respectively as इत्.

(5) षः प्रत्ययस्य (1-3-6) : ष् at the beginning of a प्रत्यय.

For example, ष्वुन् which is a प्रत्यय, has ष् as इत्.

(6) चुँटूँ (1-3-7) : वर्णs belonging to चवर्ग and टवर्ग at the beginning of प्रत्यय are इत्.

For example, in ट, ड, ण्यत् जस्, ञ्य, च्फञ् , the वर्णs ट्, ड्, ण्, ज्, ञ् and च् are इत्.

(7) लशक्वँतद्धिते (1-3-8) : ल्, श् and कवर्ग at the beginning of any प्रत्यय, which is not a तद्धित-प्रत्यय, is an इत्.

For example, ल्युट् , शि, शप्, क्त, क्तवतुँ, ग्स्नु, ङे, ङस् have ल्, श्, क् etc., as इत्.

पाणिनि provides another सूत्र at the end of this list - तस्य लोपः (1-3-9) - to specify that the इत्-वर्णs are to be ignored when looking at the content.

We shall revisit this idea of इत्-वर्णs when we look at their applications, on how they are used as meta-data in later chapters.

6 तिङन्त-पद

6.1 Introduction

In our discussion on प्रकृति-प्रत्यय-व्यवस्था, we saw that words are fundamental building blocks of a sentence and that a Saṃskṛta word has two components in it- प्रकृति and प्रत्यय. We also saw that प्रकृति is of two types - प्रातिपदिक and धातु; and that some types of प्रत्ययs are specific to प्रातिपदिकs and some to धातुs. Among those, we noted that सुप् is a set of प्रत्ययs applicable to प्रातिपदिकs and तिङ् is another set applicable to धातुs. These two sets - सुप् and तिङ् - have a unique role since technically a "पद" (Saṃskṛta "word") must necessarily have either of these to be called a "word" or a "पद". पाणिनि, in fact, defines पद as: "सुप्तिङन्तं पदम्" = पद is that which ends with either a सुप्-प्रत्यय or a तिङ्-प्रत्यय. Therefore, we have two kinds of पदs - सुबन्त-पदs and तिङन्त-पदs. (Figure 6.1)

In common parlance, the सुबन्त-पदs are understood as नामपदs, and तिङन्त-पदs as क्रियापदs. However, as we see later, this is an inaccurate mapping. Many सुबन्तपदs also refer to क्रिया, and hence are also क्रियापदs. Similarly, many तिङन्तपदs do refer to an entity in the क्रिया, and not

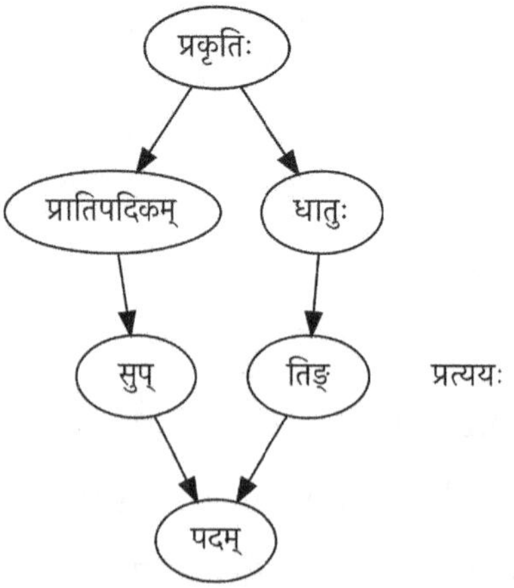

Figure 6.1: पद

just the क्रिया, and hence are also नामपदs. Therefore, this mapping is rather arbitrary, and it is better to understand them technically, as we discuss in the following sections.

6.2 तिङन्त-पद

पाणिनि has provided a set of eighteen प्रत्ययs in the सूत्रः तिप्-तस्-झि-सिप्-थस्-थ-मिप्-वस्-मस्-त-आताम्-झ-थास्-आथाम्-ध्वम्-इड्-वहि-महिङ् (3-4-78), which starts from तिप् and ends in महिङ्. Therefore, this set, taking the first and last वर्णs, is called "तिङ्". The first nine are called परस्मैपद-प्रत्ययs and the second nine are called आत्मनेपद-प्रत्ययs.

As we may recall, we have seen earlier that धातुs can be either परस्मैपदि-धातु, आत्मनेपदि-धातु or उभययपदि-धातु. These eighteen प्रत्ययs are applicable accordingly. That is, परस्मैपदि-धातुs take the परस्मैपद-प्रत्ययs (the first nine in the तिङ् set, Table 6.1), the आत्मनेपदि-धातुs take the आत्मनेपद-प्रत्ययs (the second nine in the तिङ् set, Table 6.2), and the उभयपदि-धातुs, as indicated by their very name, take both sets (all the eighteen प्रत्ययs).

This conjugation of धातु+तिङ् provides a usable word form in Saṃskṛta.

Each set of nine, refer to three वचनs and three पुरुषs, as depicted in Tables 6.1 and 6.2

Tables 6.3 and 6.4 provide examples of conjugation of धातु and तिङ्.

The concept of वचन and पुरुष is commonly seen in most languages. For example, the idea of grammatical numbers in English, as reflected in singular and plural forms, is the same as वचन in Saṃskṛta. On similar lines, the idea of "I/we" referring to the first person, "you" to the second person, and "he/she/it" to the third person, is the same idea of पुरुष in Saṃskṛta, albeit with minor differences.

Saṃskṛta, unlike modern English and current languages, classifies grammatical numbers into three - singular (एकवचन), dual (द्विवचन)

परस्मैपदप्रत्ययs			
वचन / पुरुष	एकवचन	द्विवचन	बहुवचन
प्रथमपुरुष	तिप्	तस्	झि
मध्यमपुरुष	सिप्	थस्	थ
उत्तमपुरुष	मिप्	वस्	मस्

Table 6.1: परस्मैपद-प्रत्ययs

आत्मनेपदप्रत्ययs			
वचन / पुरुष	एकवचन	द्विवचन	बहुवचन
प्रथमपुरुष	त	आताम्	झ
मध्यमपुरुष	थास्	आथाम्	ध्वम्
उत्तमपुरुष	इट्	वहि	महिङ्

Table 6.2: आत्मनेपद-प्रत्ययs

and plural (बहुवचन) - to indicate one, two, and three or more entities, respectively. For example, पठति in Table 6.3 refers to one person reading; पठतः refers to two persons reading; and पठन्ति refers to a group of people that has three or more persons reading.

वचन / पुरुष	एकवचन	द्विवचन	बहुवचन
प्रथमपुरुष	पठ्+तिप् → पठति	पठ्+तस् → पठतः	पठ्+झि → पठन्ति
मध्यमपुरुष	पठ्+सिप् → पठसि	पठ्+थस् → पठथः	पठ्+थ → पठथ
उत्तमपुरुष	पठ्+मिप् → पठामि	पठ्+वस् → पठावः	पठ्+मस् → पठामः

Table 6.3: परस्मैपदि-धातु (पठँ व्यक्तायां वाचि) + तिङ्

वचन / पुरुष	एकवचन	द्विवचन	बहुवचन
प्रथमपुरुष	वद्+त → वन्दते	वद्+आताम्→ वन्देते	वद्+झ→ वन्दन्ते
मध्यमपुरुष	वद्+थास् → वन्दसे	वद्+आथाम्→ वन्देथे	वद्+ध्वम्→ वन्दध्वे
उत्तमपुरुष	वद्+इट् → वन्दे	वद्+वहि→ वन्दावहे	वद् +महिङ् → वन्दामहे

Table 6.4: आत्मनेपदि-धातु (वदिँ अभिवादनस्तुत्योः) + तिङ्

Saṃskṛta categorises पुरुषs into three: प्रथमपुरुष, मध्यमपुरुष and उत्तमपुरुष. प्रथमपुरुष refers to "he/she/they/this/that/these" (all those that are considered the third person in English); मध्यमपुरुष refers to "you" (that is regarded as the second person in English); and उत्तमपुरुष refers to "I/we" (that is regarded as the first person in English). For example, पठति refers to someone other than me/you reading; पठसि refers to you reading; and पठामि refers to me reading.

It is to be noted that these तिङन्त-पदs in Saṃskṛta do not change their forms based on the लिङ्ग of the entity that they are referring.

For example, पठति is used for all लिङ्गs such as रामः पठति, रमा पठति or मित्रं पठति.

The eighteen तिङ्-प्रत्ययs are constant for all धातुs. However, the final form of the तिङन्त-पद varies based on four factors:

(1) The लकार (tense/mood form) that is intended to be conveyed.
(2) The गण to which a particular धातु belongs.
(3) The last and/or the penultimate वर्ण (called अन्त्यवर्ण and उपधावर्ण respectively) of the धातु.
(4) The group to which the धातु belongs: सेट्-धातु or अनिट्-धातु.

6.2.1 लकार

लकारs are a group of ten प्रत्ययs that provide the meaning of a tense (काल) or a modality (भावना)[1]. They are added to a धातु to provide that contextual meaning to the धातु. Let's see the meanings of all these ten लकार-प्रत्ययs below:

The ten लकारs are लट्, लिट्, लुट्, लृट्, लेट्, लोट्, लङ्, लिङ् (विधिलिङ् and आशीर्लिङ्), लुङ् and लृङ्. In these प्रत्ययs, ल् is the data while the अच्-वर्ण

[1]In English some of the tense forms are included as verb modifications (do-doing-did-done), and some are indicated with an additional word (is, was, will, etc.). Modalities are always indicated with a separate modal verb, such as can, may, ought, must, could, etc.

and ट्/ङ् are इत्. As we can see, six of these have ट् as the ending इत्-वर्ण and four have ङ् as their ending इत्-वर्ण.

Out of these, लट्, लिट्, लुट्, लृट्, लङ्, and लुङ् provide the meanings of different tenses; लोट्, लिङ् (विधिलिङ् and आशीर्लिङ्), and लृङ् provide the meanings of different moods; while लेट् is a special प्रत्यय used mainly in the Vedas and not in classical literature.

The Table 6.5 provides the meanings of the six लकारs indicating different tenses:

लकार	Meanings of different tenses provided by these लकारs	
लट् -	वर्तमाने	- Present
लिट् -	परोक्षभूते	- Past, that was not directly observed
लङ् -	अनद्यतनभूते	- Past beyond today
लुङ् -	भूते	- Past in general
लृट् -	भविष्यति	- Future in general
लुट् -	अनद्यतनभविष्यति	- Future beyond today

Table 6.5: लकारs having the meaning of tense

Table 6.6 provides the meanings of the four लकारs indicating the meanings of moods:[2]

लकार	Moods in which it is used
विधिलिङ्	प्रवर्तन, विधि, निमन्त्रण, आमन्त्रण, अधीष्ट, सम्प्रश्न, प्रार्थना
आशीर्लिङ्	आशीः
लोट्	प्रवर्तन, विधि, निमन्त्रण, आमन्त्रण, अधीष्ट, सम्प्रश्न, प्रार्थना, आशीः
लृङ्	To indicate that an effect did not materialise due to absence of the cause

Table 6.6: लकारs having meaning of Moods

(1) विधिलिङ् is primarily used for प्रवर्तन, that is to "suggest someone to act". There are many ways of this प्रवर्तन. It can be विधि (mandate/prescribe/motivate); निमन्त्रण (an invitation that has to be accepted); आमन्त्रण (an invitation that need not be accepted); अधीष्ट (respectful request); सम्प्रश्न (enquire) or a प्रार्थना (request).

(2) आशीर्लिङ् is used in the meaning of आशीः (wish including a blessing)

(3) लोट् can be seen as an alternative to लिङ् to mean प्रवर्तन, आशीः etc.

[2]There are some more specific instances where these लकारs are prescribed, details of which are beyond the scope of this book. Interested readers may refer to the original अष्टाध्यायी-सूत्रs.

(4) लृङ् is used argumentatively to indicate that an effect did not materialize because the cause was absent.

Putting the ideas of 9 तिङ्-प्रत्ययs and 10 लकारs together, we get 9x10=90 forms[3] for a given धातु in परस्मैपद and a similar 9x10=90 forms in आत्मनेपद. In the following sections, we provide a sample taking two examples - one परस्मैपदि-धातु and another आत्मनेपदि-धातु.

6.2.2 परस्मैपदि-धातु forms of भू सत्तायाम्

भवति	भवतः	भवन्ति
भवसि	भवथः	भवथ
भवामि	भवावः	भवामः

Table 6.7: लट्लकारः

बभूव	बभूवतुः	बभूवुः
बभूविथ	बभूवथुः	बभूव
बभूव	बभूविव	बभूविम

Table 6.8: लिट्लकारः

भविता	भवितारौ	भवितारः
भवितासि	भवितास्थः	भवितास्थ
भवितास्मि	भवितास्वः	भवितास्मः

Table 6.9: लुट्लकारः

भविष्यति	भविष्यतः	भविष्यन्ति
भविष्यसि	भविष्यथः	भविष्यथ
भविष्यामि	भविष्यावः	भविष्यामः

Table 6.10: लृट्लकारः

[3] We have not included लेट् here. However, since लिङ् is of two types, we still have 10 लकार for our discussions

भवतु , भवतात्	भवताम्	भवन्तु
भव , भवतात्	भवतम्	भवत
भवानि	भवाव	भवाम

Table 6.11: लोट्लकारः

अभवत्	अभवताम्	अभवन्
अभवः	अभवतम्	अभवत
अभवम्	अभवाव	अभवाम

Table 6.12: लङ्लकारः

भवेत्	भवेताम्	भवेयुः
भवेः	भवेतम्	भवेत
भवेयम्	भवेव	भवेम

Table 6.13: विधिलिङ्लकारः

भूयात्	भूयास्ताम्	भूयासुः
भूयाः	भूयास्तम्	भूयास्त
भूयासम्	भूयास्व	भूयास्म

Table 6.14: आशीर्लिङ्लकारः

अभूत्	अभूताम्	अभूवन्
अभूः	अभूतम्	अभूत
अभूवम्	अभूव	अभूम

Table 6.15: लुङ्लकारः

अभविष्यत्	अभविष्यताम्	अभविष्यन्
अभविष्यः	अभविष्यतम्	अभविष्यत
अभविष्यम्	अभविष्याव	अभविष्याम

Table 6.16: लृङ्लकारः

6.2.3 आत्मनेपदि-धातु forms of वदिँ अभिवादनस्तुत्योः

वन्दते	वन्देते	वन्दन्ते
वन्दसे	वन्देथे	वन्दध्वे
वन्दे	वन्दावहे	वन्दामहे

Table 6.17: लट्लकारः

ववन्दे	ववन्दाते	ववन्दिरे
ववन्दिषे	ववन्दाथे	ववन्दिध्वे
ववन्दे	ववन्दिवहे	ववन्दिमहे

Table 6.18: लिट्लकारः

वन्दिता	वन्दितारौ	वन्दितारः
वन्दितासे	वन्दितासाथे	वन्दिताध्वे
वन्दिताहे	वन्दितास्वहे	वन्दितास्महे

Table 6.19: लुट्लकारः

वन्दिष्यते	वन्दिष्येते	वन्दिष्यन्ते
वन्दिष्यसे	वन्दिष्येथे	वन्दिष्यध्वे
वन्दिष्ये	वन्दिष्यावहे	वन्दिष्यामहे

Table 6.20: लृट्लकारः

वन्दताम्	वन्देताम्	वन्दन्ताम्
वन्दस्व	वन्देथाम्	वन्दध्वम्
वन्दै	वन्दावहै	वन्दामहै

Table 6.21: लोट्लकारः

अवन्दत	अवन्देताम्	अवन्दन्त
अवन्दथाः	अवन्देथाम्	अवन्दध्वम्
अवन्दे	अवन्दावहि	अवन्दामहि

Table 6.22: लङ्लकारः

वन्देत	वन्देयाताम्	वन्देरन्
वन्देथाः	वन्देयाथाम्	वन्देध्वम्
वन्देय	वन्देवहि	वन्देमहि

Table 6.23: विधिलिङ्लकारः

वन्दिषीष्ट	वन्दिषीयास्ताम्	वन्दिषीरन्
वन्दिषीष्ठाः	वन्दिषीयास्थाम्	वन्दिषीध्वम्
वन्दिषीय	वन्दिषीवहि	वन्दिषीमहि

Table 6.24: आशीर्लिङ्लकारः

अवन्दिष्ट	अवन्दिषाताम्	अवन्दिषत
अवन्दिष्ठाः	अवन्दिषाथाम्	अवन्दिध्वम्
अवन्दिषि	अवन्दिष्वहि	अवन्दिष्महि

Table 6.25: लुङ्लकारः

अवन्दिष्यत	अवन्दिष्येताम्	अवन्दिष्यन्त
अवन्दिष्यथाः	अवन्दिष्येथाम्	अवन्दिष्यध्वम्
अवन्दिष्ये	अवन्दिष्यावहि	अवन्दिष्यामहि

Table 6.26: लृङ्लकारः

6.3 गणs

In the previous section, we saw the first parameter - लकार - that affects the तिङ् forms. We shall now see the second parameter that affects how तिङ् forms are created. This is the गण to which a धातु belongs.

We had seen in our discussion on धातुs in the chapter on प्रकृति-प्रत्यय-व्यवस्था, that the धातुs are categorized into ten groups called गणs. पाणिनि has listed धातुs under each गण, and these गणs are named after the first धातु in the respective गणs. For example, the first धातु in the first गण is "भू सत्तायाम्". Therefore the first गण is called भ्वादि-गण, literally "a group of धातुs, starting from भू". Similarly, the other गणs are called अदादि, जुहोत्यादि etc.

This classification has nothing to do with the meanings of these धातुs but is only based on how these धातुs get transformed in the final तिङन्त form.

Each गण has been mapped with a प्रत्यय called विकरण-प्रत्यय. These प्रत्ययs are to be inserted between धातु and तिङ्-प्रत्यय, thus affecting the final तिङन्त form. The विकरण-प्रत्ययs for each of these ten गणs are mentioned in Table 6.27. It is to be noted that even these विकरण-प्रत्ययs have no meaning attached to them but have a role only in transformations. We provide the प्रथम-पुरुष-एकवचन for one धातु of each गण as an example. However, the examples are given for only four लकारs viz., लट्, लोट्, लङ्, and विधिलिङ्, because the विकरण-प्रत्ययs affect only these forms. All other लकारs have a तिङन्त form that is independent of the गण (as seen in Table 6.29 and Table 6.31). Those four लकारs, which vary in their transformation because of the विकरण-प्रत्ययs are called सार्वधातुक-लकारs and the others are called आर्धधातुक-लकारs.

Tables 6.28 and 6.29 provide examples for परस्मैपदि-धातु. Table 6.30 and Table 6.31 provide examples for आत्मनेपदि-धातु.

गण	विकरण-प्रत्यय	धातु - लट्-लकार-रूपम्
भ्वादि	शप्	भू सत्तायाम् - भवति
अदादि	लुक्	अदँ भक्षणे - अत्ति
जुहोत्यादि	श्लु	हु दानादनयोः - जुहोति
दिवादि	श्यन्	दिवुँ क्रीडाविजिगीषा..... - दीव्यति
स्वादि	श्नु	षुञ् अभिषवे- सुनोति
तुदादि	श	तुदँ व्यथने - तुदति
रुधादि	श्नम्	रुधिँर् आवरणे - रुणद्धि
तनादि	उ	तनुँ विस्तारे - तनोति
क्र्यादि	श्ना	डु क्रीञ् करणे - क्रीणाति
चुरादि	णिच्	चुरँ स्तेये - चोरयति

Table 6.27: विकरण-प्रत्यय of 10 गणs

गण	वि-प्र	धातु	लट्	लोट्	लङ्	विधिलिङ्
भ्वादि	शप्	भू सत्तायाम्	भवति	भवतु	अभवत्	भवेत्
अदादि	लुक्	अदँ भक्षणे	अत्ति	अत्तु	आदत्	अद्यात्
जुहोत्यादि	श्लु	हु दानादनयोः	जुहोति	जुहोतु	अजुहोत्	जुहुयात्
दिवादि	श्यन्	दिवुँ क्रीडा...गतिषु	दीव्यति	दीव्यतु	अदिव्यत्	दीव्येत्
स्वादि	श्नु	षुञ् अभिषवे	सुनोति	सुनोतु	असुनोत्	सुनुयात्
तुदादि	श	तुदँ व्यथने	तुदति	तुदतु ,	अतुदत्	तुदेत्
रुधादि	श्नम्	रुधिँर् आवरणे	रुणद्धि	रुणद्धु	अरुणत्	रुन्ध्यात्
तनादि	उ	तनुँ विस्तारे	तनोति	तनोतु	अतनोत्	तनुयात्
क्र्यादि	श्ना	डुक्रीञ् द्रव्यविनिमये	क्रीणाति	क्रीणातु	अक्रीणात्	क्रीणीयात्
चुरादि	णिच्	चुरँ स्तेये	चोरयति	चोरयतु	अचोरयत्	चोरयेत्

Table 6.28: सार्वधातुक-लकारs of परस्मैपदि-धातुs in 10 गणs

गण	वि.प्र	धातु	लिट्	लुट्	लृट्	आशीर्लिङ्	लुङ्	लृङ्
भ्वादि	शप्	भू	बभूव	भविता	भविष्यति	भूयात्	अभूत्	अभविष्यत्
अदादि	लुक्	अदँ	जघास	अत्ता	अत्स्यति	अद्यात	अघसत्	आत्स्यत्
जुहोत्यादि	श्लु	हु	जुहाव	होता	होष्यति	हूयात्	अहौषीत्	अहोष्यत्
दिवादि	श्यन्	दिवुँ	दिदेव	देविता	देविष्यति	दीव्यात्	अदेवीत्	अदेविष्यत्
स्वादि	श्नु	षुञ्	सुषाव	सोता	सोष्यति	सूयात्	असौषीत्	असोष्यत्
तुदादि	श	तुदँ	तुतोद	तोत्ता	तोत्स्यति	तुद्यात्	अतौत्सीत्	अतोत्स्यत्
रुधादि	श्नम्	रुधिँर्	रुरोध	रोद्धा	रोत्स्यति	रुध्यात्	अरुधत्	अरोत्स्यत्
तनादि	उ	तनुँ	ततान	तनिता	तनिष्यति	तन्यात्	अतनीत्,	अतनिष्यत्

गण	वि.प्र	धातु	लिट्	लुट्	लृट्	आशीर्लिङ्	लुङ्	लृङ्
क्र्यादि	श्ना	डुक्रीञ्	चिक्राय	क्रेता	क्रेष्यति	क्रीयात्	अक्रैषीत्	अक्रेष्यत्
चुरादि	णिच्	चुरँ	चोरयामास	चोरयिता	चोरयिष्यति	चोर्यात्	अचूचुरत्	अचोरयिष्यत्

Table 6.29: आर्धधातुक-लकारs of परस्मैपदि-धातुs in 10 गणs

गण	वि.प्र	धातु	लट्	लोट्	लङ्	विधिलिङ्
भ्वादि	शप्	ईक्षँ दर्शने	ईक्षते	ईक्षताम्	ऐक्षत	ईक्षेत
अदादि	लुक्	आसँ उपवेशने	आस्ते	आस्ताम्	आस्त	आसीत
जुहोत्यादि	श्लु	डुदाञ् दाने	दत्ते	दत्ताम्	अदत्त	ददीत
दिवादि	श्यन्	ईँशुचिँर् पूतीभावे	शुच्यते	शुच्यताम्	अशुच्यत	शुच्येत
स्वादि	श्नु	षुञ् अभिषवे	सुनुते	सुनुताम्	असुनुत	सुन्वीत
तुदादि	श	मुचॢँ मोक्षणे	मुञ्चते	मुञ्चताम्	अमुञ्चत	मुञ्चेत
रुधादि	श्नम्	छिदिँर् द्वैधीकरणे	छिन्ते	छिन्ताम्	अच्छिन्त,	छिन्दीत
तनादि	उ	डु कृञ् करणे	कुरुते	कुरुताम्	अकुरुत	कुर्वीत
क्र्यादि	श्ना	ज्ञा अवबोधने	जानीते	जानीताम्	अजानीत	जानीत
चुरादि	णिच्	गण सङ्ख्याने	गणयते	गणयताम्	अगणयत	गणयेत

Table 6.30: सार्वधातुक-लकारs of आत्मनेपदि-धातुs in 10 गणs

गण	वि.प्र	धातु	लिट्	लुट्	लृट्	आशीर्लिङ्	लुङ्	लृङ्
भ्वादि	शप्	ईक्षँ	ईक्षाञ्चक्रे	ईक्षिता	ईक्षिष्यते	ईक्षिषीष्ट	ऐक्षिष्ट	ऐक्षिष्यत
अदादि	लुक्	आसँ	आसाञ्चक्रे	आसिता	आसिष्यते	आसिषीष्ट	आसिष्ट	आसिष्यत
जुहोत्यादि	श्लु	डुदाञ्	ददे	दाता	दास्यते	दासीष्ट	अदित	अदास्यत
दिवादि	श्यन्	ईँशुचिँर्	शुशुचे	शोचिता	शोचिष्यते	शोचिषीष्ट	अशोचिष्ट	अशोचिष्यत
स्वादि	श्नु	षुञ्	सुषुवे	सोता	सोष्यते	सोषीष्ट	असोष्ट	असोष्यत
तुदादि	श	मुचॢँ	मुमुचे	मोक्ता	मोक्ष्यते	मुक्षीष्ट	अमुक्त	अमोक्ष्यत
रुधादि	श्नम्	छिदिँर्	चिच्छिदे	छेत्ता	छेत्स्यते	छित्सीष्ट	अच्छित्त	अछेत्स्यत
तनादि	उ	डुकृञ्	चक्रे	कर्ता	करिष्यते	कृषीष्ट	अकृत	अकरिष्यत
क्र्यादि	श्ना	ज्ञा	जज्ञे	ज्ञाता	ज्ञास्यते	ज्ञासीष्ट	अज्ञास्त	अज्ञास्यत
चुरादि	णिच्	गण	गणयाञ्चक्रे	गणयिता	गणयिष्यते	गणयिषीष्ट	अजगणत	अगणयिष्यत

Table 6.31: आर्धधातुक-लकारs of आत्मनेपदि-धातुs in 10 गणs

6.4 तिङर्थ

In the previous we have seen the following:

(1) धातुs refer to क्रियाs. धातुs can be used in a meaningful sentence only when they are transformed into तिङन्त-पदs.

(2) There are eighteen तिङ्-प्रत्ययs that are applicable to धातुs. These प्रत्ययs carry two bits of information - वचन and पुरुष.

(3) The धातु+तिङ् combination transforms into different forms based on लकार, गण etc. Of these, लकार has a meaning, while others don't.

So, in summary, we have seen that a तिङन्त-पद carries four pieces of information: क्रिया (due to धातु); काल/भावना (due to लकार); and पुरुष and वचन (due to तिङ्).

Here, we can observe that these bits of information still need to be completed. पुरुष and वचन are always attributes of entities. Therefore, by default, most of the तिङन्त-पदs are taken to be referring to the कर्तृ in the क्रिया (indicated by the धातु).[4] In other words, when the कर्तृ is "he/she/they etc." then प्रथम-पुरुष forms should be used; when the कर्तृ is "you", then मध्यम-पुरुष forms should be used; and when the कर्तृ is "I/we", then we use उत्तम-पुरुष forms.

6.5 कर्मणि forms

We saw in the above section that most of the तिङन्त-पदs refer to कर्तृ by default. This principle applies to all लकारs of परस्मै-पदि-धातुs and सार्वधातुक-लकारs of आत्मने-पदि-धातुs. For others, it may refer to कर्तृ or कर्म or

[4]More specifically, all परस्मै-पद-प्रत्ययs in all लकारs refer to कर्तृs by default. All आत्मने-पद-प्रत्ययs too refer to the करतृs by default, in the four सार्वधातुक-लकारs. In the remaining 6 लकारs of आत्मने-पदि-धातुs , the तिङन्त-पद may refer to either कर्तृ or कर्म or भाव, contextually. We shall see more details a little later.

भाव contextually. However, with some additional transformations, even the लकारs of परस्मै-पदि-धातुs and सार्वधातुक-लकारs of आत्मने-पदि-धातुs may refer to कर्म. In such cases, the पुरुष and वचन are also attributes of कर्म.

For example, "पठति" is a प्रथम-पुरुष एक-वचन form of पठ् धातु (which is a परस्मैपदि-धातु) in लट् लकार. So, it refers to someone reading. It is in the present tense, referring to one person, and that person is a third person. Similarly, "पठतः" is a dual form, and it means that there are two कर्तृs. And, "पठन्ति" is a plural form, and it means that there are three or more कर्तृs.

Now, let's compare these with three other forms - पठ्यते, पठ्येते and पठ्यन्ते. Here all the other parameters are kept constant while adding a new transformational प्रत्यय called यक्-प्रत्यय. Now, it refers to the कर्म and not the कर्तृ. Hence, पठ्यते is a reference not to the person reading but something that is being read, say, a book. पठ्येते refers to two books, and पठ्यन्ते to three or more.

पठ्यते	पठ्येते	पठ्यन्ते
पठ्यसे	पठ्येथे	पठ्यध्वे
पठ्ये	पठ्यावहे	पठ्यामहे

Table 6.32: कर्मणि लट्-लकार

We can observe in Table 6.32 that: The final form of the तिङन्त-पद in कर्मणि is the form of an आत्मनेपदि-धातु. In fact, that is the rule. All कर्मणि forms always take the आत्मनेपद-प्रत्ययs. Additionally, the four सार्वधातुक-लकारs, viz, लट्, लोट्, लङ् and विधिलिङ् are transformed with the help of यक्-प्रत्यय.[5]

Therefore in summary,

(1) परस्मैपद-सार्वधातुक-लकारs take आत्मनेपदप्रत्ययs and यक्-प्रत्यय to refer to कर्म.

(2) परस्मैपद-आर्धधातुक-लकारs take आत्मनेपदप्रत्ययs to refer to कर्म.[6]

(3) आत्मनेपद-सार्वधातुक-लकारs take यक्-प्रत्यय to refer to कर्म.

(4) आत्मनेपद-आर्धधातुक-लकारs refer to either कर्तृ or कर्म.[7]

Tables 6.33, 6.34, 6.35, and 6.36 provide examples for each of the लकारs for these four cases, respectively:

6.6 भावे forms

One obvious question at this stage would be: What would a कर्मणि transformation of the तिङन्त-पद from an अकर्मक-धातु refer to? There is

[5]Of the remaining, the प्रथमपुरुष-एकवचन of लुङ् is transformed using चिण्-प्रत्यय.

[6]With the exception of प्रथमपुरुष-एकवचन of लुङ् which needs an additional चिण्-प्रत्यय.

[7]With the exception of प्रथमपुरुष-एकवचन of लुङ् which needs an additional चिण्-प्रत्यय if it is referring to कर्म

गण	विकरण	धातु	लट्	लोट्	लङ्	विधिलिङ्
भ्वादि	शप्	भू सत्तायाम्	भूयते	भूयताम्	अभूयत	भूयेत
अदादि	लुक्	अदँ भक्षणे	अद्यते	अद्यताम्	आद्यत	अद्येत
जुहोत्यादि	श्लु	हु दानादनयोः	हूयते	हूयताम्	अहूयत	हूयेत
दिवादि	श्यन्	दिवुँ क्रीडा...गतिषु	दीव्यते	दीव्यताम्	अदीव्यत	दीव्येत
स्वादि	श्नु	षुञ् अभिषवे	सूयते	सूयताम्	असूयत	सूयेत
तुदादि	श	तुदँ व्यथने	तुद्यते	तुद्यताम्	अतुद्यत	तुद्येत
रुधादि	श्नम्	रुधिँर् आवरणे	रुध्यते	रुध्यताम्	अरुध्यत	रुध्येत
तनादि	उ	तनुँ विस्तारे	तन्यते, तायते	तन्यताम्, तायताम्	अतन्यत	तन्येत, तायेत
क्र्यादि	श्ना	डुक्रीञ् द्रव्यविनिमये	क्रीयते	क्रीयताम्	अक्रीयत	क्रीयेत
चुरादि	णिच्	चुरँ स्तेये	चोर्यते	चोर्यताम्	अचूरोयत	चोर्येत

Table 6.33: कर्मणि - परस्मैपद-सावर्धातकु -लकारs

गण	विकरण	धातु	लिट्	लुट्	लृट्	आशीर्लिङ्	लुङ्	लृङ्
भ्वादि	शप्	भू	बभूवे	भविता	भविष्यते	भविषीष्ट	अभावि	अभविष्यत
अदादि	लुक्	अदँ	जक्षे, आदे	अत्ता	अत्स्यते	अत्सीष्ट	अघासि	आत्स्यत
जुहोत्यादि	श्लु	हु	जुहुवे	होता	होष्यते	हाषीष्ट	अहावि	अहाविष्यत
दिवादि	श्यन्	दिवुँ	दिदिवे	देविता	देविष्यते	देविषीष्ट	अदेवि	अदेविष्यत
स्वादि	श्नु	षुञ्	सुषुवे	सोता	सोष्यते	सोषीष्ट	असावि	असोष्यत
तुदादि	श	तुदँ	तुतुदे	तोत्ता	तोत्स्यते	तुत्सीष्ट	अतोदि	अतोत्स्यत
रुधादि	श्नम्	रुधिँर्	रुरुधे	रोद्धा	रोत्स्यते	रुत्सीष्ट	अरोधि	अरोत्स्यत
तनादि	उ	तनुँ	तेने	तनिता	तनिष्यते	तनिषीष्ट	अतानि	अतनिष्यत
क्र्यादि	श्ना	डुक्रीञ्	चिक्रीये	क्रेता	क् क्रेष्यते	क्रेषीष्ट	अक्रायि	अक्रेष्यत
चुरादि	णिच्	चुरँ	चुचूरे	चोरिता	चोरिष्यते	चोरिषीष्ट	अचोरि	अचोरिष्यत

Table 6.34: कर्मणि - परस्मैपद-आर्धधातुक-लकारs

no कर्म in such a क्रिया. In those circumstances, पाणिनि says that the reference is made to the very क्रिया. क्रिया is also called भाव.

For example, the very act of "reading" is the भाव of the पठ् धातु; the act of "praising" is the भाव of the वदिँ धातु; and the act of standing is

गण	विकरण	धातु	लट्	लोट्	लङ्	विधिलिङ्
भ्वादि	शप्	ईक्षँ दर्शने	ईक्ष्यते	ईक्ष्यताम्	ऐक्ष्यत	ईक्ष्येत
अदादि	लुक्	आसँ उपवेशने	आस्यते	आस्यताम्	आस्यत	आस्येत
जुहोत्यादि	श्लु	डुदाञ् दाने	दीयते	दीयताम्	अदीयत	दीयेत
दिवादि	श्यन्	ईँशुचिँर् पूतीभावे	शुच्यते	शुच्यताम्	अशुच्यत	शुच्येत
स्वादि	श्नु	षुञ् अभिषवे	सूयते	सूयताम्	असूयत	सूयेत
तुदादि	श	मुचॢँ मोक्षणे	मुच्यते	मुच्यताम्	अमुच्यत	मुच्येत
रुधादि	श्नम्	छिदिँर् द्वैधीकरणे	छिद्यते	छिद्यताम्	अच्छिद्यत	छिद्येत
तनादि	उ	डु कृञ् करणे	क्रियते	क्रियताम्	अक्रियत	क्रियेत
क्र्यादि	श्ना	ज्ञा अवबोधने	ज्ञायते	ज्ञायताम्	अज्ञायत	ज्ञायेत
चुरादि	णिच्	गण सङ्ख्याने	गण्यते	गण्यताम्	अगण्यत	गण्येत

Table 6.35: कर्मणि - आत्मनेपद-सार्वधातुक-लकारs

गण	विकरण	धातु	लिट्	लुट्	लृट्	आशीर्लिङ्	लुङ्	लृङ्
भ्वादि	शप्	ईक्षँ	ईक्षाञ्चक्रे	ईक्षिता	ईक्षिष्यते	ईक्षिषीष्ट	ऐक्षि	ऐक्षिष्यत
अदादि	लुक्	आसँ	आसाञ्चक्रे	आसिता	आसिष्यते	आसिषीष्ट	आसि	आसिष्यत
जुहोत्यादि	श्लु	डुदाञ्	ददे	दाता	दास्यते	दासीष्ट	अदीयि	अदास्यत
दिवादि	श्यन्	ईँशुचिँर्	शुशुचे	शोचिता	शोचिष्यते	शोचिषीष्ट	अशोचि	अशोचिष्यत
स्वादि	श्नु	षुञ्	सुषुवे	सोता	सोष्यते	सोषीष्ट	असावि	असोष्यत
तुदादि	श	मुचॢँ	मुमुचे	मोक्ता	मोक्ष्यते	मुक्षीष्ट	अमोचि	अमोक्ष्यत
रुधादि	श्नम्	छिदिँर्	चिच्छिदे	छेत्ता	छेत्स्यते	छित्सीष्ट	अच्छेदि	अछेत्स्यत
तनादि	उ	डुकृञ्	चक्रे	कर्ता	करिष्यते	कृषीष्ट	अकारि	अकरिष्यत
क्र्यादि	श्ना	ज्ञा	जज्ञे	ज्ञाता	ज्ञास्यते	ज्ञासीष्ट	अज्ञायि	अज्ञास्यत
चुरादि	णिच्	गण	गणयामास	गणयिता	गणयिष्यते	गणयिषीष्ट	अगणि	अगणयिष्यत

Table 6.36: कर्मणि - आत्मनेपद-आर्धधातुक-लकारs

the भाव of the ष्ठा-धातु. As we know, the first two are सकर्मक, and the third is अकर्मक. For that reason, when यक् is applied to the first two, the transformed तिङन्त-पद refers to कर्म. If applied to the third, the transformed तिङन्त-पद refers to भाव (that is, the क्रिया).

Let's take "ष्ठा गतिनिवृत्तौ" as the धातु. It is a परस्मैपदि-धातु. Its कर्तरि forms in लट्-प्रथमपुरुष would be तिष्ठति, तिष्ठतः, तिष्ठन्ति. These forms refer to singular, dual and plural कर्तृs. For example, बालः तिष्ठति, बालौ तिष्ठतः and बालाः तिष्ठन्ति.

Now, if we apply the transformational यक्-प्रत्यय, it refers to भाव/क्रिया. By convention, it is always एक-वचन and प्रथम-पुरुष. So, we get the form स्थीयते. This will be applicable to all numbers. That is, बालेन स्थीयते, बालाभ्यां स्थीयते and बालैः स्थीयते. Similarly, it is applicable to all persons - बालेन स्थीयते, त्वया स्थीयते and मया स्थीयते.

Also, similar to the कर्मणि forms, भावे forms have आत्मनेपद-प्रत्ययs only. All the rules summarised in the above section for कर्मणि transformations/references apply to भावे forms also. The only differentiator is the सकर्मक-अकर्मक status of the धातु. If it is सकर्मक it refers to कर्म, and if अकर्मक it refers to भाव.

6.7 उभयपदि-धातुs

We have seen that the प्रत्ययs applied till now are of two types. One has purely a transformational function, and the other refers to meaning. While विकरणप्रत्ययs are only for transformation, लकारs, and तिङ्-प्रत्ययs, have meanings associated with them. Even among the तिङ्-प्रत्ययs, the same meaning (i.e., वचन, पुरुष and कर्तृ/कर्म/भाव) is mapped to two प्रत्ययs - one is called परस्मैपद-तिङ्प्रत्यय and the other आत्मनेपद-तिङ्प्रत्यय.

We have also seen that for परस्मैपदि-धातुs, we use परस्मैपद-तिङ्प्रत्ययs, and for आत्मनेपदि-धातुs, we use आत्मनेपद-तिङ्प्रत्ययs. However, there are some धातुs that are उभय-पदि and can hence take either परस्मैपद-प्रत्ययs or आत्मनेपद-प्रत्ययs. Which one should we choose in those circumstances?

पाणिनि suggests that this choice is dependent on the beneficiary of the क्रिया. If the कर्तृ is the beneficiary, then आत्मनेपद-तिङ्प्रत्ययs are to be used. If anyone other than कर्तृ is the beneficiary, then परस्मैपद-तिङ्प्रत्ययs forms are to be used.

To summarize the discussion of this Chapter, we need to identify the following in any तिङन्त-पद:

(1) The धातु (and it's meaning)
(2) The लकार (and it's meaning)
(3) The तिङ् form - पुरुष, वचन and आत्मनेपद/परस्मैपद.
(4) The entity being referred - कर्तृ/कर्म/भाव

7 सुबन्त-पद

7.1 Introduction

As we have seen multiple times, there are only two sets of प्रत्ययs that can make a पद - तिङ्-प्रत्ययs and सुप्-प्रत्ययs. तिङ् is applicable to धातु and सुप् to प्रातिपदिकs. पाणिनि has defined 21 सुप्-प्रत्ययs in the सूत्रः स्वौजसमौट्छष्टाभ्याम्भिस्ङेभ्याम्भ्यस्ङसिभ्याम्भ्यस्ङसोसाम्ङ्योस्सुप् (4-1-2). They refer to three वचनs of seven विभक्तिs as depicted in Table 7.1 . The वचन refers to the grammatical number of the प्रातिपदिक. In this chapter, विभक्तिs are only named as प्रथमा, द्वितीया, etc. The meanings of those विभक्तिs shall be discussed in Chapter-11.

विभक्ति \ वचन	एकवचन	द्विवचन	बहुवचन
प्रथमा	सुँ	औ	जस्
द्वितीया	अम्	औट्	शस्
तृतीया	टा	भ्याम्	भिस्
चतुर्थी	ङे	भ्याम्	भ्यस्
पञ्चमी	ङसिँ	भ्याम्	भ्यस्
षष्ठी	ङस्	ओस्	आम्
सप्तमी	ङि	ओस्	सुप्

Table 7.1: सुप्-प्रत्ययs

These 21 प्रत्ययs (Table 7.1) are constant for all प्रातिपदिकs. However, the final form of सुबन्त-पद varies generally based on three factors:

(1) The last वर्ण of the प्रातिपदिक.
(2) The लिङ्ग of the प्रातिपदिक.
(3) Whether the प्रातिपदिक is a सर्वनाम[1] or not.

In some cases, if the प्रातिपदिक is a derived प्रातिपदिक, [2] then a fourth factor - the component प्रत्यय that is responsible for the new प्रातिपदिक - also plays a role in shaping the final form of सुबन्त-पद. For example, even though the two प्रातिपदिकs मरुत् and गच्छत् have the same last वर्ण, their declensions vary because गच्छत् is derived from शतृँ, whereas मरुत् is not.

Table 7.2 provides 21 forms of the प्रातिपदिक राम, obtained when the सुँप्-प्रत्ययs are added to it.

[1] सर्वनामs are a special type of प्रातिपदिकs. The term सर्वनाम means "a name applicable to all". In other words, it is a प्रातिपदिक that has the potential to refer to all entities with a specific property, but the context defines which distinct entity it is referring to. In that sense, it is very similar to the idea of pronouns in English. For example, : तद् (that/he/she), इदम् (this), किम् (which/who). However, some words are not understood as pronouns in English, such as पूर्व (= east), but are considered सर्वनाम in संस्कृत. The term सर्वनाम is defined and detailed in अष्टाध्यायी-सूत्रs 1.1.27 to 1.1.36.

[2] As discussed in the chapter on प्रकृति-प्रत्यय-व्यवस्था, प्रकृतिs when appended with some types of प्रत्ययs, provide a new प्रातिपदिक. We are referring to such प्रातिपदिकs as derived प्रातिपदिकs.

विभक्ति \ वचन	एकवचन	द्विवचन	बहुवचन
प्रथमा	रामः	रामौ	रामाः
द्वितीया	रामम्	रामौ	रामान्
तृतीया	रामेण	रामाभ्याम्	रामैः
चतुर्थी	रामाय	रामाभ्याम्	रामेभ्यः
पञ्चमी	रामात् / रामाद्	रामाभ्याम्	रामेभ्यः
षष्ठी	रामस्य	रामयोः	रामाणाम्
सप्तमी	रामे	रामयोः	रामेषु
सम्बोधन-प्रथमा	हे राम	हे रामौ	हे रामाः

Table 7.2: सुप्-प्रत्ययs

Memorizing the declensions of different प्रातिपदिकs[3] will be helpful for later applications, such as analyzing a word form, identifying the information embedded in it, understanding a Saṃskṛta text etc.

[3]The declensions can be found online using the link mentioned on the last page of the book.

8 अव्यय and उपसर्ग

8.1 अव्यय

Let's take a very simple sentence and analyze its word forms (and not the meanings), रामः कृष्णः च पठतः ।

Here we can observe रामः and कृष्णः as सुबन्त forms. They are प्रथमाविभक्ति-एकवचन forms of the two प्रातिपदिकs - राम and कृष्ण. We can also observe that पठतः is the तिङन्त form of the पठ् धातु. However, to which category does "च" belong?

We do know that a पद is legitimate only when it has either तिङ् or सुप्. Apparently, "च" doesn't seem to have either of them. But, the पद "च" is ubiquitously used and must be legitimate. So, where and how do we locate and understand words such as च, तु, अपि, एव, etc.?

These words are called अव्ययs. Their fundamental nature is captured in this term 'अव्यय'. It means 'that which doesn't change'. In other words, these words don't change under any circumstance. There may be a लिङ्ग, विभक्ति or वचन associated with them. But their form remains the same in all those circumstances.

This idea is captured in a popular verse:

सदृशं त्रिषु लिङ्गेषु सर्वासु च विभक्तिषु ।
वचनेषु च सर्वेषु यन्न व्येति तदव्ययम् ॥

To accommodate those words, पाणिनि has called अव्ययs a particular type of सुबन्तपद्s where सुप् is not visible. They thus get the legitimacy of a पद् while retaining their nature of "non-transformation".

There are a few सूत्रs that specify the अव्ययs. In those सूत्रs we can find two sets of अव्ययs specified:

(1) The set where अव्ययs are specifically listed.
(2) The set where a few attributes are specified. If those attributes are found, then they are to be deemed as अव्ययs.

We shall see both these sets in more detail below.

8.1.1 अव्ययs that are specifically listed

This first set is defined primarily by one सूत्र (1-1-37) and supplemented by a set of 42 सूत्रs (1-4-56 to 1-4-97).

The primary सूत्र - स्वरादिनिपातमव्ययम् - defines that any word that satisfies either of the two criteria mentioned below is an अव्यय:

(1) It is listed in the group starting from स्वर्
(2) It is labeled निपात.

The set of 42 सूत्रs is concerned with this second criterion. They specify the निपातs. In fact the first सूत्र i.e., प्राग्रीश्वरान्निपाताः (1-4-56) is a definitional सूत्र. It says that all those that are mentioned from here on up to (and including) अधिरीश्वरे (1-4-97) are to be called निपातs. So, the 41 subsequent सूत्रs list those words and specify some unique names for some subsets. Of these, two important सूत्रs, चादयोऽसत्त्वे (1-4-57) and प्रादयः (1-4-58), list the majority of the निपातs.

चादयोऽसत्त्वे mentions a गण (a group) starting from च. That गण is available in पाणिनीय-गणपाठ.[1] When these words do not refer to some entity in the physical world, they come under the category of निपातs. Examples include च, अपि, अनु, पशु (when not referring to an animal), and वा.

प्रादयः mentions another गण from गणपाठ starting from प्र. This is a short list of 22 words: प्र परा अप सम् अनु अव निस् निर् दुस् दुर् वि आङ् नि अधि अपि अति सु उत् अभि प्रति परि उप.

All words in this गण are also in the category of निपातs.

[1]These resources can be found online using the link mentioned on the last page of the book.

8.1.2 अव्ययs whose attributes are specified

The second set of अव्ययs is defined in four सूत्रs from 1-1-38 to 1-1-41. The popular ones defined in those four सूत्रs can be summarised as below:

(1) All those तद्धितान्त-पदs formed by the प्रत्ययs such as त्रल्, तसिँल्,तसिँ, शस्, चित्, चन.
Examples: यत्र, तत्र, यतः, ततः, बहुशः, कश्चित्, कुतश्चन, etc.

(2) All those कृदन्त-पदs formed by क्त्वा-प्रत्यय or प्रत्ययs ending with म् such as णमुल्, तुमुन्[2] etc.
Examples: कृत्वा, गत्वा, प्रकृत्य, आगम्य, स्मारं स्मारम्, पायं पायम्, गन्तुम्, कर्तुम्, वक्तुम् etc.,

(3) All those समस्तपदs formed by अव्ययीभाव-समास.[3]
Examples: यथाशक्ति, आसेतु, अनुरूपम्

8.2 उपसर्ग

We saw earlier that the सूत्रs between प्राग्रीश्वरान्निपाताः (1-4-56) and अधिरीश्वरे (1-4-97) list some निपातs and give some notable names to some subsets. Of those, one is particularly important for our later

[2]Here, the प्रत्यय refers only to the content and not इत्. Therefore, प्रत्ययs like णमुँल्, तुमुँन् are ending with म्. Because the actual content is only अम् and उम् in these प्रत्ययs, respectively.

[3]This will be discussed later in Chapter-16 on समास.

discussion. This is the concept of उपसर्ग defined in उपसर्गाः क्रियायोगे (1-4-59). This सूत्र specifies that the निपातs listed in प्रादि-गण get a special name called "उपसर्ग" when used with a धातु.

उपसर्गs usually change the meaning of the धातु, with which they are associated. For example, गमॢ is a popular धातु, and it refers to the action of "going". गच्छति is its लट् प्रथमपुरुष एकवचन परस्मै कर्तरि form. Now, we can add उपसर्गs to it. As we have seen earlier, आ, अव, and निर् are listed in प्रादिगण. They will get an additional label उपसर्ग, if they are attached to, say, गच्छति. Thus, we get new forms - आगच्छति, अवगच्छति and निर्गच्छति. Here, even though गच्छति was referring to someone going, आगच्छति refers to someone "coming"; अवगच्छति refers to someone "understanding"; and निर्गच्छति refers to someone "exiting".

We can see another example: हरति refers to someone "taking away". However, प्रहरति refers to someone "hitting"; आहरति refers to someone "bringing"; संहरति refers to someone "killing"; विहरति refers to someone "recreating"; परिहरति refers to someone "solving"; अपहरति refers to someone "stealing".

As a general rule, when उपसर्ग is added, the meaning of the धातु usually changes. Sometimes the new meaning may be just a minor variation of the original and sometimes completely different. In a few cases, the meaning may remain unaltered[4]. Here is a simple shloka that summarises this idea:

> उपसर्गेण धात्वर्थो बलादन्यत्र नीयते ।
> प्रहाराहारसंहारविहारपरिहारवत् ॥

Please note that the forms given in this shloka are not of तिङन्तs but of कृदन्तs. We will deal with कृदन्तs later.

[4]Details on what different उपसर्गs may or may not do to the meanings of various धातुs is available in reference books such as बृहद्धातुकुसुमाकर.

9 समानाधिकरण-पद, विशेषण

9.1 समानाधिकरण-पद

When two or more words in a sentence refer to the same entity, they are said to be समानाधिकरण-पदs. समानाधिकरण-पद means, "a word that has the same (समान) substratum (अधिकरण)". The phrase "same" always begs the question, "same as what?". Hence we need at least one other word to make sense of the term समानाधिकरण. Therefore, this idea of समानाधिकरण is applicable when we have two or more words that refer to the same entity. Such words are called समानाधिकरण-पदs, and the relationship between two such words is called सामानाधिकरण्य.

We have seen in the discussion under कारकs that the idea of अधिकरण also refers to विषय. Meaning of a word is also a type of विषय. We have also seen that all प्रातिपदिकs have a meaning. Hence, in this context, we understand अधिकरण as the meaning of a प्रातिपदिक.

All सुबन्तपदs have two components: प्रातिपदिक and सुप्. If two सुबन्तपदs are समानाधिकरण, then:

(1) Both प्रातिपदिकs will be referring to the same entity, i.e., the same अधिकरण.
(2) Both words will have the same विभक्ति and वचन (i.e., they have the same सुप्).
(3) Both words will be in the same लिङ्ग if the प्रातिपदिकs in question are not नियतलिङ्ग.

The idea of समानाधिकरण is, in principle, applicable to both सुबन्तs and तिङन्तs. However, it is primarily used in the context of सुबन्तपदs only.

Consider the sentence- "यत्र योगेश्वरः कृष्णः" - Here, the two words योगेश्वरः and कृष्णः are referring to the same entity. Hence they are समानाधिकरण to each other. Observe that they are in same विभक्ति, वचन and लिङ्ग.

Similarly, in the statement - "प्रजहाति यदा कामान् सर्वान् पार्थ मनोगतान्" - three words कामान्, सर्वान्, and मनोगतान् are समानाधिकरण-पदs.

रामस्य मित्रं सुग्रीवः - Here the words मित्रं and सुग्रीवः are समानाधिकरण to each other. The two प्रातिपदिकs are referring to the same entity, and both words have the same विभक्ति and वचन; note that they are in different लिङ्ग as मित्र cannot change its लिङ्ग because it is नियतलिङ्ग.

For a clearer appreciation, let's consider - "यत्र योगेश्वरः कृष्णः यत्र पार्थः धनुर्धरः". Here, the next two words पार्थः and धनुर्धरः are also in the same विभक्ति, वचन and लिङ्ग as योगेश्वरः and कृष्णः. However, the meanings of the प्रातिपदिकs are different. While योगेश्वरः and कृष्णः refer to वासुदेव, the other two words - धनुर्धरः and पार्थः - refer to अर्जुन. Hence योगेश्वरः and कृष्णः are समानाधिकरण to each other; धनुर्धरः and पार्थः are also समानाधिकरण to each other; but योगेश्वरः and पार्थः are not.

9.2 विशेषण and विशेष्य

The ideas of विशेषण and विशेष्य are central to understanding the relationship between objects, their properties, and the role played by them as communicated in a sentence. The grammatical idea of समानाधिकरण-पद is used as a technique to identify this relationship between विशेषण and विशेष्य.

विशेष means भेद (distinctive feature). विशेषण is something that shows the existence of a विशेष in the विशेष्य. In other words, विशेष्य may have multiple distinctive features; विशेषण points us to one unique feature of the विशेष्य. Hence, विशेषण and विशेष्य are related terms; विशेषण

is for a विशेष्य, and विशेष्य gets the name due to a विशेषण. The relationship between विशेषण and विशेष्य is called विशेषण-विशेष्य-भाव.

For example, "नीलम् उत्पलम्" means "a dark lotus". नीलम् and उत्पलम् are two समानाधिकरण-पदs, both referring to a lotus. Here, lotuses (उत्पल) are known to come in many shades, and darkness (नीलत्व) distinguishes this specific lotus from others. Hence, the word उत्पल is विशेष्य, नीलत्व is विशेष; and the word नीलम् is indicating that विशेष, hence is a विशेषण to उत्पल.

In some other instances, another entity itself may be a distinguisher. For example, let's consider a group of people, with one of them, the King (राजा), wearing a crown (किरीट). Here the किरीट distinguishes the राजा from others and is hence a विशेषण. However, in usage, we cannot just say किरीट but should link it to राजा. Therefore, we say किरीटी (the one who has a crown). Thus we use the sentence in a way that the two words are in समानाधिकरण - "किरीटी राजा". Therefore, किरीटी is विशेषण and राजा is विशेष्य.

In summary, the विशेषण is anything that distinguishes a विशेष्य. It is typically a property and sometimes even another entity. The more important one is generally the विशेष्य. The विशेषण-विशेष्य-भाव is also dependent on our intent.[1] In usage, to identify this relationship between विशेषण and विशेष्य, we use समानाधिकरण-पदs. Hence all rules applicable to समानाधिकरण-पदs apply to विशेषणs also. That is, विशेषण and विशेष्य will -

(1) Refer to the same entity.
(2) Have same विभक्ति and वचन.
(3) Have same लिङ्ग if they are not नियतलिङ्गs.

The below verse re-emphasizes this point:

> यल्लिङ्गं यद्वचनं या च विभक्तिर्विशेष्यस्य ।
> तल्लिङ्गं तद्वचनं सा च विभक्तिर्विशेषणस्य ॥

9.2.1 Functions of विशेषण

The primary function of विशेषण is to distinguish the विशेष्य. The fact that a particular विशेष्य has a certain विशेषण may sometimes be known and some other times unknown. When we don't know about that specific विशेषण of that particular विशेष्य, then the function of that विशेषण is to let us know this विशेषण. For example, "व्याकरणं वेदाङ्गम्"

[1] In a phrase such as "सुन्दरः नर्तकः", the quality of being a सुन्दर is distinguishing this नर्तक from other नर्तकs. We can, similarly, say नर्तकः सुन्दरः since the quality of being a नर्तक can again distinguish this सुन्दर from other सुन्दरs. Here, both these attributes are, in fact, properties, and there is nothing to choose between them. However, depending on our intent, we make one विशेषण and the other विशेष्य.

= "Vyakarana is Vedanga". Assume that we knew about Vyakarana but didn't know that it is a Vedanga. Thus, वेदाङ्ग, the विशेषण here, is prescribing the attribute of "being a वेदाङ्ग" to व्याकरण. This kind of विशेषण is called a विधेय.

At some other places, perhaps most often, we may be using a known attribute as a विशेषण. In such cases, the most common purpose of using the विशेषण is to distinguish the विशेष्य from others. For example, "द्वैपायनः कृष्णः". Here द्वैपायन, the विशेषण, distinguishes this कृष्ण from other कृष्णs, say वसुदेवसुतकृष्ण or धर्मसुतकृष्ण. Such a विशेषण is called व्यावर्तक-विशेषण.

Known attributes may also be used to indicate logic. For example, सर्वज्ञः शम्भुः उपायं वदति. An approximate translation would be "The all-knowing Shambhu is telling a solution." Here, सर्वज्ञ (one who knows everything) is a विशेषण. The attribute of being a सर्वज्ञ logically explains his ability to provide a solution. He can give a solution because he knows everything. Such विशेषणs are called हेतुगर्भ-विशेषणs, literally meaning "impregnated with a logic".

In summary, based on common purposes, विशेषणs can be विधेय, व्यावर्तक, or हेतुगर्भ.

10 कृदन्त

10.1 Introduction

In our discussion on प्रकृति-प्रत्यय-व्यवस्था we had seen that some प्रत्ययs apply to धातुs and some to प्रातिपदिकs. Largely, the प्रत्ययs that are applicable to a धातु are either तिङ् or कृत्. In fact, कृत्-प्रत्ययs are defined as प्रत्ययs that are not तिङ्, but applicable to धातुs and prescribed in सूत्रs occurring after धातोः(3-1-91). We may also recall that, while तिङ्-प्रत्ययs result in a पद, the कृत्-प्रत्ययs result in a प्रातिपदिक.

धातु + कृत् → कृदन्त-प्रातिपदिक

10.2 Basic Features of कृदन्तपद

A list of frequently used कृत्-प्रत्ययs and their meanings is given in Table 10.2 at the end of next section. The following points and examples help in understanding that table:

(1) कृत्-प्रत्ययs indicate two meanings:
   (i) क्रिया (भाव) or कारकs
   (ii) Modality (must/ought) or काल (generic or specific tense such as भूत, वर्तमान or भविष्यत्)

(2) Some of these कृत्-प्रत्ययान्त-पदs act as विशेषणs in some circumstances. In such cases, all the rules of विशेषण-विशेष्य discussed earlier also apply here. That is, the कृदन्त-पद and the विशेष्य-पद will always have same विभक्ति and वचन. If the कृदन्त-पद is not नियतलिङ्ग, then it takes the लिङ्ग of विशेष्य-पद.

(3) When कृदन्त-पद is indicating भाव, most often it gets नियतलिङ्ग or becomes अव्यय.

(4) Applicability of कृत्-प्रत्ययs is sometimes dependent on धातुs, अर्थ and उपपदs. That is, some प्रत्ययs apply to some धातुs only. Some are applicable in some meanings only. Some apply only in the presence of another पद.

(5) When धातु and कृत् combine, they transform the word depending on the इत्-वर्णs and content present in the कृत्-प्रत्ययs and/or

the धातुs. For example, if the content of the प्रत्यय is यु, then it transforms into अन; and if it is वु, then it transforms into अक.[1]

10.3 कृत्-प्रत्ययs

We will illustrate the above points by providing some examples.

10.3.1 कृत्-प्रत्ययs in the meaning of कर्तृ-कारक

प्रत्ययs in meaning of कर्तृ-कारक and refer to काल in general terms

(1) डुपचँष् पाके + ण्वुल् → पाचक

(i) Here the प्रातिपदिक refers to the कर्तृ in the पाक-क्रिया (action of cooking).

(ii) It refers to a time in a generic sense: "पाचक is a cook." and doesn't specifically mean that the cooking "was" done or "will be" done or "is being" done.

(iii) It acts as a विशेषण in usages such as "पाचकः भीमः", "पाचिका कृष्णा" or "पाचकम् मित्रम्". Note the features of सामानाधिकरण्य - same entity being referred, same विभक्ति, वचन and same लिङ्ग. Since the words are समानाधिकरण, it essentially means that कृदन्तपद

[1]युवोरनाकौ (7-1-1)

पाचक is indicating the कर्तृ and the विशेष्य भीम, is actually the कर्तृ. That is, भीम is the cook.

(iv) Since, the प्रत्यय has "वु", it transforms into "अक" and is visible as such in all the words created by ण्वुल् - पाचक, गायक, कारक, नायक, पूरक, and मोदक.

(2) नृतीँ गात्रविक्षेपे + ष्वुन् → नर्तक

(i) The ष्वुन्-प्रत्यय is prescribed instead of ण्वुल्, for some specific धातुs - नृतीँ गात्रविक्षेपे, खनुँ अवदारणे, रञ्जँ रागे.

(ii) This also refers to the कर्तृ and acts as a विशेषण, as in "नर्तकी बृहन्नला"

(iii) The final form is a little different from that formed by ण्वुल्. Note the दीर्घ in the first letter of पाचक and the absence of it in नर्तक. This is due to the presence (and absence) of ण् as an इत् in ण्वुल् (and ष्वुन्). We shall see the details of these rules later.

(3) गमॢ गतौ + तृच्/तृन् → गन्तृ

(i) तृच् and तृन् प्रत्ययs are also prescribed in the meaning of कर्तृकारक.

(ii) The derived प्रातिपदिकs for both the प्रत्ययs have the same form.[2] Between the two, तृन् gives one of the following additional meanings while also specifying the कर्तृ :

[2]The difference is only in pronunciations. कृदन्त with तृच् ending has to be pronounced differently than that with a तृन् ending.

(a) कर्तृ has the nature of doing the said क्रिया (तच्छील)

(b) कर्तृ believes that it is his duty to do the said क्रिया (तद्धर्म)

(c) कर्तृ can do the said क्रिया very well (तत्साधुकारि)

(iii) Some examples of तृच्/ तृन् are: गन्तृ, कर्तृ, वक्तृ, भोक्तृ

(iv) Some examples of तृन् are: काव्यं कर्ता कालिदासः ,वनं गन्ता गुहः - Here the first word is also required to mention the specific क्रिया - "composing काव्यs". In the second example, गुह's nature may not be just "going" but "going to the forest".

(4) जिज्ञास् + उ → जिज्ञासु

(i) The उ-प्रत्यय is a प्रत्यय in the meaning of कर्तृ, mainly used for सन्नन्त-धातुs. We will see the सन्नन्त-धातुs in detail later. It suffices here to know that सन्-प्रत्यय is used for primary धातुs to derive a new secondary धातु called सन्नन्त-धातु, in the meaning of 'desire to do the action indicated by the primary धातु'.

(ii) For such derived धातुs, उ-प्रत्यय is used to refer to the कर्तृ. This प्रत्यय also indicates that such a कर्तृ is either तच्छील, तद्धर्म, or तत्साधुकारि as explained above.

(iii) For example, जिज्ञासु, चिकीर्षु, विवक्षु, and पिपासु.

(5) ल्यु, णिनिँ and अच् for some predefined set of words.

(i) There are some predefined sets of words (गणs)[3] that are listed in the meaning of कर्तृ.

[3]These resources can be found online using the link mentioned on the last page of the book.

(a) A set starting from नन्दि that gets *ल्यु* in the meaning of कर्तृ.
For example, नन्दन, वासन, and मदन.

(b) A set starting from ग्रहि that gets *णिनिँ* in the meaning of कर्तृ.
For example, ग्राहिन्, मन्त्रिन्, स्थायिन्, and उत्साहिन्.

(c) A set starting from पच् that gets *अच्* in the meaning of कर्तृ.
For example, पच, वद, वस, and तप.
This specific set is said to be a sample (आकृतिगण), and many more words may be derived using *अच्*.

प्रत्ययs in the meaning of कर्तृ-कारक and refer to वर्तमानकाल or भविष्यत्काल

(1) गमॢ + *शतृँ* = गच्छत्

(i) *शतृँ*-प्रत्यय is applicable only to परस्मै-पदि-धातुs and उभय-पदि-धातुs.

(ii) It refers to कर्तृ-कारक in the क्रिया referred by the धातु.

(iii) Additionally, it refers to वर्तमान-काल, similar to how a present participle indicates continuous tense. It doesn't necessarily mean that the action is "currently happening".

(a) For example, गच्छन् पिपीलिकः याति = "A moving ant reaches". In this example, the word "गच्छन्" indicates the continuity in the act of "movement".

(b) Other examples: धारयत्, गच्छन्ती, स्पृशत्, पचत्, कुर्वत्.

(c) *शतृँ* is also used to indicate future tense (in the meaning of लृट्). In those usages, we also see an additional प्रत्यय - स्य (this is usually transformed to ष्य).

For example, धरिष्यत्, गमिष्यत्, स्पर्क्ष्यत्, पचिष्यत्, and करिष्यत्.

(2) वदिँ + *शानच्* = वन्दमान

(i) This is exactly similar to *शतृँ* in its meaning. However, it is applicable only to आत्मने-पदि-धातुs and उभय-पदि-धातुs.

For example, वन्दमान, लभमान, पचमान, कुर्वाण

(ii) *शानच्* will indicate कर्म/भाव, when the धातु is added with यक्. Also, since *यक्* can be added to all धातुs, *यक्* + *शानच्* can be applied to all, परस्मै-पदि, आत्मने-पदि and उभय-पदि धातुs. For example, गम्यमान, क्रियमाण, दृश्यमान, पच्यमान, and लभ्यमान. By definition, in this usage, they refer to कर्म/भाव and not to कर्तृ.

(iii) In the meaning of future tense, it gets the forms such as, वन्दिष्यमाण, लप्स्यमान, पक्ष्यमाण and करिष्यमाण.

प्रत्ययs in the meaning of कर्तृ-कारक and refer to भूतकाल

(1) डुकृञ् + *क्तवतुँ* → कृतवत्

(i) This प्रत्यय is applicable to all धातुs; refers to कर्तृ; and indicates that the क्रिया is done (भूतकाल).

For example, गतवत्, उक्तवत्, पठितवत्, and लिखितवत्.

(2) गमॢ + क्त = गत

(i) This प्रत्यय refers to भूतकाल. Popularly it refers to कर्म, which we will discuss later. However, in some special cases (3-4-71, 72) it refers to कर्तृ. Some such cases are :

(a) if the धातु is अकर्मक

E.g., आसित, उपविष्ट, स्थित, शयित, and जात.

(b) if the meaning of the धातु is movement(गत्यर्थ)

E.g., गत, यात, इत, and अटित.

(c) to indicate that the क्रिया has begun.

E.g., प्रकृतः पठनं कृष्णः, प्रभुक्तः पायसं बालकः.

प्रत्ययs that refer to कर्तृ, refer to काल in general terms and are applicable only when there are specific उपपदs.

(1) कुम्भम् + डुकृञ् + *अण्* → कुम्भकार [कर्मणि उपपदे, *अण्*-प्रत्ययः]

(i) The *अण्*-प्रत्यय is applicable to most of the धातुs in the meaning of कर्तृ, provided there is a उपपद[4] referring to कर्म in that क्रिया

In कुम्भकार, डुकृञ् धातु gets *अण्* प्रत्यय to indicate the कर्तृ of that क्रिया, since we do have a कर्म, that is कुम्भ, associated there as उपपद.

For example, : शास्त्रकार, वेदाध्याय, चर्चापार

[4]For information on उपपद, refer to the सूत्र - तत्रोपपदं सप्तमीस्थम् (3-1-92)

(2) सर्वम् + ज्ञा + *क* → सर्वज्ञ [उपपदे, *क*-प्रत्ययः]

(i) *क*-प्रत्यय is also in the meaning of कर्तृ and is applicable only when there is a सुबन्त-उपपद, if the धातु is आकारान्त (such as ज्ञा, दा, ला, पा, ष्ठा) and generally when those धातुs do not have a उपसर्ग.

For example, सर्वज्ञ, वरद, वातल, मधुप, स्वस्थ, समस्थ, स्थितप्रज्ञ, वरप्रद

(3) धर्मम् + चर् + *णिनिँ* = धर्मचारिन् [उपपदे, *णिनिँ*-प्रत्ययः]

(i) *णिनिँ*-प्रत्यय is applied in the presence of सुबन्त-उपपद, in the meaning of a कर्तृ, if engaging in that क्रिया is in the very nature of the कर्तृ or if the कर्तृ does the क्रिया perfectly.

For example, धर्मचारिन्, शीतभोजिन्, ब्रह्मवादिन्, साधुकारिन्, धनदायिन्

(4) शास्त्रम् + विद् + *क्विप्* → शास्त्रविद् [*क्विप्*-प्रत्ययः]

(i) This प्रत्यय is also applied in the meaning of कर्तृ. It is usually applied in the presence of a सुबन्त-उपपद, rarely even without.

For example, वेदविद्, उपनिषद्, विश्वजित्, राज्, ईश्

10.3.2 कृत्-प्रत्ययs in the meaning of कर्म-कारक or भाव

(1) कृत्यप्रत्ययs

(i) The प्रत्ययs- *तव्य, तव्यत्, अनीयर्, यत्, ण्यत्, क्यप्* are called कृत्य-प्रत्ययs.

(ii) These प्रत्ययs indicate कर्म-कारक or भाव, and refer to काल in general. These प्रत्ययs provide an additional sense that the कर्तृ is eligible (अर्ह) or suitable (योग्य) for this activity and he considers this activity as a means (साधन) to achieve his desires

(इष्ट)[5]. Sometimes, they also provide an additional sense of capability of the कर्तृ (शक्य) in doing that क्रिया.
For example, - कर्तव्य, करणीय, कार्य, गन्तव्य, गमनीय, गम्य, गेय, पेय, भक्ष्य, भोज्य, लेह्य, चोष्य, विद्या, शय्या, भृत्या.

(iii) Here, if we take an example "रामेण वनं गन्तव्यम्" (Rama should go to forest.) the word गन्तव्य is a कृत्य-प्रत्ययान्त-पद. It refers to कर्म-कारक, namely वन. It also means that राम is capable of going to वन and that this act is a means for his desire of pleasing दशरथ, or following धर्म (पितृवाक्यपरिपालन).

(2) क्त-प्रत्यय

(i) This प्रत्यय is by default used in the meaning of कर्म-कारक or भाव and refers to भूतकाल. For example, कृत, गत, श्रुत, नीत, विक्रीत, दृष्ट, ज्ञात, पूत.

(ii) Here, if the धातु is सकर्मक, then क्त-प्रत्यय may refer to either कर्म or भाव. If the धातु is अकर्मक, it can refer only to भाव.

(iii) There are some exceptional cases. We have already seen that the reference can be to कर्तृ in some cases.

(a) If the धातु has the meaning of moving, eating, or any क्रिया that has stillness in it, then the क्त-प्रत्यय may even refer to अधिकरण. For example, यातः मार्गः, भुक्तं स्थलम्, आसितः मञ्चः.

[5]This sense of अर्हता + इष्टसाधनता is similar to the meaning of लिङ्-लकार or लोट्-लकार.

(b) If the धातु is of the meaning - to desire, to know or to respect, then क्त-प्रत्यय can refer to वर्तमान-काल. It may be so even in some other usages. For example: मत, इष्ट, बुद्ध, ज्ञात, पूजित, शीलित, रक्षित, सुप्त, तृप्त.

(iv) In summary, क्तप्रत्यय has different possible meanings depending on the meaning of the धातु and whether it is सकर्मक/अकर्मक

(a) All सकर्मक धातुs have कर्म and भाव meanings. In addition,

(I) Those धातुs referring to movement can additionally get the meaning of कर्तृ and अधिकरण.

(II) Those धातुs referring to eating can additionally get the meaning of अधिकरण.

(b) All अकर्मक धातुs have कर्तृ and भाव meanings. In addition,

(I) Those धातुs referring to क्रियाs in which there is stillness, can additionally get अधिकरण meaning.

10.3.3 कृत्-प्रत्ययs in the meaning of करण or अधिकरण

(1) क्त-प्रत्यय

(i) We have already seen that क्त-प्रत्यय is also applied in some cases to refer to अधिकरण.

For example, आसित, भुक्त, यात

(2) ल्युट्-प्रत्यय

(i). ल्युट्-प्रत्यय is applicable in the meaning of करण, अधिकरण or भाव. We will discuss भावार्थ later.

(a) Examples of ल्युट्-प्रत्यय in the meaning of करण - नयन, प्रमाण, दर्शन, करण, व्याकरण, चरण, वाहन.

(b) Examples of ल्युट्-प्रत्यय in the meaning of अधिकरण - आसन, शयन, स्थान, अधिकरण, पान.

10.3.4 कृत्-प्रत्ययs in the meaning of भाव (क्रिया)

These प्रत्ययs refer to the क्रिया, which is the very meaning of the धातु to which they are applied. We have seen above that क्त, and ल्युट् do provide those meanings. We shall see these, among others, below. Generally, their final form, that is, the प्रातिपदिक derived by adding कृत्-प्रत्यय, is in a specified लिङ्ग. We will categorize them under each लिङ्ग for easy reference.

भावार्थक-कृत्-प्रत्ययs that result in a स्त्रीलिङ्ग-प्रातिपदिकs

(1) *क्तिन्-प्रत्यय*

(i) Applicable to all धातुs and generally provides the meaning of भाव. E.g., भक्ति, सृष्टि, नति, दृष्टि, व्याप्ति

(ii) For some specific धातुs (श्रु, यज, स्तु), क्तिन् can also indicate करण-कारक. E.g., श्रुति, इष्टि, स्तुति

(2) *अ-प्रत्यय*

(i) This is applicable to those धातुs that have a प्रत्यय at their end, such as सन्-प्रत्यय, यङ्-प्रत्यय, यङ्-लुगन्त (these will be discussed later).

For example, जिज्ञासा, चिकीर्षा, लोलूया, कण्डूया, पुत्रकाम्या

(3) *अङ्-प्रत्यय*

(i) This is applicable for some types of धातुs or for some specific धातुs[6]:

(a) Those that have ष् as इत्-वर्ण such as जॄष् वयोहानौ, त्रपूँष् लज्जायाम्.

E.g., जरा, त्रपा

(b) Those that have आ at their ending (दा, धा) and have a उपसर्ग

E.g., प्रदा, उपधा

(ii) Some other examples are: भिदा, छिदा, गुहा, मेधा, श्रद्धा, चिन्ता, पूजा, कथा, and चर्चा

(4) *युच्-प्रत्यय*

(i) It is mainly seen for धातुs that have णिच् attached.

E.g., प्रार्थना, कल्पना, योजना, कारणा, हारणा, वेदना

(ii) It is also used in some other cases, in पुंलिङ्ग and in the meaning of कर्तृ.

E.g., वर्धन, दुर्योधन, ज्वलन, पवन, पतन, भूषण

[6]Refer सूत्र 3-3-104 to 106

भावार्थक-कृत्-प्रत्ययs that result in a नपुंसक-प्रातिपदिकs

(1) ल्युट्-प्रत्यय

  (i) We have seen this प्रत्यय earlier also, in other meanings. It also comes in the meaning of भाव.
  E.g., दर्शन, करण, and गमन.

(2) क्त-प्रत्यय

  (i) We have seen क्त-प्रत्यय also in other meanings such as कर्तृ, कर्म, and अधिकरण. This would vary depending on whether the धातु is सकर्मक, अकर्मक and the meaning of the धातु. However, क्त-प्रत्यय in the meaning of भाव applies to almost all धातुs.
  E.g., कृतम्, भूतम्, मतम्, हुतम्, दत्तम्, इष्टम्

भावार्थक-कृत्-प्रत्ययs that result in a पुंलिङ्ग-प्रातिपदिकs

(1) घञ्-प्रत्यय

  (i) This is applicable to most of the धातुs.
  E.g., पाक, त्याग, and राग.

  (ii) In some cases, घञ्-प्रत्यय is seen in the meaning of कर्तृ.
  E.g., पाद, रोग, and स्पर्श.

  (iii) In other cases, where the reference is to a label/name which is a कारक other than कर्तृ, घञ्-प्रत्यय is applied.
  E.g., आहार, विहार, and राम.

(2) अप्-प्रत्यय

(i) It is applicable for धातुs that have ऋ/ॠ or उ as the last वर्ण, such as कृ करणे, शॄ हिंसायाम्, गॄ निगरणे, यु मिश्रणेऽमिश्रणे च
E.g., कर, शर, गर, and यव.

(ii) It is also seen in some specific words such as ग्रह, वर, दर, निश्चय, and गम.

10.3.5 कृत्-प्रत्ययs in the meaning of भाव and result in an अव्यय

(1) तुमुँन्-प्रत्यय

(i) This is applicable to all धातुs.

(ii) This is seen only when we have two क्रियाs and if the कर्तृ is the same for both क्रियाs.

(iii) It is applicable in four instances:

(a) If the purpose of a क्रिया is another future क्रिया, then the धातु referring to that future क्रिया gets तुमुन्-प्रत्यय. For example, "रामः फलानि आहर्तुं वनं गच्छति" = "Rama is going to forest to get fruits". Here, "going to the forest" is one क्रिया, and "getting the fruits" is another क्रिया. The first act is done for the second act. Hence the धातु of the second act, which is the purpose, gets तुमुन्-प्रत्यय.

(b) If a धातु is associated with a क्रियापद that has a meaning of इच्छा, then sucha a धातु gets तुमुन्-प्रत्यय.
E.g., भोक्तुम् इच्छति, भोक्तुं कामयते.

(c) it is applied to a धातु if that धातु is associated with any क्रियापद form of these धातुs - शक, धृष, ज्ञा, ग्ला, घट, रभ, लभ, क्रम, सह, अर्ह or any धातु in the meaning of अस्ति - when suggesting meaning other than the apparent meaning of these धातुs.
E.g., सः पठितुं शक्नोति or सः पठितुं जानाति. These do not mean that the person is capable of reading or knows how to read. These usages suggest that he is skilful in reading.

(d) It is applied to a धातु that is associated with a word referring to काल. For example, कालः स्नातुम्, समयः भोक्तुम्.

(2) क्त्वा-प्रत्यय

(i) This प्रत्यय is also applicable only when two क्रियाs have the same कर्तृ. It provides the meaning that this action is done prior to another action.
E.g., देवं नत्वा व्याकरणं पठामि; पुस्तकं गृहीत्वा शालां गच्छामि.

(ii) In some cases where a क्त्वा-प्रत्ययान्त-पद is compounded (समास) with a उपसर्ग or a few other elements, this प्रत्यय is replaced by ल्यप्.
E.g., नत्वा → प्रणम्य, आनम्य; गत्वा → आगत्य.

(3) णमुँल्-प्रत्यय

(i) This प्रत्यय is similar to क्त्वा and is an alternative for क्त्वा. However, this is applicable only if the prior action is done repeatedly.
E.g., स्मृत्वा स्मृत्वा वदति can also be denoted as स्मारं स्मारम् वदति. Both these forms indicate that the action of स्मरण is done repeatedly, prior to the other action of वदन (कथन).

Table 10.2 summarises essential information related to all the कृत्प्रत्ययs discussed in this chapter. Readers can use this for a quick reference.

कृत्प्रत्यय	Meaning	Tense	Example	Comment
ण्वुल्	कर्तृ		पाचक	
ष्वुन्	कर्तृ		रजक	
तृच्	कर्तृ		कर्तृ	
तृन्	कर्तृ		कर्तृ	Also gives an additional meaning of- तच्छील/ तद्धर्म/ तत्साधुकारि
उ	कर्तृ		जिज्ञासु	This प्रत्यय is applicable only to derived धातुs obtained after adding सन्-प्रत्यय.
शतृँ	कर्तृ	Present/ Future	गच्छत्/ गमिष्यन्	Only for परस्मैपदि-धातुs and उभयपदि-धातुs

कृत्प्रत्यय	Meaning	Tense	Example	Comments
शानच्	कर्तृ	Present/ Future	वन्दमान/ वन्दिष्यमाण	Only for आत्मनेपदि-धातुs and उभयपदि-धातुs
ल्यु	कर्तृ		नन्दन	Applicable only to नन्द्यादि-गण[7]
णिनिँ	कर्तृ		ग्राहिन्	Applicable only to ग्रहादि-गण
अच्	कर्तृ		पच	Applicable only to पचादि-गण
क्तवतुँ	कर्तृ	Past tense	गतवत्	
क्त	कर्तृ/ कर्म/ भाव/ अधिकरण	Past tense	गत	It refers to कर्तृ only in the case of गत्यर्थ/ अकर्मक धातुs. It can refer to अधिकरण only if the धातु is गत्यर्थक (in the meaning of going)/प्रत्यवसानार्थक(in the meaning of eating)/ ध्रौव्यार्थक(in the meaning of being still)
यक् + शानच्	कर्म	Present/ Future	पठ्यमान/ पठिष्यमाण	
अण्	कर्तृ		कुम्भकार	In the presence of उपपद
क	कर्तृ		गोद	In the presence of उपपद

[7]The गण-पाठ can be found online using the link mentioned on the last page of the book.

कृत्प्रत्यय	Meaning	Tense	Example	Comments
णिनिँ	कर्तृ		धर्मचारी	In the meaning of having that as a habit, in the presence of उपपद
क्विप्	कर्तृ		वेदविद्	In the presence of उपपद
तव्यत्/ तव्य	कर्म/ भाव		कर्तव्य	These are also called कृत्य-प्रत्ययs. These additionally mention capability/ eligibility/suitability of the कर्तृ
अनीयर्	कर्म/ भाव		करणीय	These are also called कृत्य-प्रत्ययs. It additionally mentions capability/ eligibility/suitability of the कर्तृ
यत्/ ण्यत्/ क्यप्	कर्म/ भाव		जेय	These are also called कृत्य-प्रत्ययs. It additionally mentions capability/ eligibility/suitability of the कर्तृ
ल्युट्	करण/ अधिकरण/ भाव		प्रहरण, शयन, गमन	
घञ्	भाव		पाठ	These प्रातिपदिकs are in पुंलिङ्ग
क्तिन्	भाव		नति	These प्रातिपदिकs are in स्त्रीलिङ्ग
युच्	भाव		योजना	These प्रातिपदिकs are in स्त्रीलिङ्ग

कृत्प्रत्यय	Meaning	Tense	Example	Comments
अङ्	भाव		चिन्ता	These प्रातिपदिकs are in स्त्रीलिङ्ग
अ	भाव		जिज्ञासा	This प्रत्यय is applicable only to derived धातुs obtained after adding सन्-प्रत्यय. These प्रातिपदिकs are in स्त्रीलिङ्ग.
अप्	भाव		गम	These प्रातिपदिकs are in पुंलिङ्ग
तुमुँन्	भाव		पठितुम्	If a क्रिया is done for the purpose of another future क्रिया, then the धातु of that future क्रिया gets तुमुँन्. This always results in an अव्यय.
त्त्वा	भाव		कृत्वा	If the same कर्तृ performs two क्रियाs done one after another, the धातु of the first क्रिया gets त्त्वा. This always results in an अव्यय.
ल्यप्	भाव		उपकृत्य	When an उपसर्ग is present, ल्यप् replaces त्त्वा.
णमुँल्	भाव		स्मारं स्मारं	Indicates the meaning of repetition

Table 10.2: कृत्-प्रत्ययs and their meaning

10.4 Transformations

The final form of the derived प्रातिपदिक (derived from the combination of धातु + प्रत्यय) is dependent on many factors, इत्-वर्णs in the प्रत्यय.

Before we discuss the transformations related to कृदन्त. It is required to understand the idea of आदेश and the meanings of the terms गुण and वृद्धि. These are detailed in the section on सन्धि. In a nutshell, आदेश is a replacement of a वर्ण with a सदृश-वर्ण. सदृश-वर्ण is the most similar वर्ण, similarity based on उच्चारणस्थान. गुण and वृद्धि are specific types of आदेशs, in the case of कृदन्तs and तद्धितान्तs. The term "गुण" denotes the set of वर्णs - अ, ए, and ओ; and the term वृद्धि refers to the set of three other वर्णs - आ, ऐ and औ.

The कृदन्त-related transformation can be on (1) धातु or (2) प्रत्ययs.

10.4.1 धातु-transformations

(1) अन्त्यगुण

Here, अन्त्यगुण refers to the replacement of the last इक्-वर्ण of the धातु by a सदृश-गुण-वर्ण (ए for इ and ओ for उ, अर् for ऋ). This is the most common transformation. It occurs when the कृत्-प्रत्यय DOESN'T have क्, ङ्, ञ् or ण् as इत्.

(i) For example, कृ + तृच् → कर् + तृ → कर्तृ. Here ऋ at the end of धातु, is replaced with a गुण-वर्ण and has resulted in अर्.

(ii) Counter-example: कृ + क्त → कृत. Here, since the प्रत्यय has क् as इत्, the अन्त्यवर्ण of धातु doesn't get गुण or वृद्धि, but remains as is.

(2) अन्त्यवृद्धि

अन्त्यवृद्धि refers to the replacement of the last इक्-वर्ण of the धातु by a सदृश-वृद्धि-वर्ण (आ for अ, ऐ for इ, औ for उ and आर् for ऋ). It occurs when the कृत्-प्रत्यय HAS ञ् or ण् as इत्.

(i) Example: कृ + ण्यत् → कार् + य → कार्य. Here, ऋ is replaced with वृद्धि-वर्ण and has resulted in आर्.

(ii) Counter-example: कृ + क्त → कृत. (See explanation above).

(3) उपधागुण

उपधा is a technical term referring to the penultimate वर्ण. A ह्रस्व-इक् in the position of उपधा, gets replaced by a सदृश-गुण-वर्ण. This occurs only when the कृत्-प्रत्यय DOESN'T have क् or ङ् as इत्.

(i) Example : युज् + तुमुन् → योज् + तुम् → योक्तुम्. Here उ which is at the उपधा of युज्, gets ओ, its सदृश-गुण-वर्ण.

(ii) Counter-example: युज् + क्त्वा → युक्त्वा (See explanation above)

(4) उपधावृद्धि

If ह्रस्व-अवर्ण is in the position of उपधा, then it gets replaced by सदृश-वृद्धि-वर्ण. It occurs when the कृत्-प्रत्यय HAS ञ् or ण् as इत्.

(i) Example : पच् + घञ् → पाच् + अ → पाक. Note that the ह्रस्व-अवर्ण in the position of उपधा gets replaced by आ, its सदृश-वृद्धि-वर्ण.

(ii) Counter-example: पच् + क्तवत् → पक्तवत्

Please note that no change in अन्त्यवर्ण or उपधावर्ण of धातु occurs if the प्रत्यय has क् or ङ् as इत्. The counter-examples given above, such as कृत, युक्त्वा, and पक्तवत् are examples of this "no-change".

10.4.2 प्रत्यय-transformations

There are many प्रत्यय-transformations listed in अष्टाध्यायी. As an illustration, we describe two common ones.

(1) यु or वु of कृत्-प्रत्ययs get replaced by अन and अक respectively.

(2) वि in क्विप्-प्रत्यय is completely omitted.

For example,

(1) गम् + ल्युट् → गम् + यु → गम् + अन → गमन

(2) पठ् + ण्वुल् → पाठ् + वु → पाठ् + अक → पाठक

(3) वेद + विद् + क्विप् → वेद+ विद् + वि → वेदविद्

11 सुबर्थ

11.1 Introduction

In Chapter 7, we observed that twenty-one सुप्-प्रत्ययs correspond to seven विभक्तिs and three वचनs. We saw their forms differ based on certain features of the प्रातिपदिक - its last वर्ण, लिङ्ग, from which प्रत्यय it is derived and whether it is a सर्वनाम or not.

We shall now understand what these विभक्तिs mean. पाणिनि has prescribed विभक्तिs in three different contexts:

(1) To provide the meaning of a कारक.
(2) To provide the meaning of something other than a कारक.
(3) In association with some specific words/instances.

11.2 कारक-meanings of विभक्तिs

In our previous discussions, we have seen different kinds of पदs indicating कारकs. Some forms of तिङन्त-पदs indicated कर्तृ and some others indicated कर्म. Similarly, some specific कृत्-प्रत्ययs were applied in different contexts to mean कर्तृ, कर्म, करण and अधिकरण. We will see later how some समासs, especially the ones in बहुव्रीहि-समासs, indicate कर्तृ, कर्म and other कारकs. Some rare examples exist of तद्धित-पदs (another type of derived words to be discussed later) that indicate some कारकs.

In these instances, we say in व्याकरण termininology that कारकs are "अभिहित" (mentioned) by तिङ्, कृत्, समास and तद्धितs, as the case may be.

For example, the word गच्छति, a तिङन्त-पद, mentions कर्तृकारक. Hence, कर्तृकारक is अभिहित by this तिङ्-प्रत्यय. पठ्यते, another तिङन्त-पद, mentions कर्मकारक. Hence, कर्मकारक is अभिहित by this तिङ्-प्रत्यय. पाचक, a कृदन्त-पद, mentions कर्तृकारक. Hence, कर्तृकारक is अभिहित by this कृत्-प्रत्यय - ण्वुल्. पठित, another कृदन्त-पद, mentions कर्मकारक. Hence, कर्मकारक is अभिहित by this कृत्-प्रत्यय -क्त.

This concept of अभिहित is important for the following reason: पाणिनि has prescribed सुप्-प्रत्ययs to provide the meaning of a कारक only if that कारक is अनभिहित (not अभिहित) by तिङ्, कृत्, समास and तद्धितs.

Let's consider a simple case of a boy reading a book. Here, as we can see, the act of reading is क्रिया. In this क्रिया, the boy is कर्तृ, and the book is कर्म. The act of reading can be represented in different ways: पठति, पठ्यते, अपठत्, पठितः, अपठ्यत, पठितवान् etc.

We know from our discussions on तिङन्त and कृदन्त that, while each of these forms represent पठन-क्रिया, some of them mention कर्तृ and some others कर्म. Additionally, tense indicated by these words may also vary. Specifically,

(1) पठति represents कर्तृ and वर्तमानकाल
(2) पठ्यते represents कर्म and वर्तमानकाल
(3) अपठत् represents कर्तृ and भूतकाल
(4) पठितः represents कर्म and भूतकाल
(5) अपठ्यत represents कर्म and भूतकाल
(6) पठितवान् represents कर्तृ and भूतकाल

We see कर्तृ is अभिहित in some forms and कर्म in some other forms.

11.2.1 विभक्तिs for कर्तृ and कर्म

The choice of the तिङन्त-पद form, such as the ones mentioned above, used to express the idea of "boy reading a book" in a sentence determines the appropriate prescription of विभक्तिs. पाणिनि has prescribed द्वितीया-विभक्ति for अनभिहित-कर्म and तृतीया-विभक्ति for अनभिहित-कर्तृ. If that कर्तृ or कर्म is अभिहित, then there is no prescription of a विभक्ति to indicate कारक. In such cases,

(1) if कर्तृ/कर्म is अभिहित by तिङन्त, then the कर्तृ/कर्म gets प्रथमा-विभक्ति, which is actually a default विभक्ति when no other विभक्ति is prescribed.

(2) if कर्तृ/कर्म is अभिहित by कृत्/तद्धित/समास then the कृदन्त/तद्धितान्त/समस्तपद will be विशेषण to the विशेष्य which actually refers to the respective कर्तृ/कर्म. That कृदन्त/तद्धितान्त/समस्तपद gets the same विभक्ति as their विशेष्य.

Therefore, if we use पठति, then कर्तृ is अभिहित, while कर्म is अनभिहित. Hence, द्वितीया is prescribed for कर्म, and कर्तृ gets the default प्रथमा. Hence we get the form: "बालकः ग्रन्थं पठति". Similarly, in forms such as अपठत् and पठितवान्, the same rules apply. Thus, we get the forms "बालकः ग्रन्थम् अपठत्" and "बालकः ग्रन्थं पठितवान्".

However, if we use a कर्म-indicating form, such as पठ्यते, then the structure changes. In पठ्यते, कर्म is अभिहित while कर्तृ is अनभिहित. Since तृतीया-विभक्ति is prescribed for an अनभिहित-कर्तृ, कर्तृ gets तृतीया-विभक्ति, while कर्म gets the default प्रथमा. Thus, we have the forms such as "बालकेन ग्रन्थः पठ्यते" "बालकेन ग्रन्थः पठितः" "बालकेन ग्रन्थः अपठ्यत".

Here, we should note one important idea. "बालकः ग्रन्थं पठति" and "बालकेन ग्रन्थः पठ्यते" are representing the same fact. There is no change in reality, but only the expression in the language is different. And both these forms represent that fact in वर्तमानकाल. Similarly, four other forms represent another fact, and there is no difference in the fact represented by any of those four forms. Why do we even need these variations if there is no difference in reality? These variations provide the user of a language with different options to emphasize his intent. For example, we may use a कर्म-indicating क्रियापद without mentioning कर्तृ, to emphasize what has happened to कर्म, in which the कर्तृ is not in our focus. Other such utilities can be appreciated by looking at classical literature.

It is worth noting that the concept of अनभिहित is primarily helpful in determining the appropriate विभक्ति for कर्तृकारक and कर्मकारक, and not as much for other कारकs at this point. In certain instances of करण-कारक and अधिकरण-कारक, it might seem that the कृत्-प्रत्ययs already signify the कारकs, which means that a विभक्ति may not be necessary to indicate the same कारक. Still, in reality, the कृत्-प्रत्यय would have been typically for some other क्रिया than the one indicated by विभक्ति. We will see this clearly when we see an example of अधिकरण-कारक-विभक्ति a little later.

In summary, we have now seen that, कर्तृ is indicated by तृतीया if कर्तृ is अनभिहित; similarly कर्म is indicated by द्वितीया if कर्म is अनभिहित. However, if अभिहित by a तिङन्त, the कर्तृ/कर्म gets the default प्रथमा. If कर्तृ/कर्म is अभिहित by a तिङन्त, the कर्तृ/कर्म will be in समानाधिकरण with its विशेष्य.

षष्ठी-विभक्ति is also prescribed for कर्तृ and कर्म, if the क्रिया is mentioned by a कृदन्त-पद, and if they are अनभिहित. Here, there are multiple possibilities, and we shall see them one by one:

(1) कर्तृ-indicating कृदन्त-पदs such as स्रष्टृ and गायक: Here, the कर्म in these क्रियाs will be अनभिहित and hence gets षष्ठी-विभक्ति. For example, जगतः स्रष्टा, भगवद्गीतायाः गायकः.

(2) कर्म-indicating कृदन्त-पदs such as सृज्य, गेय and वक्तव्य: Here, the कर्तृ in these क्रियाs will be अनभिहित, and gets षष्ठी-विभक्ति. For example, ब्रह्मणः सृज्यम्, गोपिकानां गेयम्, मित्रस्य वक्तव्यम्. In case the प्रत्यय is a कृत्य प्रत्यय, then this षष्ठी is optional. तृतीया is prescribed if षष्ठी is not used. For example, ब्रह्मणा सृज्यम्, गोपिकाभिः गेयम्, मित्रेण वक्तव्यम्.

(3) भाव-indicating कृदन्त-पदs such as अनुशासन and कृति: Here, both कर्तृ and कर्म are अनभिहित. In such cases, षष्ठी is prescribed for कर्म-कारक. For example, आचार्येण शब्दानाम् अनुशासनम्, पाणिनिना सूत्रस्य कृतिः. Within the Pāṇinian School, some commentators say that, in such cases, षष्ठी may be used optionally for कर्तृ-कारक. That is, आचार्यस्य शब्दानाम् अनुशासनम्, पाणिनेः सूत्रस्य कृतिः, are also valid usages.

(4) There are some exceptions to the prescription of षष्ठी-विभक्ति when a कृदन्त is used. If शतृँ, शानच्, उ, क्त्वा, ल्यप्, तुमुँन्, क्त, क्तवतुँ, तृन् are used, then अनभिहित कर्तृ and कर्म will not get षष्ठी-विभक्ति and will instead get तृतीया and द्वितीया respectively. For example, कृष्णेन गीतम्, कटं चिकीर्षुः.

We have seen that द्वितीया is prescribed for अनभिहित-कर्म. Additionally, if the क्रिया is indicating a displacement (गत्यर्थ with चेष्टा) then चतुर्थी-

विभक्ति is also prescribed optionally for कर्म. For example: ग्रामाय गच्छति or ग्रामं गच्छति.

In some cases where a तुमुन्-प्रत्ययान्त-पद is omitted, then the कर्म in the क्रिया referred by तुमुन्, gets चतुर्थी-विभक्ति. For example, consider someone going to the forest to bring fruits. This can be said as फलानि आहर्तुं वनं गच्छति. Here, फल is कर्म in आहरणक्रिया. If the word आहर्तुम् is omitted, then that कर्म (फल) gets चतुर्थी. Hence, we say फलेभ्यः वनं गच्छति.

11.2.2 विभक्तिs for other कारकs (करण, सम्प्रदान, अपादान, अधिकरण)

(1) तृतीया-विभक्ति is prescribed for करणकारक
E.g., रामः परशुना वृक्षं छिनत्ति

(2) चतुर्थी-विभक्ति is prescribed for सम्प्रदानकारक
E.g., राजा भृत्याय धनं ददौ, राधा पुष्पेभ्यः स्पृहयति, द्रोणः द्रुपदाय क्रुद्ध्यति,

(3) पञ्चमी-विभक्ति is prescribed for अपादाकारक
E.g., वृक्षात् फलं पतति, हिमालयात् गङ्गा प्रभवति, बालकः व्याघ्रात् बिभेति

(4) सप्तमी-विभक्ति is prescribed for अधिकरणकारक
E.g., कृषिकः ग्रामे वसति, वररुचेः व्याकरणे ज्ञानमस्ति, भीमः स्थाल्याम् ओदनं पचति

There is one popular usage called ल्यब्लोपनिमित्ता पञ्चमी, which is an exception for the above said rules on कर्म and अधिकरण. ल्यब्लोप refers to omission of ल्यप्-प्रत्ययान्त-पद. If the ल्यप्-प्रत्ययान्त-पद is omitted, then the कर्म or अधिकरण of the क्रिया indicated by the omitted ल्यप्-प्रत्ययान्त-पद, gets पञ्चमी विभक्ति.

For example, consider the sentence "हरिः प्रासादम् आरुह्य प्रेक्षते" (Hari is watching, after climbing the terrace). Here, प्रासाद is कर्म in the क्रिया of आरोहण. And, if we do not use the ल्यबन्त-पद, that is आरुह्य, then that कर्म will be mentioned in पञ्चमी. Hence the sentence will be: "हरिः प्रासादात् प्रेक्षते". Similarly, "आसने उपविश्य प्रेक्षते" can be said as "आसनात् प्रेक्षते".

11.3 Non-कारक-meanings of विभक्तिs

11.3.1 Meanings of प्रथमा-विभक्ति

प्रथमाविभक्ति doesn't give any extra meaning other than the very meaning of the प्रातिपदिक, its gender (लिङ्ग), and grammatical number (वचन).

A variant of प्रथमाविभक्ति called सम्बोधना-प्रथमा-विभक्ति is used while addressing someone. Its final forms are very similar to the प्रथमा-विभक्ति, with a slight change only in the एकवचन forms. For example, "अच्युत, सेनयोः मध्ये रथं स्थापय", "क्लैब्यं मा स्म गमः पार्थ", "हरे राम हरे राम राम राम हरे हरे","हे कृष्ण हे यादव हे सखेति", "सदेव सौम्य इदमग्रे आसीत्, "अहम् आगच्छामि पितरौ", "भवति" भिक्षां देहि", "भोः मित्राणि".

11.3.2 Meanings of द्वितीया-विभक्ति

In the meaning of a continuous association with an activity for a specific time or space (कालाध्वनोरत्यन्तसंयोग):

For example, if a बालक is studying continuously for one whole संवत्सर (year), without any break, then द्वितीया-विभक्ति is prescribed for that unit of time (संवत्सर) - बालकः भगवद्गीतां संवत्सरम् अधीते. If this association is not continuous, then the word संवत्सर gets सप्तमी-विभक्ति, since it is an अधिकरण - बालकः संवत्सरे अधीते. Similarly if बालक is continuously speaking while travelling a distance of क्रोश, we say, "बालकः क्रोशं वदति". Else, it would have been बालकः क्रोशे वदति.

11.3.3 Meanings of तृतीया-विभक्ति

(1) In the meaning of successful completion of an activity while associating continuously with it (अपवर्ग + कालाध्वनोरत्यन्तसंयोग):

In the same example of the studious student given above, if he completes his studies successfully, then तृतीया-विभक्ति is used. Hence the usage will be बालकः संवत्सरेण भगवद्गीताम् अधीते.

(2) In the meaning of a cause/reason (हेतु):

To indicate the cause or reason behind an action, use the तृतीया-विभक्ति. For example, "गौरी विद्यया यशः प्राप्नोति" means that गौरी gets यशस् because of विद्या. Here, विद्या is the cause, and यशस् is the result;

hence, विद्या gets तृतीया-विभक्ति. Similarly, "पुण्येन हरिः दृष्टः" means that हरि was seen due to पुण्य. पुण्य is the cause for seeing हरि, hence पुण्य gets तृतीया. On similar lines, when David is residing in भारत because of studies, we say "डेविड् अध्ययनेन भारते वसति".

Here, it is helpful to note that करण and हेतु are similar entities, and both are denoted by तृतीया. How does one differentiate the two? Commentators have indicated a helpful feature to differentiate them. Consider two examples involving an axe - "कुमारः परशुना दारुं छिनत्ति". "कुमारः परशुना कलहं करोति". In the first case, Kumara is chopping wood using an axe, in the second case, he is fighting for an axe. The first example is of करण, where there is an activity (व्यापार) seen in the axe. He has to move the axe forcefully towards the wood. In the second case, the axe is the cause of the fight - possibly because someone snatched it from him. In that second case, the axe is an idle thing (निर्व्यापार). Thus the presence or absence of व्यापार helps us to differentiate करण and हेतु.

The difference between हेतु and उद्देश/फल is very subtle. Typically the हेतु exists even before the क्रिया is begun, while उद्देश/फल is something that appears after the क्रिया. It is possible to consider उद्देश/फल also as a हेतु, as that उद्देश may be the reason for someone to do that क्रिया in the first place. However, not all हेतुs can be called उद्देश/फल.

(3) In the meaning of an identifier that indicates a speciality (इत्थम्भूतलक्षण):

When an identifier indicates the speciality of an entity, then that identifier gets तृतीया-विभक्ति. For example, consider the usage - "शुक्लनिचुलेन वैद्यः दृष्टः" "काषायवस्त्रेण आरक्षकः आगच्छति" "दण्डेन सन्न्यासी स्नाति". Here a doctor belongs to a special group of human beings. Similarly, a policeman is special, and an ascetic is special. Their identifiers indicate the specialities of being a doctor, policeman, or ascetic. A white coat is an identifier of a doctor; a khaki dress identifies a police officer; and a stick identifies an ascetic. Hence those words - शुक्लनिचुल, काषायवस्त्र and दण्ड - get तृतीया-विभक्ति.

11.3.4 Meanings of चतुर्थी-विभक्ति

(1) In the meaning of purpose (तादर्थ्य/तुमुनर्थ):
An entity indicating purpose gets चतुर्थी-विभक्ति. For example, "रविः घटाय मृद् गृह्णाति" means रवि takes mud for making a घट (pot). Here, घट is the purpose for this action; hence, घट gets चतुर्थी-विभक्ति. Other examples are "मुक्तये भजति", "पाठाय सन्नद्धः", "छेदनाय परशुम् आदत्ते" "वाताय व्यञ्जनं क्रीणाति", "ज्ञानाय यतते", "पाकाय गच्छति".

11.3.5 Meanings of पञ्चमी-विभक्ति

(1) In the meaning of हेतु:

We saw that तृतीया-विभक्ति is prescribed in the meaning of हेतु. However, पञ्चमी is also prescribed in that meaning. Generally, पञ्चमी is used if that हेतु is a गुण (property) and if it is not in स्त्रीलिङ्ग. Eg: विनयाद् याति पात्रताम्, पात्रत्वाद् धनमाप्नोति.

(2) In the meaning of identifying a particular entity (निर्धारण):

निर्धारण is defined as the process of determining a special element. This speciality may be in the form of its properties - its category, characteristic, or function. Also, to call something special, we need a reference group against which (sometimes, within which) this becomes special. If the element is not part of that group, then the group gets पञ्चमी.

E.g., भारतदेशस्थाः चीनादेशस्थेभ्यः विलक्षणाः(भारतदेशस्थs does not belongs to the group of चीनादेशस्थs), सुवर्णः रजतात् श्रेष्ठः (सुवर्ण does not belongs to the group of रजत), जम्बीरफलम् आम्रफलात् आम्लरसकम्(जम्बीरफल does not belongs to the group of आम्रफल) .

11.3.6 Meanings of षष्ठी-विभक्ति

(1) In the meaning of relation (सम्बन्ध):

षष्ठी-विभक्ति is prescribed for indicating a relationship between entities. These relationships are typically in the form of: creator and created; cause and effect; whole and part; lord and servant; owner and owned; possessor and possessed; object and its characteristics.

Eg; कुम्भकारस्य घटः, तन्तूनां पटः, पशोः पादः, महाराजस्य सेवकः, बालस्य पुस्तकम्, कृष्णस्य गृहम्, रामस्य सौन्दर्यम्.

षष्ठी-विभक्ति is most commonly used in this meaning which is also referred to as "शेष-षष्ठी".

(2) In the meaning of निर्धारण:

As discussed above, when निर्धारण is intended and if the entity is not a part of the group, then the group gets पञ्चमी. However, if that entity is a part of the group, then the group receives षष्ठी or सप्तमी.

Eg: पाणिनिः वैय्याकरणानां प्रथितयशाः (पाणिनि belongs to the group of वैय्याकरणs), भक्तानां ज्ञानी उत्तमः (ज्ञानी is a भक्त), स्थावराणां हिमालयः अत्युत्कृष्टः (हिमालय is a स्थावर). We can also use सप्तमी. Then the same examples can be: पाणिनिः वैय्याकरणेषु प्रथितयशाः, भक्तेषु ज्ञानी उत्तमः, स्थावरेषु हिमालयः अत्युत्कृष्टः.

11.3.7 Meanings of सप्तमी-विभक्ति

(1) In the meaning of निर्धारण:

As discussed above, सप्तमी is also prescribed in निर्धारण.

Eg: पाणिनिः वैय्याकरणेषु प्रथितयशाः, भक्तेषु ज्ञानी उत्तमः, स्थावरेषु हिमालयः अत्युत्कृष्टः.

(2) In the meaning of indicating the time of another क्रिया:

Suppose two actions (प्रसिद्ध-क्रिया and अप्रसिद्ध-क्रिया) are happening at the same time, and that we know the time of only one of them (प्रसिद्ध-क्रिया). Then we can indicate the time of another क्रिया (अप्रसिद्ध-क्रिया), by adding सप्तमी to the कारक (कर्तृ or कर्म only) which is अभिहित by the कृदन्त representing this प्रसिद्ध-क्रिया. Since the कृदन्त is a विशेषण to कर्तृ or कर्म of the प्रसिद्ध-क्रिया, the कृदन्त also gets सप्तमी-विभक्ति.

Sometimes, to make this meaning explicit, we see words such as सति, सतोः, सत्सु or सत्याम्, सतोः, सतीषु. These words indicate the present-continuous tense in that क्रिया. For this reason, this kind of सप्तमी is popularly known as सति-सप्तमी.
Eg: Lakshmana was born when the Sun rose in Karkataka. Here, "Sun rising in Karkataka" is the प्रसिद्ध-क्रिया. Hence, we say: "रवौ कर्काटके उदिते लक्ष्मणः जातः". Note that उदय is the प्रसिद्ध-क्रिया, and the corresponding कृदन्त, that is उदित, is referring to रवि. Hence,

रवि gets सप्तमी, so does उदित. Some other examples are: "गोषु दुह्यमानासु बालकः शालां गतः", "अध्यापके पाठे ब्रुवति छात्राः लिखन्ति".

Sometimes this सति-सप्तमी may not refer to the क्रिया that occurred at the same time but at a very close time (imminent क्रिया). For example, in this extract from the first chapter of भगवद्गीता - "प्रवृत्ते शस्त्रसम्पाते पाण्डवः हृषीकेशम् आह", two क्रियाs are mentioned -

(i) Arjuna telling Krishna (अप्रसिद्ध-क्रिया), and
(ii) the beginning of the war (प्रसिद्ध-क्रिया).

Here, प्रसिद्ध-क्रिया is represented by प्रवृत्त which is in सप्तमी, to indicate that the अप्रसिद्ध-क्रिया took place at the same time. However, when Arjuna started speaking with Krishna, the war had not yet begun in the real sense but was just about to begin. Hence, सति-सप्तमी should be interpreted as referring to the imminent क्रिया if not a simultaneous क्रिया. Other examples include: धर्मे नष्टे अधर्मः अभिभवति, कुलक्षये कुलधर्माः प्रणश्यन्ति, क्षीणे पुण्ये मर्त्यलोकं विशन्ति etc.

(3) In the meaning of निमित्त:

सप्तमी-विभक्ति is also prescribed in the meaning of a purpose, provided that purpose is physically connected to the कर्म. Consider this popular verse quoted as an example in this usage: "चर्मणि द्वीपिनं हन्ति दन्तयोर्हन्ति कुञ्जरम्". Here, a hunter kills a tiger and an elephant for skin and tusks. The skin is physically attached to the tiger and the tusks to the elephant. Hence, the words चर्म and दन्त are mentioned in सप्तमी-विभक्ति.

11.4 In association with words

In the above sections, we have seen two kinds of meanings for the विभक्तिs, namely, कारक-meanings, and non-कारक-meanings. There are some other instances where विभक्तिs are prescribed not with a specific meaning but only as accompanying विभक्तिs when some types of words are associated. These are sometimes called उपपद-विभक्तिs - literally, "a विभक्ति because of an associated पद". Here, association (योग) refers to a meaningful relationship. In other words, these उपपदs typically expect another word to complete/close their meanings, and their associated words provide completion/closure. For example, the word विना means "without", and the word "without" is incomplete if the corresponding entity is not specified: without what? That associated entity is prescribed to be mentioned in either द्वितीया, तृतीया or पञ्चमी-विभक्ति. There is no specific meaning for such विभक्ति, but it only helps in associating it with the corresponding word. More examples are given in Table 11.2.

There is one special case where तृतीया-विभक्ति is prescribed to a set of words: प्रकृति, प्राय, गोत्र, सम, विषम, द्विद्रोण, पञ्चक, साहस्र, सुख, दुःख etc. Here, the

विभक्ति is attached to these very words and not to associated words. Hence, we see usages such as प्रकृत्या साधुः, प्रायेण पठति etc. Note that the तृतीया here is not in any particular कारक or non-कारक meanings.

पद	Prescribed विभक्ति	Example
अन्तरा, अन्तरेण	द्वितीया	अन्तरा/अन्तरेण त्वां च मां च कमण्डलुः, अन्तरेण पुरुषकारं न किञ्चित् लभ्यते
पदs with कर्मप्रवचनीय-संज्ञा (1-4-83 to 97)	द्वितीया	शाकल्यस्य संहिताम् अनु प्रावर्षत्
अप, आङ्, परि (1-4-88 to 1-4-90)	पञ्चमी	अप हरेः संसारः, परि हरेः संसारः, आमुक्तेः संसारः
नमः, स्वस्ति, स्वाहा, स्वधा, अलं, वषट्	चतुर्थी	नमो देवेभ्यः, स्वस्ति प्रजाभ्यः, स्वाहा अग्नये, स्वधा पितृभ्यः, अलं मल्लो मल्लाय, वषट् अग्नये
सह, सार्धम्, साकम्, समम्	तृतीया	रामः कृष्णेन सह आगच्छति
हेतु	षष्ठी	अन्नस्य हेतोर्वसति (If a सर्वनाम is used, then any विभक्ति can be used. E.g., किं निमित्तं पठति, केन निमित्तेन वसति, etc.).
अन्य, आरात्, इतर, ऋते, दिक्, शब्द, अञ्चु, उत्तरपद, आच्, आहि	पञ्चमी	अन्यः देवदत्तात्, आरात् देवदत्तात्, इतरः देवदत्तात्, ऋते देवदत्तात्, पूर्वः ग्रामात्, प्रत्यग् ग्रामात्, उत्तरा ग्रामात्, उत्तराहि ग्रामात्

पद	Prescribed विभक्ति	Example
पृथक्, विना, नाना	तृतीया/ पञ्चमी/ द्वितीया	पृथग् देवदत्तेन/देवदत्तात्/देवदत्तम्, विना देवदत्तेन/ देवदत्तात्/देवदत्तम्, नाना देवदत्तेन/देवदत्तात्/देवदत्तम्
अभितः, परितः, समया, निकषा, हा, प्रति	द्वितीया	अभितः ग्रामम्, परितः ग्रामम्, समया ग्रामम्, निकषा ग्रामम्, हा देवदत्तम्, बुभुक्षितं न प्रतिभाति किञ्चित्

Table 11.2: विभक्तिs based on associated words

12 तद्धितप्रत्ययs, स्त्री-प्रत्ययs

12.1 Introduction

We had mentioned about two specific types of प्रत्ययs that result in the formation of new/derived प्रातिपदिकs - कृत् प्रत्ययs and तद्धित-प्रत्ययs. Of these, कृत् are applicable to धातुs and तद्धितs to प्रातिपदिकs. We have already seen in detail about the कृत् प्रत्ययs. In this chapter, we deal with the तद्धितप्रत्ययs. These are prescribed in the fourth and fifth अध्यायs of अष्टाध्यायी.

Essentially, तद्धित-प्रत्ययs have the following features:

(1) They are applied to a प्रातिपदिक. Hence, प्रातिपदिक + तद्धित $\rightarrow$ a derived तद्धितान्त-प्रातिपदिक.
(2) They have specific meanings. Hence the meaning of the तद्धितान्त-पद will be a combination of meanings of the original प्रातिपदिक and तद्धित.
(3) The तद्धितप्रत्ययान्त-पदs typically behave as विशेषणs and they get the लिङ्ग of विशेष्य.
(4) Some of the तद्धित-प्रत्ययs result in the formation of अव्यय (mentioned earlier in the discussion on अव्ययs).

(5) The final forms of the तद्धितान्त -पदs are dependent on the transformations defined by the इत्-वर्णs in the तद्धित-प्रत्ययs. We will deal with these in the chapter on transformations.

We will start by describing the meanings of some popular तद्धित-प्रत्ययs and provide examples for the same. The readers can apply the same approach to understand other तद्धित-प्रत्ययs.

12.2 अपत्यार्थ

अण् is the most commonly used तद्धित-प्रत्यय in the meaning of अपत्य ("a descendant of").

For example:

(1) विवस्वत् + *अण्* → वैवस्वत (a son of विवस्वत्)
(2) पाण्डु + *अण्* → पाण्डव (a son of पाण्डु)
(3) रघु + *अण्* → राघव (a descendant of रघु)
(4) हिमवत् + *अण्* → हैमवती (a daughter of हिमवत्)

Here, it is to be noted that the word अपत्य usually refers to a son/daughter. However, sometimes it may refer to any descendant in one's pedigree. Words such as राघव referring to राम or यादव referring to कृष्ण are examples of that meaning.

Also, note that the default derivative is in पुंलिङ्ग. To get स्त्रीलिङ्ग word, in the meaning of a daughter, an additional स्त्री-प्रत्यय is to be used. We will discuss those प्रत्ययs in detail later in this chapter.

There are some exceptions to अण्. If the original प्रातिपदिक is an अकारान्त, then a different तद्धित - इञ्, and not अण्, is prescribed in अपत्यार्थ. The following words serve as examples:

(1) दशरथ + इञ् → दाशरथि (a son of दशरथ)
(2) सोमदत्त + इञ् → सौमदत्ति (a son of सोमदत्त)

ढक् is another similar तद्धित-प्रत्यय in the meaning of अपत्य. This is prescribed if the original प्रातिपदिक is derived after adding a स्त्री-प्रत्यय. Such प्रातिपदिकs, for example, are विनता, सुपर्णी, कुन्ती, गङ्गा etc. ढक्-प्रत्ययान्त words derived from these are:

(1) विनता + ढक् → वैनतेय
(2) सुपर्णी + ढक् → सौपर्णेय
(3) कुन्ती + ढक् → कौन्तेय
(4) गङ्गा + ढक् → गाङ्गेय

12.3 मत्वर्थ

मतुँप् is the most commonly used प्रत्यय in the meaning of "this belongs to (is possessed by) someone/something". The name "मत्वर्थ"

means "the meaning of मतुँप्" ("a possessor of"). This possession is not a simple possession of anything in any quantity but a possession that has some significance. It means the possession is of some extraordinary nature that is uncommon to others.

Some types of significance can be:[1]

(1) Abundance
(2) Praiseworthiness
(3) Blameworthiness
(4) Permanent presence
(5) Excess
(6) Contact

These examples may help in clarifying these meanings:

(1) गो + मतुँप् → गोमत् (one who has cows in abundance)
(2) विद्या + मतुँप् → विद्यावत् (one who has knowledge, a praiseworthy quality)
(3) क्रोध + मतुँप् → क्रोधवत् (one who has anger, a blameworthy quality)
(4) क्रिया + मतुँप् → क्रियावत् (one who is engaged in an action, always)
(5) उदर + मतुँप् → उदरवत् (one who has obese belly)
(6) शङ्ख + मतुँप् → शङ्खवत् (one who has a conch in his hand)

In these examples, we may notice that some words end as "..मत्" and some others as "..वत्". This variation is because of the following rule:

[1]भूमिनिन्दाप्रशंसासु नित्ययोगेऽतिशायने । संसर्गेऽस्ति विवक्षायां भवन्ति मतुबादयः ॥

"If अ (or its variations) or म् is the last or penultimate वर्ण of the प्रातिपदिक, then मत् changes to वत्." E.g., धनवत्, विद्यावत्, शंवत्, यशस्वत्, लक्ष्मीवत् etc.

Otherewise, मत् is retained. E.g.,: गोमत्, बुद्धिमत्, धीमत् etc.

The above mentioned मतुबर्थs, can also be obtained by using some other तद्धित-प्रत्ययs other than मतुँप् itself. Some of them are: ठन्, इनिँ and विनिँ. These are prescribed with special conditions. ठन् and इनिँ are prescribed for ह्रस्व-अकारान्त-प्रातिपदिकs; and, विनिँ is prescribed for असु-अन्त-प्रातिपदिकs and माया, मेधा and स्रज्.

(1) धन + *इनिँ* ⟶ धनिन्; दण्ड + *इनिँ* ⟶ दण्डिन्;

(2) धन + *ठन्* ⟶ धनिक; दण्ड + *ठन्* ⟶ दण्डिक;

(3) यशस् + *विनिँ* ⟶ यशस्विन्; मनस्+ *विनिँ* ⟶ मनस्विन्; माया + *विनिँ* ⟶ मायाविन्; मेधा+ *विनिँ* ⟶ मेधाविन्; स्रज् + *विनिँ* ⟶ स्रग्विन्;

12.4 भावार्थ

In this context, भाव is defined as the characteristic (a quality, action, category, etc.) of an entity that gives it a name. These are also called प्रवृत्ति-निमित्त. It refers to - "the reason for using a specific word to a specific entity". It can crudely be translated to the meaning conveyed in English by suffixes such as "-ness" or "-ity". For example, humans are called humans because of "humanity" in them. Similarly, a pot is called a pot because of the "pot-ness" in it. A driver is called a driver because of the "driver-ness" in them. Essentially, these refer to a fundamental characteristic that can act as an entity's exclusive identifier (or the essence).

There are three popular तद्धित-प्रत्ययs in Saṃskṛta that give the meaning of भाव: *त्व, तल्* and *ष्यञ्*. For example,

(1) मनुष्य + त्व → मनुष्यत्व; सुन्दर + त्व → सुन्दरत्व

(2) मनुष्य + तल् → मनुष्यता; सुन्दर + तल् → सुन्दरता

(3) मनुष्य + ष्यञ् → मानुष्य; सुन्दर + ष्यञ् → सौन्दर्य

Out of these, the प्रातिपदिकs formed with *त्व* and *ष्यञ्* are नपुंसकलिङ्ग-प्रातिपदिकs, while those formed by *तल्* become स्त्रीलिङ्ग-प्रातिपदिकs.

12.5 अतिशयार्थ

Another popular set of तद्धित-प्रत्ययs is of those used while comparing entities based on their quality in them. To compare two entities, we use either *ईयसुन्* or *तरप्*; for comparison among a group of three or more, we use *इष्ठन्* or *तमप्*. This idea is very similar to the concept of comparative and superlative degrees in English (similar to "more/most")

Examples:

(1) गुरु (heavy) + *ईयसुन्* → गरीयस् (heavier)
लघु (light) + *ईयसुन्* → लघीयस् (lighter)

(2) गुरु (heavy) + इष्ठन् → गरिष्ठ (heaviest)
लघु (light) + इष्ठन् → लघिष्ठ (lightest)

(3) गुरु + *तरप्* → गुरुतर (heavier); लघु + *तरप्* → लघुतर(lighter)

(4) गुरु + *तमप्* → गुरुतम (heaviest); लघु + *तमप्* → लघुतम (lightest)

12.6 पूरणार्थ

Numbers are used in two ways: one as cardinal numbers and the other as ordinal numbers. Cardinal numbers are used to count, while ordinal numbers are used to note the order/position of an object in that count. In other words, one, two, three, etc., are cardinal numbers; first, second, third, etc., are ordinal numbers. Similarly in Saṃskṛta, we use numbers for गणन (counting) - एक, द्वि, त्रि etc., and for पूरण (to fill a position) - प्रथम, द्वितीय, तृतीय etc.[2] These पूरणार्थक-पदs are created by adding one of these two तद्धित-प्रत्ययs: *तीय,* डट् *and sometimes along with आगमs, मट्* or *तमट्.*

(1) *तीय* applies to द्वि and त्रि to result in two words: द्वितीय and तृतीय.

[2]These resources can be found online using the link mentioned on the last page of the book.

(2) डट् applies to numbers greater than or equal to four (चतुर्). These result in words such as एकादश, द्वादश, एकोनविंश, विंश, त्रिंश, पञ्चाश etc. However, for some numbers, after applying डट्-प्रत्यय, an additional आगम (insertion) such as *मट्*, *तमट्* or *थुक्* is added in the following way:

(i) *थुक्* is added to चतुर् and षट् to result in चतुर्थ and षष्ठ.[3]

(ii) मट् is added to पञ्चन्, सप्तन्, अष्टन्, नवन् and दशन् and result in पञ्चम, सप्तम, अष्टम, नवम and दशम

(iii) *तमट्* is added optionally for all numbers between विंशति (20) and एकोनशत(99). Hence, we get forms such as विंशतितम as an option for विंश or विंशतितम, एकविंशतितम as an option for एकविंश, एकोनशततम as an option for एकोनशत etc.

(iv) However, *तमट्* is added mandatorily for all numbers greater than or equal to शत (100) and also for four other numbers - षष्टि, सप्तति, अशीति, and नवति.

Note that the word प्रथम denotes "first" and is not derived using the above प्रत्यय.

Two other words, कति (how many) and कतिपय (how many ever), also get an ordinal meaning in Saṃskṛta with the addition of डट्-प्रत्यय and थुक्-आगम, resulting in कतिथ and कतिपयथ. These words do not

[3]चतुर्थ has another similar form after losing its first वर्णs - तुरीय/तुर्य also meaning "the fourth".

have an exact equivalent in English. Some examples: कतिथायां कक्ष्यायां पठसि? (In which grade are you studying?); कतिपयथायां कक्ष्यायां पठामि, तत्र संस्कृतपाठाः सन्ति (In whichever grade I am studying, there are Saṃskṛta lessons in it.).

12.7 A few more तद्धित-प्रत्ययs

(1) अभूततद्भावार्थ (*च्वि*): This प्रत्यय indicates that an entity has acquired or is in the process of acquiring a new state or characteristic. For example, when an impure (अशुचि) entity is purified (शुचि), then we create the term शुची and use it as शुचीभूतः, शुचीकृतः, शुचीभवति, शुचीकरोति, शुचीकृत्य, शुचीभूय, शुचीस्यात् etc. Note that this प्रत्यय is not seen at the end since it is always suffixed with a form of one of the three धातुs - अस्, भू or कृ.

(2) समूहार्थ (*तल्*): This प्रत्यय is used in the meaning of a group, for the words - ग्राम, जन, बन्धु and सहाय. For example, a group of villages is called ग्रामता; and a group of people is called जनता.

(3) परिमाणार्थ (*वतुँप्*): वतुँप् is used in the meaning of quantity, and is applied to only three popular सर्वनामs - यद्, तद् and एतद्, and generate यावत्, तावत्, and एतावत् respectively. Literally speaking, यावत् means "as much", तावत् "that much", and एतावत् "this much".

(4) सञ्जात (*इतच्*): This प्रत्यय is used to indicate that a new entity has appeared. For example, when पुष्प (flowers) appears in a tree, we suffix इतच् to पुष्प and say that the वृक्ष is now पुष्पित.

(5) विकार (*मयट्*): This प्रत्यय is widely used in the meaning of a transformation. For example, लोहमय refers to something made of लोह (a metal). मयट् is also used in other meanings, such as:

(i) प्राचुर्य (abundance): जलमय = having water in abundance

(ii) अवयव (part): मूर्वामय = part of मूर्वा (Elephant creeper).

12.8 तद्धितप्रत्ययs forming अव्ययs

There are a few तद्धित-प्रत्ययs that transform प्रातिपदिकs into अव्ययs. We shall discuss some of them as examples below:

(1) *तसिः / तसिँल्* : These two प्रत्ययs are used in the meaning of पञ्चमी-विभक्ति. For example, रामतः → रामात्; अतः → अस्मात्; ततः → तस्मात्; रमातः → रमायाः; वनतः → वनात्.

(2) त्रल् : This प्रत्यय is used in the meaning of सप्तमी-विभक्ति, and is applicable mainly for सर्वनाम-पदs. For example, तत्र → तस्मिन्; यत्र → यस्मिन्; अत्र → अस्मिन्; कुत्र → कस्मिन्; अन्यत्र → अन्यस्मिन्.

(3) *दा*: This प्रत्यय is prescribed for the प्रातिपदिकs- सर्व, एक, अन्य, किम्, यत्, and तद् in the meaning of सप्तमी-विभक्ति, but only to indicate time. When we want to indicate time, then दा is an option, but not

त्रल्. For example, तदा = तस्मिन् काले = at that time; कदा = कस्मिन् काले = at what time

(4) *थाल्*: This is used to indicate a type or manner. For example, तथा = in that manner; अन्यथा = in another manner / otherwise; सर्वथा = by all means / at any cost.

(5) *धा*: This is used to indicate the number of types of doing/being. For example, एकधा = "is of one type"; द्विधा = "is of two types"; बहुधा = "is of more than two types"; अनेकधा = "is of more than one type".

(6) साति: This प्रत्यय is usually used to indicate that an entity has been modified completely. For example, भस्मसात् = fully turned into ashes.

(7) *वति*: This is a very popular प्रत्यय used to indicate similarity. For example, राजवत् करोति = does like a king; चैत्रवत् मैत्रस्य गावः = Cows of Maitra are similar to those of Chaitra; महानसवत् पर्वतः अग्निमान् = The mountain has fire, similar to that in kitchen.

12.9 स्त्रीप्रत्ययs

We have seen earlier that in Saṃskṛta vocabulary लिङ्ग is typically mapped with प्रातिपदिकs and not with the entity that they are referring to. In other words, लिङ्ग is one of the features of all प्रातिपदिकs. Among the स्त्रीलिङ्ग-प्रातिपदिकs, some words are inherently स्त्रीलिङ्ग, and others are derived using a स्त्री-प्रत्ययs. Of all the स्त्रीलिङ्ग-प्रातिपदिकs, those that are ending with इ, उ, ऋ or any हल् do not have a स्त्री-प्रत्यय in them. However, most of the others, viz, those ending with आ, ई, or ऊ, would have a स्त्रीप्रत्यय. (There are very few exceptions, such as लक्ष्मी, श्री, and स्त्री, which do not have a स्त्री-प्रत्यय in them).

These स्त्री-प्रत्ययs are generally applied in two situations where we change the gender of a प्रातिपदिक into its feminine form:

(1) When the default is पुंलिङ्ग or नपुंसकलिङ्ग, and we intend to indicate its feminine form.
    E.g., अज is converted to अजा when referring to a female goat.
(2) When the विशेष्य is feminine and we intend to use a विशेषण that has विशेष्यनिघ्नलिङ्ग
    E.g., consider the phrase "सुन्दरः पुरुषः". Here सुन्दर is विशेषण to पुरुष, and सुन्दर does take the gender of its विशेष्य. Now, if we want to talk about a स्त्री, then this phrase transforms into "सुन्दरी स्त्री".

12.9.1 Derive स्त्रीलिङ्ग-प्रातिपदिकs with स्त्री-प्रत्ययs

It is for the purposes mentioned above that we need a mechanism to derive स्त्रीलिङ्ग-प्रातिपदिकs. This derivation is accomplished by employing स्त्रीप्रत्ययs. स्त्री-प्रत्ययs are prescribed in अष्टाध्यायी 4-1-3 to 4-1-82. They are a total of eight in number - *टाप्*, *डाप्*, *चाप्*, *ङीप्*, *ङीष्*, *ङीन्*, *ऊङ्* and *ति*. All these प्रत्ययs can be categorized into four groups based on their actual content, that is, the component after removing all इत्-वर्णs.[4] They are - आ, ई, ऊ and ति.

(1) आ-प्रत्यय:

आ-प्रत्यय is applied for:

(i) All ह्रस्व-अकारान्त-प्रातिपदिकs. E.g., खट्वा, मेधा, गङ्गा, पाचिका, अध्यापिका[5]

(ii) All words in the set starting from अजा. E.g., अजा, एडका, अश्वा.[6]

(iii) All मन्नन्त-स्त्रीलिङ्ग-प्रातिपदिकs (optionally). E.g., सीमन् or सीमा, पामन् or पामा

(iv) All अन्नन्त-स्त्रीलिङ्ग-प्रातिपदिकs derived in बहुव्रीहि-समास (optionally). E.g., बहुराजा or बहुराजन्

(2) *ई-प्रत्यय*:

This is a very common स्त्री-प्रत्यय and is applicable for many types of प्रातिपदिकs. Some of them are:

(i) All प्रातिपदिकs ending with ऋ. E.g., कर्तृ → कर्त्री, हर्तृ → हर्त्री.

(ii) All प्रातिपदिकs ending with न्. E.g., दण्डिन् → दण्डिनी, छत्रिन् → छत्रिणी.

[4]The इत्-वर्णs, in this case, are used only to specify the स्वर (उदात्त, अनुदात्त, स्वरित) in which these words are to be pronounced. These स्वरs are not in use in contemporary Saṃskṛta. Therefore, we ignore them for the discussion here.

[5]If the word is ending with a प्रत्यय-derived-क and has an आप् at the end, then अ in the previous वर्ण gets इ (please see 7.3.44), E.g., पाचक → पाचिका, अध्यापक → अध्यापिका

[6]These resources can be found online using the link mentioned on the last page of the book.

(iii) All प्रातिपदिकs derived from प्रत्ययs that have उ or ऋ as इत् (such as मतुँप् or शतृ). E.g., गुणवत् → गुणवती. कुर्वत् → कुर्वती, गच्छत् → गच्छन्ती[7]

(iv) All प्रातिपदिकs derived from ढ, अण्, ठक् and प्रत्ययs that have ट् as इत् (such as ल्युट्). E.g., वैनतेय → वैनतेयी, कुम्भकार → कुम्भकारी, आस्तिक → आस्तिकी, साधन → साधनी.

(v) All प्रातिपदिकs mentioned in the list starting from गौर. E.g., गौरी, मत्स्यी, मनुष्यी[8]

(vi) All प्रातिपदिकs derived from प्रत्ययs that have ष् as इत् (such as ष्वुन् or ष्कन्). E.g., नर्तक → नर्तकी.

(vii) All प्रातिपदिकs that are derived from पुंलिङ्ग-प्रातिपदिक, in the sense of "a woman related to". E.g., गोप → गोपी, इन्द्र → इन्द्राणी, भव → भवानी, आचार्य → आचार्यानी[9]

(viii) All प्रातिपदिकs ending with ह्रस्व-अ, and derived with द्विगु-समास. E.g., अष्टाध्यायी.

(ix) All प्रातिपदिकs in the set starting from बहु (optionally). E.g., बहु → बहु/बह्वी

[7]Here, note a small difference between the forms कुर्वती and गच्छन्ती. The additional "न्" is applied for the धातुs in 1st, 4th, and 10th गणs, and optionally for those in 6th गण. This is prescribed by आच्छीनद्योर्नुम् (7-1-80) and शप्श्यनोर्नित्यम् (7-1-81).

[8]These resources can be found online using the link mentioned on the last page of the book.

[9]Here, some words such as इन्द्र, भव, etc., get an extra "आन्" before "ई" at the end due to आनुक् -आगम mentioned in 4.1.49.

(3) ऊ-प्रत्यय: This is applied to only one category of words - those that are ending with उ and referring to a clan of people. E.g., कुरु → कुरू, यदु → यदू.

(4) ति-प्रत्यय: This is applied to only one special word - युवन् to derive युवति

12.10 Transformations

We had discussed earlier that the final form of the derived तद्धितान्त-प्रातिपदिक (derived from the combination of प्रातिपदिक + तद्धित-प्रत्यय) is dependent on many factors, including the इत्-वर्णs in the तद्धित-प्रत्यय.

Before we discuss the transformations related to तद्धितान्तs, it is required to understand the idea of आदेश and the meanings of the terms गुण and वृद्धि. These are detailed in the section on सन्धि. In a nutshell, आदेश is a replacement of a वर्ण with a सदृश-वर्ण. सदृश-वर्ण is the most similar वर्ण, similarity based on उच्चारणास्थान. गुण and वृद्धि are specific types of आदेशs, in the case of कृदन्तs and तद्धितान्तs. The term "गुण" denotes the set of वर्णs - अ, ए, and ओ; and the term वृद्धि refers to the set of three other वर्णs - आ, ऐ, and औ.

At a broad level, each derivative has two components - the प्रातिपदिक and the प्रत्यय. Some transformations happen in, प्रातिपदिक or प्रत्ययs. We describe these transformations separately.

12.10.1 प्रातिपदिक-transformations

(1) आदिवृद्धि

If a तद्धित-प्रत्यय has either ञ्, ण् or क् as one of the इत्-वर्णs, then it leads to आदिवृद्धि in the प्रातिपदिक. आदिवृद्धि refers to the process in which the first अच्-वर्ण gets the आदेश of a सदृश-वर्ण from the set of वृद्धिवर्णs.(आ for अ, ऐ for इ, औ for उ and आर् for ऋ)

Examples:

(i) दशरथ + इञ् → दाशरथि (Note the change from द to दा)

(ii) विवस्वत् + अण् → वैवस्वत (Note the change from वि to वै)

(iii) कुन्ती + ढक् → कौन्तेय (Note the change from कु to कौ)

(2) अन्त्यलोप

If प्रातिपदिक is ending with अ or इ, then that last वर्ण is omitted in the presence of any तद्धित-प्रत्यय.

For example,

(1) दशरथ + इञ् → दाशरथि. Here, अ at the end of दशरथ is omitted in the presence of इञ्, leading to दाशरथि

(2) मुनि + अण् → मौन. Here, इ at the end of मुनि is omitted in the presence of अण्, leading to मौन.

(3) अन्त्यगुण

If a प्रातिपदिक is ending with उ, then it gets गुण (ओ for उ) in the presence of any तद्धित-प्रत्यय added to it.

(i) For example, रघु + अण् results in राघव. Here, अण्, being a णित्, has affected आदिवर्ण and has resulted in आदिवृद्धि, leading to

राघ् + उ + अ. Now, उ gets गुण, and thus we get राघ् + ओ + अ. Then, using the basic principles of सन्धि which we shall see later, ओ + अ changes to अव् + अ. At the end, we get, राघ् + अव् + अ → राघव.

(ii) Similarly, पाण्डु + *अण्* → पाण्डव, is another example for उ getting अन्त्य-गुण.

12.10.2 प्रत्यय-transformations

Although it's easy to understand that the इ at the end of दाशरथि is due to the इ of इञ्, you may wonder how we ended up with एय at the end of कौन्तेय, even though the प्रत्यय was ढक्.

This happens due to a rule that prescribes mandatory replacements for some of the तद्धित-प्रत्ययs. According to the rule, फ् is replaced by आयन्, ढ् by एय्, ख् by ईन्, छ् by ईय्, घ् by इय्, and ठ् by इक्.[10] Therefore, in the above example, ढ्-प्रत्यय is replaced by एय् resulting in कौन्तेय.

[10]आयनेयीनीयियः फढखछघां प्रत्ययादीनाम् (7.1.2), ठस्य इकः (7.3.50)

13 सनादिप्रत्ययs

13.1 Introduction

The label "धातु" is prescribed in अष्टाध्यायी at two instances. First is भूवादयो धातवः (1.3.1) that gives the label "धातु" to the list mentioned in धातु-पाठs. These can be called primary धातुs. Second is सनाद्यन्ता धातवः (3.1.32) that gives the label "धातु" to those ending with any of these प्रत्ययs - सन्, णिच्, यङ्, यङ्लुक्, क्यच्, काम्यच्, क्यङ्, क्यष्, णिङ्, क्विप्, यक्, आय, ईयङ्. These are called सनादि-प्रत्ययान्त-धातुs or derived धातुs / secondary धातुs.

These धातुs behave in the same way as the primary धातुs. Therefore, all प्रत्ययs prescribed for धातुs are applicable to these सनाद्यन्त-धातुs also.

The सनादि-प्रत्ययs are prescribed from 3-1-5 (गुप्तिज्किद्भ्यः सन्) to 3-1-31 (आयादय आर्धद्धातुके वा).

These can be categorised into two types:

(1) सनादिप्रत्ययs applicable to धातुs.
    E.g., सन्, णिच्

(2) सनादिप्रत्ययs applicable to प्रातिपदिकs.
    E.g., क्विप्, क्यच् (धातुs thus derived are popularly known as "नामधातु"s.)

13.2 सन्-प्रत्यय

This प्रत्यय is applicable to all धातुs. It provides the meaning that "the कर्ता is desiring to perform the act". e.g., the धातु "पा" (to drink), when added with सन्, is converted to "पिपास" (to desire to drink). The new धातु, retains the आत्मनेपदित्व/परस्मैपदित्व of the original धातु.

For example, पिपास takes the forms पिपासति, पिपासतः, पिपासन्ति, in लट्-लकार.

This new धातु is also the basis for common कृदन्त terms such as - पिपासा/पिपासुः, जिज्ञासा/जिज्ञासुः, चिकीर्षा/चिकीर्षुः, बुभुक्षा/बुभुक्षुः, मुमुक्षा/मुमुक्षुः. Here the first word in each pair refers to the act of desiring (भाव, अ प्रत्यय) and the second word refers to the entity with that desire(कर्तृ, उ प्रत्यय). We may recollect that these specific कृदन्तs were discussed in the chapter on कृदन्तs.

The सन्-प्रत्ययान्त-धातु is similar to the desiderative verb form in English

13.3 णिच्-प्रत्यय

This प्रत्यय is also applicable to all धातुs. It is used to mean "making another entity perform an activity".

The णिच्-प्रत्ययान्त-धातु is similar to the causative verb form in English. E.g., "going" is a simple verb form. Sometimes we add words like "have, let, help, and make" to these forms to create phrases such as "making him go". Those are called causative verb forms.

In Saṃskṛta, we use णिच्-प्रत्यय to derive a new धातु to indicate the "causative" role. For example, the primary धातु "पच्" (to cook) is converted to "पाचि" (to make someone cook) when appended with णिच्-प्रत्यय. While the original forms are पचति, पचतः, पचन्ति, the forms of णिच्-प्रत्ययान्त-धातु are पाचयति/पाचयते, पाचयतः/पाचयेते, पाचयन्ति/पाचयन्ते.

Note that there are two forms in the णिजन्त-धातु in the example above. In fact, all धातुs after adding णिच् behave as उभय-पदि-धातुs, and as belonging to the 10th गण.

The above described meaning of णिच्, implies that the action indicated by the णिजन्त-धातु will have two कर्तृs - a प्रयोज्य-कर्तृ and a प्रयोजक-कर्तृ. For example, in the case of "पाचयति", प्रयोज्य-कर्तृ is the one who is actually cooking, while the other who is making him cook is called प्रयोजक-कर्तृ. The प्रयोज्य-कर्तृ may also be referred as अणिजन्त-कर्तृ and the प्रयोजक-कर्तृ as णिजन्त-कर्तृ.

At this point, it helps to revisit and expand our understanding of कर्तृ and कर्म-कारकs.

We have seen that the primary entity that performs a given action is called 'कर्तृ'. However, the प्रयोजक-कर्तृ discussed here is also given the label "कर्तृ" in the context of कारकs in तत्प्रयोजको हेतुश्च(1-4-55). प्रयोजक-कर्तृ is also given the label "हेतु".

Similarly, the प्रयोज्य-कर्तृ in some specific actions is considered as "कर्म-कारक". Those are listed in 1-4-52[1] as follows:

(1) Actions of going, knowing, and eating.
Consider the example with going (गम्लृ) as the action: "हनूमान् लङ्कां गच्छति". This sentence is without णिच्. It means that "Hanumān is going to Laṅkā". Here (i) हनूमत् is कर्तृ and (ii) लङ्का is कर्म. Now, if we include Sugrīva, who sent Hanumān to Laṅkā, in this sentence to mean "Hanumān is being made to go to Laṅkā, by Sugrīva", then we say, "सुग्रीवः हनूमन्तं लङ्कां गमयति". Here, (i) the प्रयोजक-कर्तृ, namely सुग्रीव is considered कर्तृ-कारक; (ii) प्रयोज्य-कर्तृ, i.e., हनूमत् is considered कर्म-कारक; and (iii) लङ्का also remains as कर्म-कारक. Similarly, "शिष्यः धर्मं जानाति" is without णिच्, while "गुरुः शिष्यं धर्मं ज्ञापयति" is with णिच्. Similarly, herre is an example with the action of 'knowing'. "बालकः गजं पश्यति" → "पिता बालकं गजं दर्शयति". An example for the action of 'eating' would be, शिशुः ओदनं भुङ्क्ते → माता शिशुम् ओदनं भोजयति.

(2) All actions where the कर्म-कारक is in the form of a शब्द.

---

[1] गतिबुद्धिप्रत्यवसानार्थशब्दकर्माकर्मकाणामणि कर्ता स णौ

Example: कृष्णः गीतां गायति → सान्दीपनिः कृष्णं गीतां गापयति.

(3) All अकर्मक-धातुs. For example,

(i) रथः तिष्ठति → कृष्णः रथं स्थापयति,

(ii) आत्मा प्रसीदति → मुनिः आत्मानं प्रसादयति.

In all the above cases, we have two कर्म-कारकs, viz कर्तृरीप्सिततम and प्रयोज्यकर्तृ; and one कर्तृ-कारक, viz प्रयोजककर्तृ.[2]

In all other cases, the प्रयोज्य-कर्तृ doesn't get the label "कर्म-कारक". Therefore, in a way, we can treat these sentences as having two कर्तृs and one कर्म. For example,

(i) अर्जुनः बाणेन कर्णं हन्ति → कृष्णः अर्जुनेन बाणेन कर्णं घातयति ।

(ii) कर्णः अर्जुनेन बाणेन हतः → कर्णः कृष्णेन अर्जुनेन बाणेन घातितः ।

(Note that in the above examples two or three words may be in तृतीया-विभक्ति but they are not समानाधिकरण. In the second form in second example, कृष्णेन is referring to प्रयोजक-कर्तृ, अर्जुनेन to प्रयोज्य-कर्तृ and बाणेन to करण.)

It is helpful to note that this णिच् is also used as a विकरण-प्रत्यय for धातुs in चुरादिगण (10th गण). In those situations, it doesn't necessarily give the meaning of a causative verb. E.g., "भीष्मः कथां कथयति" can

[2]For this reason, some refer to these as द्विकर्मक. However, technically द्विकर्मक is a term for a given set of धातुs listed earlier.

mean both "Bhishma is telling a story" and "Bhishma is making someone else tell the story".

The term "स्वार्थे णिच्" refers to a type of णिच् where the धातु retains its original meaning and णिच् does not add any meaning of causation.

13.4 यङ् and यङ्लुक्

यङ्-प्रत्यय is prescribed for those धातुs that have only one अच् and are starting with a हल्. It gives the meaning of either repetition or intensity/greatness.[3]. For example,

(1) "पच्" धातु gets the forms such as पापच्यते (cooks repetitively)
(2) "दीप्" → देदीप्यते (shines intensively).

Note that these forms have two critical changes to the धातु - a repetition of the first वर्ण and an addition of य at the end. Therefore, we have got धातुs such as पापच्य and देदीप्य in the above examples.

The य at the end may be deleted to result in another form called यङ्-लुक्-धातुs, in the same meaning as यङ्. Examples are पापच्, देदीप्, लेलिख् etc. Their forms include पापक्ति, देदीपकः, लेलिखितव्यम् etc.

[3]This is prescribed in धातोरेकाचो हलादेः क्रियासमभिहारे यङ् (3.1.22). The following two सूत्रs also prescribe यङ्-प्रत्यय prescribed in the meanings of convoluted movement and shameful activity. Those usages are rare but can be found in सूत्रs

All यङन्त-धातुs are आत्मने-पदि, while यङ्-लुगन्तs are परस्मै-पदि.

13.5 क्यच्-प्रत्यय and काम्यच्-प्रत्यय

These two प्रत्ययs are prescribed to a कर्म-कारक in the action of desiring when that कर्म is desired for self.

Consider the example of someone desiring a cloth for themselves: "आत्मनः वस्त्रम् इच्छति". The same meaning can be communicated using क्यच्-प्रत्यय. Here the new धातु is "वस्त्रीय". So, we can say "वस्त्रीयति" to mean "आत्मनः वस्त्रम् इच्छति". Similarly, काम्यच्-प्रत्यय results in the धातु "वस्त्रकाम्य". Its corresponding form would be "वस्त्रकाम्यति".

Similarly, "आत्मनः सिद्धिं इच्छति" = "सिद्धीयति" = "सिद्धिकाम्यति".

13.6 क्यङ्-प्रत्यय

This प्रत्यय is prescribed in the context of comparison. The object with which we make a comparison gets this प्रत्यय. For example, if a child is behaving like an adult, then we say, "बालकः प्रौढवत् आचरति". The same can be conveyed by using क्यङ्-प्रत्यय on प्रौढ. This results in a new धातु "प्रौढाय". Then, we can say, "बालकः प्रौढायते". The प्रत्यय being a ङित्, these धातुs are आत्मने-पदि-धातुs .

Examples: "अमराः भ्रमरायन्ते", "दरिद्रः राजायते" etc.

13.7 क्विप्-प्रत्यय

This प्रत्यय is prescribed for all प्रातिपदिकs based on the वार्तिक (3.1.11) "सर्वप्रातिपदिकेभ्यो क्विब् वा वक्तव्यः". This प्रत्यय is used in the meaning of "behaving like". Therefore, all प्रातिपदिकs can act as धातुs too.

E.g., बलरामः कृष्ण इव आचरति = बलरामः कृष्णति ।

13.8 क्यष्-प्रत्यय

This प्रत्यय is prescribed in the meaning of becoming what the entity was previously not (e.g., तत् लोहितायते - It becomes red).

There are other less used सनादि-प्रत्ययs - णिङ् (e.g., कामयते), यक् (e.g., कण्डूयति), आय (e.g., पणायति), ईयङ् (e.g., ऋतीयते). All these are prescribed in स्वार्थ, i.e., the original meaning is unaltered.

14 अष्टाध्यायी

14.1 Introduction

अष्टाध्यायी is a work on Saṃskṛta Grammar by पाणिनि. It is today's oldest comprehensive work available on Saṃskṛta grammar. पाणिनि quotes many grammarians in his work, such as सेनक, स्फोटायन, etc., and hence it is clear that the tradition of grammar existed even before him. It is also believed that there are nine traditions of Saṃskṛta grammar, of which Pāṇini's is one. Most of them are now extinct. Only a few are available in traces such as चान्द्रव्याकरणसूत्र, काशकृत्स्नधातुपाठ etc.

पाणिनि's अष्टाध्यायी has approximately 4000 सूत्रs, arranged in eight अध्याय (chapters). In fact, it gets the name अष्टाध्यायी for that reason: अष्टानाम् अध्यायानां समाहारः = अष्टाध्यायी. These सूत्रs, supplemented with माहेश्वरसूत्रs, धातुपाठ and गणपाठ, become the primary texts of Pāṇinian Grammar. They are also supplemented by the amendments given by Vararuchi, known as "वार्तिक"s. These वार्तिकs expand or limit the scope of अष्टाध्यायी-सूत्रs.

सूत्र is a popular textual tool in Saṃskṛta literature. It is commonly translated as "formula", "algorithm", "rule", or "aphorism". However, a technical definition of सूत्र is found in traditional texts and means that सूत्र is a form of textual writing that is concise, unambiguous, fundamental, comprehensive (universally applicable), noise-less, and flaw-less.

"अल्पाक्षरम् असन्दिग्धं सारवद् विश्वतोमुखम् । अस्तोभम् अनवद्यं च सूत्रं सूत्रविदो विदुः ॥"

पतञ्जलि's महाभाष्य is the first explanation/elaboration on the सूत्रs. It also provides conceptual clarity and logical justifications for theoretical ideas of व्याकरण.

These three authors - पाणिनि, वररुचि, and पतञ्जलि - are considered the "मुनित्रयs" (the trio) of Saṃskṛta grammar.

The concise nature of the सूत्रs helps in memorizing them. However, we do need commentaries to make total sense of them in the form of complete sentences. Such commentaries are called वृत्तिs. Even though महाभाष्य elaborates on ideas, it assumes that we understand the basic meaning of the सूत्रs and वार्तिकs.

काशिका jointly authored by वामन and जयादित्य is the first comprehensive वृत्ति on अष्टाध्यायी. It also provides a lot of examples and counterexamples to illustrate how each सूत्र operates.

It is believed that काशिका was written before any commentaries were written on महाभाष्य. Later, कैय्यट wrote a commentary on महाभाष्य by the name प्रदीप. Making use of this commentary, two other commentaries came on काशिका - हरदत्तमिश्र's पदमञ्जरी and जिनेन्द्रबुद्धि's न्यास. Later, a sub-commentary, उद्योत, was written on प्रदीप by नागोजिभट्ट.

This set of works - अष्टाध्यायी, वार्तिक, महाभाष्य, प्रदीप, उद्योत, काशिका, पदमञ्जरी and न्यास - form the main corpus of classical Pāṇinian tradition.

Though not part of a main grammar tradition, another classical work worth mentioning here is वाक्यपदीय of भर्तृहरि. It deals with linguistics and the philosophy of grammar.

The सूत्रs are composed by organizing topics and making use of the principles of interpreting सूत्रs (such as अनुवृत्ति, discussed later). While this made them concise and rigorous, using the सूत्रs to derive a word was hard. It needed familiarisation with all the सूत्रs. During medieval times, to facilitate the derivation of words, a new set of commentaries was written that reorganized the सूत्रs. Two popular works written in that approach are रामचन्द्र's प्रक्रियाकौमुदी and भट्टोजिदीक्षित's सिद्धान्तकौमुदी. On the same lines, वरदराजाचार्य wrote a further simplified version for initial studies, called "लघुसिद्धान्तकौमुदी".

With this brief introduction to the main corpus of texts in the tradition of Pāṇinian grammar, let's go into the specifics of structure and methods of understanding अष्टाध्यायी.

14.2 Big Picture of अष्टाध्यायी

We saw that अष्टाध्यायी has eight अध्यायs. Each अध्याय is subdivided into four पादs (sub-chapters), and each पाद has a varying number of सूत्रs generally arranged as different प्रकरणs (modules). At a broader level, the important topics covered in the chapters (ignoring some overlaps) include:

(1) अध्यायs 1 and 2 cover सञ्ज्ञा, परिभाषा, कारक, विभक्ति and समास.

(2) अध्याय 3 deals with प्रत्यय prescribed on धातुs, i.e., तिङ्-प्रत्ययs and कृत्-प्रत्ययs.

(3) अध्यायs 4 and 5 discuss प्रत्ययs on प्रातिपदिकs such as सुप्-प्रत्ययs, तद्धित-प्रत्ययs and समासान्त-प्रत्ययs.

(4) अध्यायs 6, 7 and 8 talk about प्रकृति-प्रत्यय-विकार (transformations of प्रकृति and प्रत्यय) and सन्धि.

14.3 Types of सूत्रs and their functions

Based on the functions अष्टाध्यायी-सूत्रs are divided into 6 types.[1] Three of them (विधि, नियम and अतिदेश) deal with transformations and the three other (सञ्ज्ञा, परिभाषा and अधिकार) provide background to make sense of the transformational सूत्रs.

सञ्ज्ञा-सूत्रs define labels. These are usually technical labels and have a meaning only within grammar texts. For example, the very first सूत्र "वृद्धिरादैच्" is a सञ्ज्ञा-सूत्र. It provides the name वृद्धि to these three वर्णs- आ, ऐ and औ.

परिभाषा-सूत्रs specify conventions used in अष्टाध्यायी, that are required to interpret other सूत्रs.

अधिकार-सूत्रs are similar to topic heads. These सूत्रs should be read together with the relevant सूत्रs under this अधिकार, unlike regular topic headings. They don't carry meaning on their own. For example, the first two सूत्रs of the third chapter, "प्रत्ययः" and "परश्च" are अधिकार-सूत्रs and are applicable till the end of the fifth chapter. They mean "प्रत्यय" and "after". But they should be read with each of the following सूत्रs. Then they provide the meaning that "X is a "प्रत्यय" defined on Y, and is to be applied after Y".

[1]"सञ्ज्ञा च परिभाषा च विधिर्नियम एव च । अतिदेशोऽधिकारश्च षड्विधं सूत्रलक्षणम् ॥"

विधि-सूत्रs prescribe transformations/actions while also indicating conditions and meanings under which those transformations would be allowed. नियम-सूत्रs restrict the scope of विधि-सूत्रs. अतिदेश-सूत्रs extend the scope of विधि-सूत्रs. Therefore a detailed discussion on the विधि-सूत्रs help us in understanding the operations dealt in अष्टाध्यायी.

14.4 Understanding विधि-सूत्रs

"विधि" means a "prescription". The विधि-सूत्रs prescribe transformations on building blocks of words (such as धातुs, प्रातिपदिकs, प्रत्ययs, etc.), how they combine, and what form they take at the end. Typically these transformations are of three types: आदेश, आगम, and लोप. Replacing/substituting existing वर्ण(s) with other वर्ण(s) is called आदेश. The addition of new वर्ण(s) is called आगम. लोप refers to the deletion of वर्ण(s).

The स्थानिन् is the base for these transformations, while the conditions that govern them are called निमित्त(s). Therefore, a general template of a विधि-सूत्र is:

"A स्थानिन् undergoes a कार्य, i.e., a आदेश/आगम/लोप,
in the presence of निमित्त(s)"

There are some conventions (परिभाषाs) used in अष्टाध्यायी to indicate स्थानिन्, कार्य and निमित्त:

(1) The पद in षष्ठी-विभक्ति indicates the स्थानिन्.[2]

(2) पद(s) in पञ्चमी-, सप्तमी- or तृतीया-विभक्तिs indicate the निमित्त(s).

 (i) पञ्चमी-विभक्ति specifies that the निमित्त should precede the स्थानिन्. Such निमित्त is called पूर्वनिमित्त.

 (ii) सप्तमी-विभक्ति mentions that the निमित्त should follow the स्थानिन्. Such निमित्त is termed परनिमित्त.

 (iii) If the निमित्त can be either preceding or following the स्थानिन्, then such निमित्तs are indicated by तृतीया-विभक्ति.

(3) कार्य is indicated by a पद in प्रथमा-विभक्ति. By default, कार्य is an आदेश unless it is specifically marked by one of these three इत्s - ट्, क् or म्. In such cases, the कार्य is an आगम. लोप is further specified by one of these words - लुक्, श्लु, लुप् or लोप.

Let's illustrate all these concepts using a simple example:

"इकः यण् अचि" (6-1-77) is a सूत्र that talks about a type of सन्धि, popular as यण्-सन्धि.[3]

[2]In some सूत्रs, we find सप्तमी or पञ्चमी also indicating स्थानिन्.

[3]We shall use this only for illustrating how a सूत्र operates, but not for understanding सन्धि, which we shall discuss in Chapter-15 on सन्धिs.

Here, note that (a) इकः is षष्ठी-विभक्ति of इक्, (b) यण् is प्रथमा-विभक्ति of यण् and (c) अचि is सप्तमी-विभक्ति of अच्. Therefore, इक् is स्थानिन्, यण् is आदेश, and अच् is परनिमित्त. Hence, the meaning of the सूत्र is "यण् replaces इक् if इक् is followed by अच्"

In the above example, the कार्य was आदेश. We see more examples of आदेश later too. Therefore, before moving into more such details, especially in the discussion on सन्धि, we will briefly describe the other two कार्यs viz, आगम and लोप with a few examples.

आगम - As noted above, when the प्रथमा-विभक्ति-पद, which is indicating कार्य is marked by either ट्, क् or म्, then it suggests आगम (=insertion). If the mark is ट्, i.e., if the word indicating कार्य has ट् as इत्, (or in even simpler terms, the word indicating कार्य is टित्), it mandates that the insertion must be before स्थानिन्. When the word is कित्, then the insertion must be after the स्थानिन्. Lastly, if the word is मित्, then the insertion must be after the last अच् within स्थानिन्. For example,

(1) According to the सूत्र, नान्तादसङ्ख्यादेर्मट् (5-2-49), a प्रातिपदिक that ends with न, indicates a number, and doesn't have a number at the beginning, is the पूर्वनिमित्त. डट् (which is carried over from a previous सूत्र, and has अ as its content) is the स्थानिन्. मट् (that has म् as

its content) is कार्य. Here, since मट् is टित्, the insertion is before the स्थानिन्. Hence, पञ्चन् +डट् = पञ्चन् + मट् + डट् = पञ्चम.

(2) In the सूत्र, "ह्रस्वस्य पिति कृति तुक्" (6-1-71), धातु ending with a ह्रस्व-वर्ण, is स्थानिन्. कृत्-प्रत्यय that has प् as इत् is परनिमित्त. तुक् (that has त् as its content) is कार्य, and is कित्. Now, since तुक् is कित्, the insertion must be after the स्थानिन्. Therefore, परिहृ(धातु) + ल्यप् (कृत्) = परिहृ + त् + ल्यप्. Here note that the insertion त् is after the स्थानिन्.

(3) In the सूत्र, "इदितो नुम् धातोः" (7-1-58), धातु that has इ as इत् is स्थानिन्. नुम् (that has न् as content) is कार्य. Here, since नुम् is मित्, the insertion must be after the last अच्-वर्ण. Therefore, the धातु वदिँ (that has वद् as its content and इ as इत्) gets नुम् after its last अच् (अ after व्) and becomes वन्द्. We thus have forms, वन्दते,...

लोप - लोप means deletion. It is a kind of transformation when a वर्ण disappears from being pronounced. It occurs for a few specific वर्णs in संहिताs. For example, द्वौ + अत्र = द्वाव् + अत्र = द्वा अत्र. Here we can observe लोप of व्. More examples can be seen in tables in the next chapter.

We will use this discussion on सन्धि in the next chapter to appreciate the principles of understanding अष्टाध्यायी-सूत्रs. In fact, for that reason, we will try to stick to सूत्र-based explanations of सन्धिs as much as possible rather than just a conceptual description.

15 सन्धि

15.1 Introduction

सन्धि refers to transformations that are prescribed when two वर्णs are to be pronounced without any gap. Such pronunciation is called संहिता. This संहिता is compulsory when two वर्णs are in the same word (including a simple word, a word that has a उपसर्ग, or a compound word also called समस्तपद). संहिता is optional between two words in a sentence. Thus, संहिता is applicable in many places, including pronouncing two independent words together, joining two प्रातिपदिकs within one compound word, or even in the process of deriving a word.

We don't see the word "सन्धि" in अष्टाध्यायी itself. It is a later term to indicate the transformations that happen in संहिता. There is no classification of सन्धिs either, that अष्टाध्यायी explicitly mentions. However, for ease of identification, later works have classified सन्धिs into two approaches. One is based on the स्थानिन्, and the other is based on आदेश.

In the first approach, सन्धिs are classified as अच्-सन्धि, हल्-सन्धि and विसर्ग-सन्धि indicating that the स्थानिन् is correspondingly a स्वर, a व्यञ्जन, or a विसर्ग.

In the second approach सन्धिs can be categorised as यण्-सन्धि, गुण-सन्धि, जश्त्व-सन्धि, णत्व-सन्धि etc., indicating that यण्, गुण, जश्, ण etc., are respectively substituting another वर्ण(s).

We will use the first one for broader classification and indicate the second one as and when it applies.

As we discussed in the section on अष्टाध्यायी, we use this section on सन्धिs not only to explain the सन्धिs themselves, but also to help readers understand the formation, structure, and interpretation of सूत्रs.

15.2 अच्-सन्धि

(1) यण् सन्धि

(i) सूत्र - इको यणचि (6-1-77)
(ii) वृत्ति - इकः स्थाने यण् आदेशः भवति, अचि परे।
(iii) Meaning - "यण् replaces इक्, if इक् is followed by अच्"

Here, all three notations इक्, यण् and अच् are प्रत्याहारs. For a detailed understanding, it is useful to refer to the section on

प्रत्याहारs. Briefly, इक् refers to इ, उ, ऋ and ऌ; यण् refers to य्, व्, र् and ल्; and अच् refers to all स्वरs. So, in other words, the सूत्र can be explained as "य्, व्, र्, and ल् replace इ, उ, ऋ, and ऌ, when इ, उ, ऋ, and ऌ are followed by स्वरs".

Here, one can notice that the स्थानिन् has four elements, and the आदेश too, has four elements. Thus, the सूत्र may seem vague since it doesn't explicitly say which exact वर्ण of those four आदेशs replaces which other exact वर्ण among the four स्थानिन्s.

This ambiguity is resolved by a परिभाषा-सूत्र – यथासङ्ख्यमनुदेशः समानाम् (1-3-10). It means that if the number of स्थानिन्s and the number of आदेशs are equal, then the replacements (आदेश) should be done in the order of their prescription. Therefore, the current सूत्र means that, "य् , व् , र् and ल् replace इ, उ, ऋ and ऌ respectively, when इ, उ, ऋ and ऌ are followed by स्वरs"

In cases where the number of स्थानिन्s and the number of आदेशs are not equal, then this convention is insufficient to solve the ambiguity. In such cases, another सूत्र (स्थानेऽन्तरतमः 1-1-50) is applied. This सूत्र says that if स्थानिन् has multiple options for आदेश, then the most similar वर्ण should be taken while replacing. Since this is a परिभाषा-सूत्र, it is applied as a general convention (परिभाषा) in all similar circumstances, where स्थानिन् has multiple options for आदेश.

Now, how does one know that two वर्णs are similar? The similarity is found by analyzing the features of वर्णs, such as उच्चारण-स्थान (anatomical part of articulation) and प्रयत्न (आभ्यन्तर-प्रयत्न = internal effort; and बाह्यप्रयत्न = external effort). Both these ideas are discussed under the topic of वर्णs.

As a side note, one can see that this second rule may also help in understanding this सूत्र - इको यणचि. य् and इ have similar उच्चारण-स्थान, i.e., तालु, and are hence similar to each other. In the same way, व् is similar to उ, र् to ऋ and ऌ् to ऌ. Hence, य् replaces इ, व् replaces उ etc.

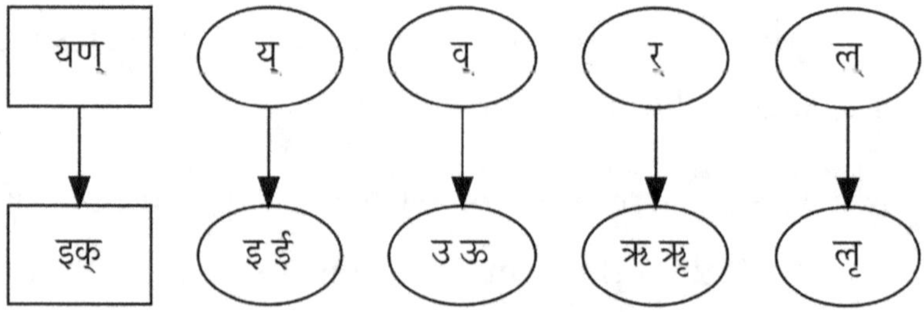

Figure 15.1: यण्-सन्धि - इको यणचि(6-1-77)

For example,

(i) दधि + अत्र → दध्यत्र

दधि + अत्र → दध् इ अ त्र → दध् य् अ त्र → दध्यत्र

(ii) गुरु + अनुग्रह → गुर्वनुग्रह

गुरु + अनुग्रह → गुर् उ अ नुग्रह → गुर् व् अ नुग्रह → गुर्वनुग्रह

(iii) मातृ + इच्छा → मात्रिच्छा

मातृ + इच्छा → मात् ऋ इ च्छा → मात् र् इ च्छा → मात्रिच्छा

(iv) ऌ + आकार → लाकार

ऌ + आकार → ऌ आ कार → ल् आ कार → लाकार

(2) अयादि-सन्धि (अय्-अव्-आय्-आव्-सन्धि)

(i) सूत्र - एचोऽयवायावः (6-1-78)

(ii) वृत्ति - एचः स्थाने अय्-अव्-आय्-आवः आदेशाः भवन्ति, अचि परे।

(iii) Meaning - "अय् , अव् , आय् and आव् replace एच्, if एच् is followed by अच्"

The सूत्र has two words: one mentions स्थानिन्s and the other आदेशs. However, a विधि-सूत्र generally needs to mention the condition under which a prescription is mandated. If such conditions are not explicitly mentioned in the सूत्र, then one should look for conditions mentioned in the preceding सूत्रs and extend the same condition to the current सूत्र. This idea of bringing words from previous सूत्रs, called अनुवृत्ति, is a very common principle applied in designing the सूत्रs. This makes the सूत्रs short, by avoiding repetitions.

In the current case, "अचि" is the condition mentioned in the previous सूत्र (6-1-77). We bring that forward and interpret 6-1-78 also. Hence we get the वृत्ति discussed above.

Now, एच्, the स्थानिन्, is a प्रत्याहार for four वर्णs - ए, ओ, ऐ and औ. And, आदेश also has four options- अय्, अव्, आय् and आव् . Thus we can apply the परिभाषा of "यथासङ्ख्यमनुदेशः समानाम्".

Thus using अनुवृत्ति and this परिभाषा, we get the meaning of this सूत्र as: "अय् , अव् , आय् and आव् replace ए, ओ, ऐ and औ respectively,, if एच् is followed by अच्".

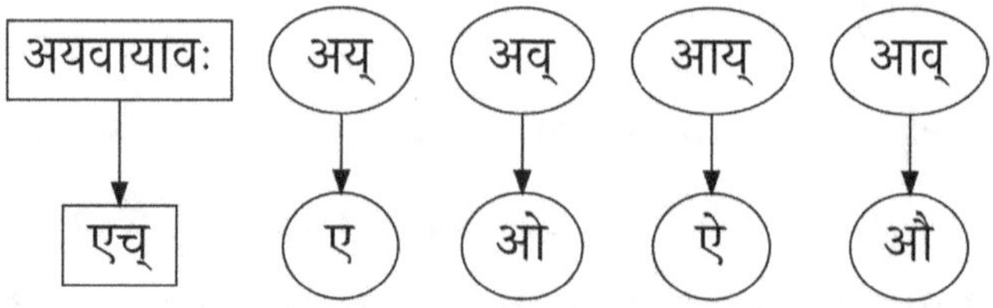

Figure 15.2: अयादि-सन्धि - एचोऽयवायावः (6-1-78)

For example,

(i) के + एते → कयेते

के + एते → क् ए ए ते → क् अय् ए ते → कयेते

(ii) गुरो + एव → गुरवेव

गुरो + एव → गुर् ओ ए व → गुर् अव् ए व → गुरवेव

(iii) बालौ + इति → बालाविति

बालौ + इति → बाल् औ इ ति → बाल् आव् इ ति → बालाविति

(iv) तस्मै + आह → तस्मायाह

तस्मै + आह → तस्म् ऐ आ ह → तस्म् आय् आ ह → तस्मायाह

(3) **गुण-सन्धि**

(i) सूत्र - आद् गुणः (6-1-87)

(ii) वृत्ति - अवर्णात् अचि परे पूर्वपरयोः एकः गुणः आदेशः भवति।

(iii) Meaning - When अ is followed by अच्, then a गुण-वर्ण replaces both अ and अच्.

Here the सूत्र mentions two components - the पूर्वनिमित्त (which is अवर्ण) and आदेश (which is a गुण). However, the meaning of this सूत्र is much more than what it appears to say. Three सूत्रs prior to this, there is another सूत्र : एकः पूर्वपरयोः (6-1-84). This is an अधिकार-सूत्र. As we saw earlier, अधिकार-सूत्रs don't prescribe anything on their own but are to be read along with the सूत्रs that are within the scope of this अधिकार. This सूत्र means that "One आदेश replaces two स्थानिन्s taken together - the preceding वर्ण (पूर्ववर्ण) and the following वर्ण (परवर्ण)". This अधिकार-सूत्र suggests that the prescriptions that come between 6-1-85 and 6-1-111 should apply to two वर्णs (both पूर्व and पर) taken together as स्थानिन्, not just one. Unlike the two सन्धिs that we discussed earlier (यण् and अयादि) where स्थानिन् is a single वर्ण. These सूत्रs (between 6-

1-85 and 6-1-111) need only mention the पूर्वनिमित्त and परनिमित्त, not the स्थानिन् separately, as the two together are considered the स्थानिन् according to 6-1-84.

Now, coming to the current सूत्र "आद्गुणः", only पूर्वनिमित्त is mentioned directly here. Hence, we use the idea of अनुवृत्ति discussed earlier to supply the परनिमित्त, i.e., "अचि". This comes from 6-1-77 (इको यणचि).

Thus we derive the whole meaning of the सूत्र as: "When अ is followed by अच्, then a गुण-वर्ण replaces both अ and अच्."

"गुण" is a technical label (सञ्ज्ञा) used in व्याकरण-शास्त्र. This along with another label, "वृद्धि", are the most commonly used labels in व्याकरण-शास्त्र. It is possibly for this reason, that the two terms are defined in the very first two सूत्रs of Pāṇini's अष्टाध्यायी : वृद्धिरादैच् (1-1-1) (वृद्धिः आत् ऐच् - are the three पदs) and अदेङ्गुणः (1-1-2) (अत् एङ् गुणः). The first सूत्र means that, "आ, ऐ and औ are called वृद्धि". The second one says that "अ, ए and ओ are called गुण".

In these two सूत्रs, one may notice the usage of "अत्" and "आत्". This notion of using a "त्" at the end is called "तपरकरण". It is done to indicate an exception. While अ, इ, अच् and such references to स्वराक्षरs suggest that we should take all eighteen (or twelve as applicable) variants of them, तपरकरण limits it to only the mentioned variant. For example, "अत्" is used to refer to the six variations of ह्रस्व-अ-वर्ण (and not all the eighteen); "आत्" refers to six variations of दीर्घ-आ-वर्ण. This idea is mentioned in परिभाषा-सूत्र 1-1-70: "तपरस्तत्कालस्य".

We can thus understand the गुण-सन्धि सूत्र as: "When अ is followed by अच्, then ह्रस्व-अ, ए or ओ replaces both अ and अच्"

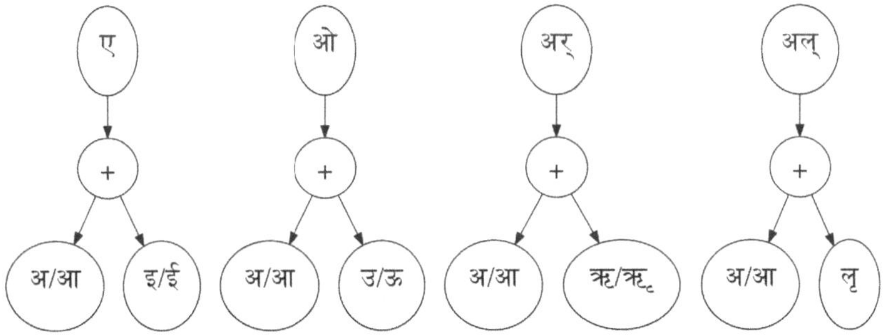

Figure 15.3: गुण-सन्धि - आद् गुणः (6-1-87)

For example,

(i) तव + इदम् ⟶ तवेदम्

तव + इदम् ⟶ तव् अ इ दम् ⟶ तव् ए दम् ⟶ तवेदम्

(ii) रमा + ईश ⟶ रमेश

रमा + ईश ⟶ रम् आ ई श ⟶ रम् ए श ⟶ रमेश

(iii) तव + उदकम् ⟶ तवोदकम्

तव + उदकम् ⟶ तव् अ उ दकम् ⟶ तव् ओ दकम् ⟶ तवोदकम्

(iv) सप्त + ऋषि ⟶ सप्तर्षि

सप्त ऋषि ⟶ सप्त् अ ऋ षि ⟶ सप्त् अर् षि ⟶ सप्तर्षि

Which among the three गुण-वर्णs (अ, ए, ओ) replaces two स्थानिन्-वर्णs is determined by the परिभाषा of स्थानेऽन्तरतमः discussed earlier. The उच्चारण-स्थानs of the three गुण-वर्णs अ, ए and ओ are कण्ठ, कण्ठ-तालु and कण्ठ-ओष्ठ respectively.

In the first example above, स्थानिन्s are अ and इ and their उच्चारण-स्थानs are कण्ठ and तालु respectively. Hence, they are replaced by ए, whose उच्चारण-स्थान (कण्ठ-तालु) is similar to that of अ and इ. For the same reason, अ and उ in the second example are replaced by ओ. We may recollect that the उच्चारण-स्थान of उ is ओष्ठ.

In the third example, अ and ऋ are replaced by "अर्". This आदेश has made use of an additional rule: उरण् रपरः (1-1-51). This सूत्र states that when an अण्-वर्ण (अ, इ, or उ) is directed as an आदेश while ऋ is the स्थानिन्, it must always be followed by a र्.

Thus, the स्थानेऽन्तरतमः rule is also satisfied in the third example. Because the स्थानिन्s अ and ऋ and their आदेशs अ and र् both have the same उच्चारण-स्थानs, i.e., कण्ठ and मूर्धन्.

(4) वृद्धि-सन्धि

(i) सूत्र - वृद्धिरेचि (6-1-88)

(ii) वृत्ति - अवर्णात् एचि परे पूर्वपरयोः एकः वृद्धिः आदेशः भवति ।

(iii) Meaning - When अ is followed by एच्, then a वृद्धि-वर्ण (आ, ऐ, औ) replaces both अ and एच्.

In this सूत्र too, the अधिकार-सूत्र and the अनुवृत्ति are applied in a way similar to the previous discussion, to derive this meaning.

As discussed above, the अधिकार-सूत्र mentions that पूर्व-निमित्त and पर-निमित्त are to be considered as one स्थानिन्, and that such a स्थानिन् will be replaced by one आदेश. However, this सूत्र has mentioned only परनिमित्त (i.e., एच्) and आदेश (i.e., वृद्धि) but not पूर्वनिमित्त. Hence, we bring "आत्" from पूर्वसूत्र, by अनुवृत्ति, and thus get the full meaning.

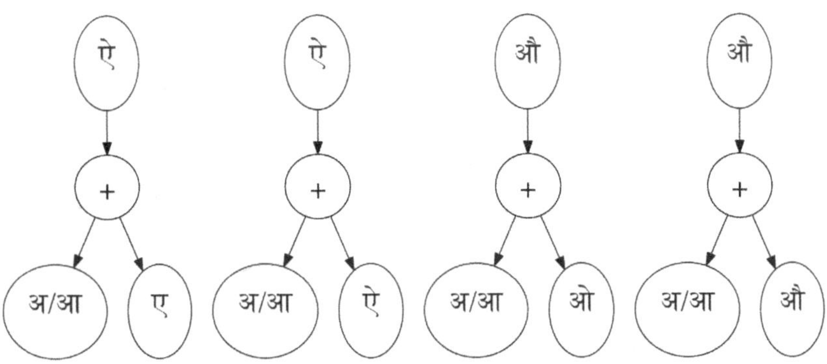

Figure 15.4: वृद्धि-सन्धि - वृद्धिरेचि (6-1-88)

For example,

(i) मम + एव → ममैव

मम + एव → मम् अ ए व → मम् ऐ व → ममैव

(ii) यथा + ऐक्यम् → यथैक्यम् यथा + ऐक्यम् → यथ् आ ऐ क्यम् → यथ् ऐ क्यम् → यथैक्यम्

(iii) तथा + ओदन → तथौदन तथा + ओदन → तथ् आ ओ दन → तथ् औ दन → तथौदन
(iv) वन + औषध → वनौषध वन + औषध → वन् अ औ षध → वन् औ षध → वनौषध

It is clear in these examples too, that the principle of स्थानेऽन्तरतमः is used in deciding which वृद्धि-वर्ण replaces the स्थानिन्s.

(5) सवर्ण-दीर्घ-सन्धि

(i) सूत्र - अकः सवर्णे दीर्घः (6-1-101)
(ii) वृत्ति - अकः सवर्णे अचि परे पूर्वपरयोः एकः दीर्घः आदेशः भवति।
(iii) Meaning - When an अक्-वर्ण is followed by सवर्ण-अच्, then a दीर्घ replaces both of them.

Here, the अधिकार-सूत्र "एकः पूर्वपरयोः" (6-1-84) and अनुवृत्ति of "अचि" from 6-1-77(इको यणचि), give the complete वृत्ति.

To understand the meaning of the सूत्र, we need the definition of सवर्ण, a concept used at multiple instances in अष्टाध्यायी. The सूत्र "तुल्यास्यप्रयत्नं सवर्णम्" (1-1-9) provides that definition: "Any two वर्णs that have the same उच्चारण-स्थान and आभ्यन्तर-प्रयत्न are called सवर्ण to each other". We have discussed the उच्चारण-स्थान and आभ्यन्तर-प्रयत्न in detail in the chapter on वर्णमाला.

Thus, all अच्-वर्णs have सवर्णs within their group of twelve or eighteen variant वर्णs. For example, अ and आ are सवर्ण to each other since they both have कण्ठ-स्थान and विवृत-प्रयत्न. Similarly, इ and ई are सवर्णs, उ and उँ are सवर्णs etc.

In the same way, among the हल्-वर्णs, those in the same वर्ग (i.e., कवर्ग, चवर्ग, etc.) are सवर्ण to each other. For example, प and ब are सवर्णs to each other since they both have ओष्ठ-स्थान and स्पृष्ट-प्रयत्न.

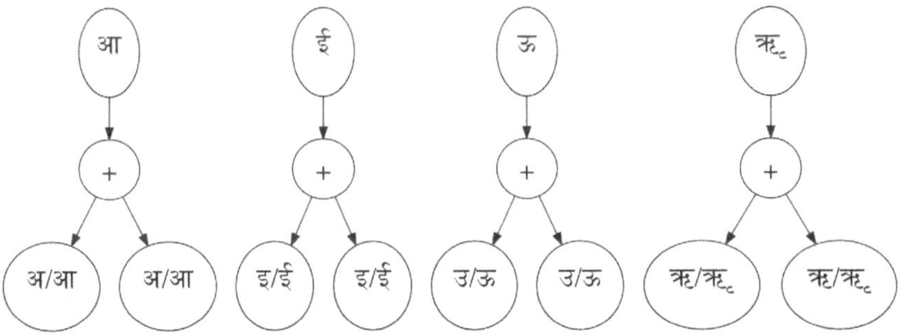

Figure 15.5: सवर्णदीर्घ-सन्धि - अकःसवर्णे दीर्घः (6-1-101)

We can now apply this सूत्र and understand the below examples:

(i) देव + आलय → देवालय
देव + आलय → देव् अ आ लय → देव् आ लय → देवालय

(ii) सीता + अशोक → सीताशोक सीता + अशोक → सीत् आ अ शोक → सीत् आ शोक → सीताशोक

(iii) हरि + ईश → हरीश हरि + ईश → हर् इ ई श → हर् ई श → हरीश

(iv) गुरु + उपदेश → गुरूपदेश गुरु + उपदेश → गुर् उ उ पदेश → गुर् ऊ पदेश → गुरूपदेश

(v) मातृ + ऋण → मातॄण मातृ + ऋण → मात् ऋ ऋ ण → मात् ॠ ण → मातॄण

(6) **पूर्व-रूप-सन्धि**

(i) सूत्र - एङः पदान्तादति (6-1-109)

(ii) वृत्ति - पदान्तात् एङः अति परे पूर्वपरयोः एकः पूर्वः आदेशः भवति।

(iii) Meaning - When ए or ओ at the end of a पद is followed by a ह्रस्व-अ, then only the पूर्व-वर्ण comes in the place of पूर्व and पर. In effect, it means that only the पूर्व-वर्ण remains. Hence the popular name "पूर्वरूप-सन्धि", For example :

(a) नमो + अस्तु → नमोस्तु

नमो + अस्तु → नम् ओ अ स्तु → नम् ओ स्तु → नमोस्तु

(b) हरे + अजित → हरेजित

हरे + अजित → हर् ए अ जित → हर् ए जित → हरेजित

In modern practice, some prefer to write these पूर्वरूप-सन्धिs with a notation of "ऽ" (अवग्रह) to indicate that "अ" exists when we split the सन्धि. For example, नमोस्तु is written as नमोऽस्तु and हरेजित is written as हरेऽजित.

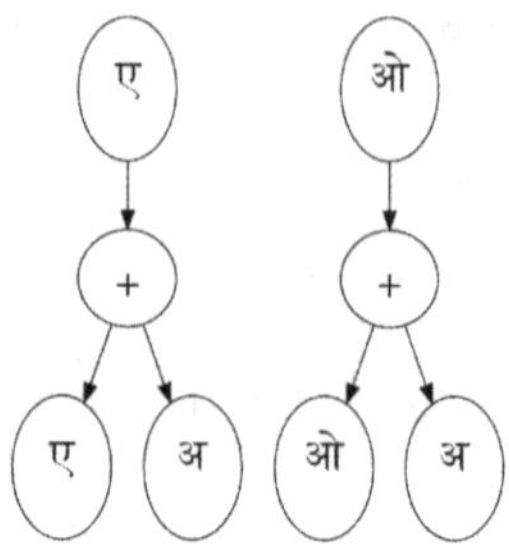

Figure 15.6: पूर्वरूप-सन्धि - एङः पदान्तादति (6-1-109)

Table 15.2 summarizes the अच्-सन्धिs.

सूत्र	निमित्त	फल	परिभाषा/अधिकार	उदाहरण
इको यणचि	*इक् अच्*	**यण्** *अच्*	स्थानेऽन्तरतमः	सुधी उपास्यः → सुध्युपास्यः
एचोऽयवायावः	*एच् अच्*	**अय्/अव्/आय्/आव्** *अच्*	यथासङ्ख्यमनुदेशः	गुरो ए → गुरवे
आद् गुणः	*अ अच्*	**एकः गुणः**	एकः पूर्वपरयोः	भास्कर उदयः → भास्करोदयः
वृद्धिरेचि	*अ एच्*	**एकः वृद्धिः**	एकः पूर्वपरयोः	मम एव → ममैव
अकः सवर्णे दीर्घः	*अक् सवर्ण_अच्*	**एकः दीर्घः**	एकः पूर्वपरयोः	देव आलयः → देवालयः
एङः पदान्तादति	*पदान्त_एङ् अत्*	**एकः पूर्वः**	एकः पूर्वपरयोः	वायो अत्र → वायोऽत्र

Table 15.2: अच्-सन्धि

The स्थानिन् and आदेश are highlighted in bold in the निमित्त and फल columns, respectively.

15.3 उत्सर्ग-अपवाद-व्यवस्था

It is time to introduce a new concept - the concept of उत्सर्ग-अपवाद (general-specific).

In some cases discussed above, conditions for more than one rule may be met in a given situation. Consider the below examples:

(1) यदि + इमे. Here, इ is followed by इ. This satisfies the condition for applicability of these two सूत्रs - इको यणचि and अकः सवर्णे दीर्घः.
(2) रामे + अस्ति. Here, conditions for both एचोऽयवायावः and एङः पदान्तादति are satisfied.
(3) वन + ओषधि. Here again, conditions for both आद् गुणः and वृद्धिरेचि are met.

Applying different सूत्रs gives different results. So, how does one decide which one to apply?

The concept of उत्सर्ग and अपवाद decides this. The terms can be translated as "general" and "specific". If there are two rules, one with broader applicability than the other, then we call the former "general" or "उत्सर्ग" and the latter "specific" or "अपवाद". In other words, उत्सर्ग applies to the whole set, while अपवाद applies to a subset of it. In that subset, we have two options (a) उत्सर्ग overruling अपवाद; or (b) अपवाद overruling उत्सर्ग. However, in the case of the former,

अपवाद is deemed redundant since there is no object on which it can be applied. But, if we choose the latter, then अपवाद only limits the scope of उत्सर्ग, but both retain some applicability. To summarize, in cases of both उत्सर्ग and अपवाद, the rule is that अपवाद functions as an exception to the general rule and overrules उत्सर्ग.

We can appreciate this idea with a simple example, popular as "तक्र-कौण्डिन्य-न्याय" in Saṃskṛta literature. Let Kaundinya be a student, and consider these two statements: "छात्रेभ्यो दधि दीयताम्" and "तक्रं कौण्डिन्याय". These mean "Let curd be given to the students" and "buttermilk to Kaundinya". When one uses these two statements, we understand that curd should be given to all students except Kaundinya, while he should be given buttermilk. The logic behind this interpretation is, in fact, the उत्सर्ग-अपवाद-व्यवस्था. Here, the first statement is general (उत्सर्ग) since it applies to all students. The second one is specific (अपवाद) since it speaks about only one student, Kaundinya. Thus, the second one, which has an application only on a subset, overrules the former.

Now, if we look back at the examples given above, we can find that one of them is उत्सर्ग and the other is अपवाद.

In the first case, the conflict is between यण्-सन्धि and सवर्ण-दीर्घ-सन्धि. One says that इ, उ, ऋ or ऌ followed by अच् (that has nine possibilities) results in यण्; and the other says that अ, इ, उ, ऋ or ऌ followed by सवर्ण results in दीर्घ. We can see that the former has more वर्ण-pairs considered as स्थानिन् and परनिमित्त and apply to a larger number of cases (4*9= 36 cases) and the latter has less वर्ण-pairs considered as स्थानिन् and परनिमित्त and applicable to a smaller domain (5*1 = 5 cases). In other words, the conditions for सवर्ण-दीर्घ-सन्धि are more specific, and hence this rule overrules यण्.

Similarly, if the conflict is between अयादि-सन्धि and पूर्व-रूप-सन्धि, then पूर्वरूप overrules the other for the same reason. In the same way, वृद्धि overrules गुण when there is a conflict between the two. This concept of उत्सर्ग-अपवाद is applicable across अष्टाध्यायी, and we will refer back to the topic wherever necessary.

15.4 हल्-सन्धि

(1) श्चुत्व-सन्धि

(i) सूत्र : स्तोः श्चुना श्चुः (8-4-40)

(ii) वृत्ति : सकार-तवर्गयोः शकार-चवर्गाभ्यां योगे शकार-चवर्गौ आदेशौ भवतः ।

(iii) Meaning: When स्, त्, थ्, द्, ध् or न् are followed or preceded by श्, च्, छ्, ज्, झ् or ञ्, then श्, च्, छ्, ज्, झ् or ञ् come as replacements correspondingly.

Here, सकार and तवर्ग are स्थानिन्s. शकार and चवर्ग are निमित्त. It is important to note that the निमित्त is mentioned in तृतीया-विभक्ति. Typically, the one mentioned in पञ्चमी refers to पूर्वनिमित्त and that mentioned in सप्तमी refers to परनिमित्त. However, to allow for both possibilities, i.e., पूर्वनिमित्त or परनिमित्त, this सूत्र has used तृतीया-विभक्ति. For example,

(i) मनस् + चाञ्चल्य → मनश्चाञ्चल्य

मनस् + चाञ्चल्य → मन स् च् आञ्चल्य → मन श् च् आञ्चल्य → मनश्चाञ्चल्य

(ii) यज् + न → यज्ञ

यज् + न → य ज् न् अ → य ज् ञ् अ → यज्ञ

(2) ष्टुत्व-सन्धि

(i) सूत्र - ष्टुना ष्टुः (8-4-41)

(ii) वृत्ति - सकार-तवर्गयोः षकार-टवर्गाभ्यां योगे षकार-टवर्गौ आदेशौ भवतः ।

(iii) Meaning - When स्, त्, थ्, द्, ध् or न् are followed or preceded by ष्, ट्, ठ्, ड्, ढ् or ण्, then ष्, ट्, ठ्, ड्, ढ् or ण् come as replacements correspondingly.

This सूत्र is very similar to the previous one. "स्तोः" is applicable here too by अनुवृत्ति. For example,

(i) तत् + टीका → तट्टीका

तत् + टीका → त त् ट् ईका → त ट् ट् ईका → तट्टीका

(ii) नष् + तम् → नष्टम्

नष् + तम् → न ष् त् अम् → न ष् ट् अम् → नष्टम्

(3) श्चुत्व-ष्टुत्व-निषेध

The two prescriptions discussed above - the श्चुत्व-सन्धि and the ष्टुत्व-सन्धि- are two consecutive सूत्रs in अष्टाध्यायी. The next three सूत्रs, that immediately follow these two, prohibit these prescriptions under special circumstances: न पदान्ताट्टोरनाम् (8-4-42), तोः षि (8-4-43) and शात् (8-4-44). Those circumstances are:

(i) टवर्ग-वर्ण is पूर्वनिमित्त AND at the end of a पद (except when परनिमित्त is नाम्)

(ii) तवर्ग-वर्ण is स्थानिन् AND परनिमित्त is ष्

(iii) तवर्ग-वर्ण is स्थानिन् AND पूर्वनिमित्त is श्

We can see that the first and second are prohibiting ष्टुत्व and the third is prohibiting श्चुत्व. For example,

(i) षट् + सन्तः → षड्सन्तः (Note that स् hasn't changed to ष्)

(ii) षट् + नाम् → षण्णाम्

(iii) सन् + षष्ठः → सन्षष्ठः (Note that न् hasn't changed to ण्)

(iv) प्रश् + न → प्रश्न (Note that न् hasn't changed to ञ्)

(4) **Remaining हल्-सन्धि सूत्रs**

Remaining सूत्रs about हल्-सन्धिs follow a similar pattern of prescribing an आदेश for a स्थानिन्, under some specific conditions. No new conventions or labels are used in these सूत्रs. Since these do not require detailed explanations, we have summarized them in Tables 15.4, 15.6, and 15.8. The स्थानिन् and आदेश/आगम are highlighted in bold in the 'Conditions' and 'Result' columns, respectively. Whatever precedes the स्थानिन् is पूर्वनिमित्त and whatever follows the स्थानिन् is परनिमित्त.

सूत्र	निमित्त	फल	उदाहरण
रषाभ्यां नो णः समानपदे (8-4-1)	र् न्	र् **ण्**	चतुर् नाम् → चतुर्णाम्
	ष् न्	ष् **ण्**	पुष् नाति → पुष्णाति
	(पूर्वनिमित्त and न् must be in the same पद)		
अट्कुप्वाङ्नुम्व्यवायेऽपि (8-4-2)	र् <अट्/कुँ/पुँ/आङ्/नुम्> न्	र् <अट्/कुँ/पुँ/आङ्/नुम्> **ण्**	हरिना → हरिणा
	ष् <अट्/कुँ/पुँ/आङ्/नुम्> न्	ष् <अट्/कुँ/पुँ/आङ्/नुम्> **ण्**	पुष्पानि → पुष्पाणि
चोः कुः (8-2-30)	**चुँ** झल्/पदान्त	**कुँ** झल्/पदान्त	पच् तुम् → पक्तुम्
झलां जशोऽन्ते(8-2-39)	पदान्त-झल्	**जश्**	रामात् → रामाद्
मोऽनुस्वारः(8-3-23)	पदान्त-म् हल्	**अनुस्वार** हल्	वनम् गतः → वनं गतः
नश्चापदान्तस्य झलि (8-3-24)	अपदान्त-न्/अपदान्त-म् झल्	**अनुस्वार** झल्	आक्रम् स्यते → आक्रंस्यते
			पयान् सि → पयांसि
आदेशप्रत्यययोः (8-3-59)	इण्/कुँ अपदान्त-स्	इण्/कुँ **ष्**	हरिसु → हरिषु
	(The अपदान्त-स् of an आदेश or प्रत्यय)		वाक् सु → वाक् षु

सूत्र	निमित्त	फल	उदाहरण
स्तोः श्चुना श्चुः (8-4-40)	श्चुँ स्तुँ	श्चुँ **श्चुँ**	यज् न → यज् ञ (यज्ञ)
	स्तुँ श्चुँ	**श्चुँ** श्चुँ	उत् चारणम् → उच्चारणम्
ष्टुना ष्टुः (8-4-41)	ष्टुँ स्तुँ	ष्टुँ **ष्टुँ**	पेष् तुम् → पेष्टुम्
	स्तुँ ष्टुँ	**ष्टुँ** ष्टुँ	राजन् डयसे → राजण्डयसे
यरोऽनुनासिकेऽनुनासिको वा (8-4-45)	यर् *अनुनासिक*	**अनुनासिक** अनुनासिक यर् अनुनासिक	सुहृत् मित्रम् → सुहृन्मित्रम् or सुहृत् मित्रम्
झलां जश् झशि (8-4-53)	झल् झश्	**जश्** झश्	लभ् धुम् → लब्धुम्
खरि च (8-4-55)	झल् *खर्*	**चर्** खर्	भगवद् पूजा → भगवत्पूजा
वाऽवसाने (8-4-56)	झल् *अवसान*	**चर्** अवसान	वाग् → वाक्/वाग्
अनुस्वारस्य ययि परसवर्णः (8-4-58)	अनुस्वार *यय्*	**सवर्ण-to-यय्** यय्	अलं कारः → अलङ्कारः
वा पदान्तस्य (8-4-59)	पदान्त-अनुस्वार यय्	**सवर्ण-to-यय्** यय्	तं कथम् → तङ्कथम्
तोर्लि (8-4-60)	तुँ ल्	**सवर्ण-to-ल्** ल्	तत् लयः → तल्लयः
झयो होऽन्यतरस्याम् (8-4-62)	*झय्* ह्	झय् **सवर्ण-to-झय्**	वाग् हसति → वाग्घसति or वाग् हसति

सूत्र	निमित्त	फल	उदाहरण
शश्छोऽटि (8-4-63)	झय् श् अट्	झय् **छ्** अट्	वाक् शेते → वाक्छेते or वाक् शेते

Table 15.4: हल्-सन्धि - आदेश

सूत्र	निमित्त	फल	उदाहरण
छे च (6-1-73)	ह्रस्व छ्	ह्रस्व **त्** छ्	इ छति → इ त् छति
दीर्घात् (6-1-75)	दीर्घ छ्	दीर्घ **त्** छ्	ही छति → ही त् छति
पदान्ताद्वा (6-1-76)	पदान्त-दीर्घ छ्	पदान्त-दीर्घ **त्** छ् पदान्त-दीर्घ छ् (optional)	लक्ष्मी छाया → लक्ष्मी त् छाया or लक्ष्मी छाया
इदितो नुम् धातोः (7-1-58)	इदित्-धातु	इदित्-धातु + **नुम्**	वदिँ → वन्द्
शि तुक् (8-3-31)	पदान्त-न् श्	पदान्त-न् **त्** श्/ पदान्त-न् श् (Optional)	भवान् शेते → भवान् त् शेते
ङमो ह्रस्वादचि ङमुण्नित्यम् (8-3-32)	ह्रस्व पदान्त-ङम् अच्	ह्रस्व **ङम्** ङम् अच् (Mandatory)	कुर्वन् इति → कुर्वन् न् इति

सूत्र	निमित्त	फल	उदाहरण
अचो रहाभ्यां द्वे (8-4-46)	अच् र्/ह् यर्	अच् र्/ह् **यर् यर्**	अर् क → अर्क्क/अर्क
		अच् र्/ह् यर् (optional)	ब्रह्म → ब्रह्म्मा /ब्रह्म
अनचि च (8-4-47)	अच् यर् अनच्	अच् **यर् यर्** अनच्	मत् यत्र → मत्त्यत्र / मत्यत्र
		अच् यर् अनच् (optional)	

Table 15.6: हल्-सन्धि - आगम

सूत्र	निमित्त	फल	उदाहरण
एतत्तदोः सुलोपोऽकोरनञ्समासे हलि (6-1-132)	एतद्/तद् सुँ हल्	एतद्/तद् हल्	स सुँ हरिः → स हरिः
लोपः शाकल्यस्य (8-3-19)	अ पदान्त-य् अश्	अ अश्	तय् इमे → त इमे
	अ पदान्त-व् अश्	अ अश्	वाव् अत्र → द्वा अत्र
		अ य्/व् अश् (optional)	तयिमे/ द्वावत्र
झरो झरि सवर्णे (8-4-65)	हल् झर् सवर्ण-झर्	हल् सवर्ण-झर्	कृष्णर् द् धिः → कृष्णर् धिः
		हल् झर् सवर्ण-झर् (optional)	कृष्णर् द् धिः → कृष्णर् द् धिः

Table 15.8: हल्सन्धि -लोप

15.5 असिद्ध

Before moving into the next section on विसर्ग सन्धि, we need to familiarise ourselves with a new concept called असिद्ध used in the application of विसर्ग सन्धि.

असिद्ध is a specific technical concept used in अष्टाध्यायी. It means "unaware of". Some सूत्रs may not be aware of the existence or action of some other सूत्रs. Because of this "unawareness," the way these सूत्रs function differs.

For example, consider two विधि सूत्रs V1 and V2, where V1 is unaware of V2. Let's see how its function differs because of its unawareness. Typically, a विधि -सूत्र would be in the following template:

"If condition C is present, then a transformation T should happen to स्थानिन् S1 resulting in a new form S2."

Assume that both V1 and V2 are looking for condition C. We know that V1 is unaware of V2's existence because V2 is असिद्ध to V1. Therefore, V1 undeterred by V2 operates on S1 resulting in S2. Once S2 is reached, V2 cannot operate anymore since condition C has been altered.

Similarly, consider another situation where V1 is looking for condition C1, and V2 is looking for condition C2. Suppose V2 satisfies its condition C2 and transforms S1 to S2. Also, consider that condition C1 for V1 is satisfied after this transformation. Under normal circumstances (without the concept of असिद्ध), both V1 and V2 operate consecutively, leading to the transformation of S1 to S2 and then to S3. However, since V2 is असिद्ध to V1, the transformed state S2, which is obtained by the application of V2, is not known to V1. Therefore, the condition for V1 is not satisfied. Hence only V2 operates, and V1 is prevented.

Consider one more situation where both V1 and V2 are unaware of each other. In other words, the transformation resulting from applying either of them is not known to the other. However, if the condition is satisfied at the initial state, both operate on it as if the other hasn't changed the state. In the absence of the concept of असिद्ध, only one of them could operate, change the state and thus make the condition not satisfied for the other to operate.

Therefore, the idea of असिद्ध is providing space for a सूत्र that would otherwise not have been applicable.

In summary, असिद्ध-

(i) helps in resolving conflict when two सूत्रs (one of them being असिद्ध to the other) are competing for applications.
(ii) prevents the application of an otherwise applicable सूत्र.
(iii) enables the application of an otherwise inapplicable सूत्र.
The last two are technically referred to as आदेशलक्षणप्रतिषेध (prevent the सूत्र which requires the transformed state) and उत्सर्गलक्षणभाव (enable the सूत्र which requires the state)

There are three सूत्रs that specify the असिद्ध-सूत्रs:

(1) पूर्वत्रासिद्धम् (8-2-1) : This says that the सूत्रs in the last three पादs of the last अध्यायs (i.e, 8.2, 8.3 and 8.4), called "त्रिपादी", are असिद्ध to all the previous सूत्रs (i.e., the first seven अध्यायs and 8.1), called "सपादसप्ताध्यायी". Even within the त्रिपादी, each सूत्र is असिद्ध to all of its previous सूत्रs.
(2) असिद्धवदत्राभात् (6-4-22): This mentions that all the सूत्रs from 6-4-23 to 6-4-175, are असिद्ध to each other.
(3) षत्वतुकोरसिद्धः (6-1-86) : This specifies that the सूत्रs from 6-1-87 to 6-1-111 are असिद्ध to षत्व सूत्रs (8-3-55 to 8-3-119) and तुक् सूत्रs (6-1-71 to 6-1-76)

Here are a few examples of how the idea of असिद्ध is put to use.

(1) Example for preventing an application:

Consider this Sandhi: द्वौ + अत्र.

Now, एचोऽयवायावः (6-1-78) applies on this, resulting in द्वाव् + अत्र. This situation satisfies condition for another सूत्र- लोपः शाकल्यस्य (8-3-19). If this सूत्र does apply, it results in the deletion of व्, and we get द्वा + अत्र. Now, it appears that the condition is right to apply अकः सवर्णे दीर्घः (6-1-101). However, since लोपः शाकल्यस्य (8-3-19) is in त्रिपादी, and अकः सवर्णे दीर्घः (6-1-101) is in सपादसप्ताध्यायी, the former is असिद्ध to latter. Hence, the result of "लोपः शाकल्यस्य" is unknown to "अकः सवर्णे दीर्घः". Therefore, "अकः सवर्णे दीर्घः" is only aware of the previous state, i.e., "द्वाव् + अत्र" and not "द्वा + अत्र". In that previous state, conditions for "अकः सवर्णे दीर्घः" are not met and thus the application of this सूत्र is prevented.

In this way, the idea of असिद्ध prevents the application of some सूत्रs.

(2) Example for defining the order:

Consider this case: कुर्वन् + ति.

Here, conditions are met for two सूत्रs: नश्चापदान्तस्य झलि (8-3-24) and अट्कुप्वाङ्नुम्व्यवायेऽपि (8-4-2). In normal circumstances, the latter

सूत्र takes precedence over the former सूत्र. However, in this example, the latter is असिद्ध to the former. Thus undeterred by the latter, the former proceeds first and applies. Thus, the result is कुर्वं + ति. Now, conditions for अनुस्वारस्य ययि परसवर्णः (8-4-58) are met, and this सूत्र is aware of नश्चापदान्तस्य झलि (8-3-24), because सूत्र 8-3-24 is not असिद्ध to सूत्र 8-4-58. Hence, we get the result कुर्वन् + ति. Again, the conditions are met for the previously discussed two सूत्रs: नश्चापदान्तस्य झलि (8-3-24) and अट्कुप्वाङ्नुम्व्यवायेऽपि (8-4-2). However, अनुस्वारस्य ययि परसवर्णः (8-4-58) is असिद्ध to both of them. Thus their application is prevented.

Hence, the final form is कुर्वन्ति.

In summary, असिद्ध helps to define the order of precedence by making one of the competing सूत्रs unknown to the other. That is the असिद्ध सूत्रs take lower precedence than the सूत्रs to which they are असिद्ध.

(3) Example for enabling an application:

Consider this case: शास् हि

Here the conditions are met for the two सूत्रs, शा हौ (6-4-35) and हुझल्भ्यो हेर्धिः (6-4-101). For the former, the condition is "हि as परनिमित्त of शास्", and the resultant is शा +हि. For the latter, the condition is "स् as पूर्वनिमित्त of हि", and the resultant is शास्+धि. So, in normal circumstances, we should either get शा + हि or शास् + धि. On application of either of the two सूत्रs, the conditions are lost for the other सूत्र. As these two सूत्रs are defined as असिद्ध to each other, they lack visibility into the results of each other's application. Hence, both सूत्रs apply, as if they are applied simultaneously and get the form "शाधि".

In this way, सूत्रs that would otherwise have no application are enabled by the concept of असिद्ध.

15.6 विसर्ग-सन्धि

The विसर्ग-सन्धि is a special type within हल्-सन्धिs that deal with words ending with स् or र्. It is called विसर्ग-सन्धि (more accurately, विसर्ग-related सन्धि) in modern classification since some of these स्s or र्s are converted to विसर्गs in the usual course. In some earlier texts, सन्धिs dealing with स्-ending-words are called स्वादि-सन्धिs and others विसर्ग-सन्धिs.

For easier comprehension, we can classify the set of these सूत्रs into three broad groups:

(1) रुँ-ending स्थानिन् with अ as the preceding वर्ण (विसर्ग-सन्धि type 1)

(2) रुँ-ending स्थानिन् OR र्-ending स्थानिन् with any preceding वर्ण - followed by खर् or at the end. (विसर्ग-सन्धि type 2)

(3) रुँ-ending स्थानिन् with any वर्ण other than अ as the preceding वर्ण followed by अश्- वर्ण (विसर्ग-सन्धि type 3)

As we can see above, there are two kinds of स्थानिन्s that we are dealing with:

(1) रुँ-ending स्थानिन्

This is derived from the सूत्र : ससजुषो रुँः (8-2-66). This सूत्र prescribes रुँ (with र् as the content, and उँ as इत्) as आदेश for स् in all स्-ending-पदs and specifically for the ष् in सजुष्.

Note that the prescription is not for प्रातिपदिकs or धातुs but for पदs. In other words, it applies to स्-ending सुप् and तिङ् प्रत्ययs since पदs are formed only after appending either सुप् and तिङ् प्रत्ययs. Therefore, it is appropriate to revisit the table of सुप् and तिङ् प्रत्ययs (without the इत्-वर्णs) as applied to a प्रातिपदिक (Table 15.10) or धातु (Table 15.12) as examples:

	एकवचन	द्विवचन	बहुवचन	एकवचन	द्विवचन	बहुवचन
प्रथमा	स्	औ	अस्	पचन्	पचन्तौ	पचन्तः
द्वितीया	अम्	औ	अस्	पचन्तम्	पचन्तौ	पचतः
तृतीया	आ	भ्याम्	भिस्	पचता	पचद्भ्याम्	पचद्भिः
चतुर्थी	ए	भ्याम्	भ्यस्	पचते	पचद्भ्याम्	पचद्भ्यः

	एकवचन	द्विवचन	बहुवचन	एकवचन	द्विवचन	बहुवचन
पञ्चमी	अस्	भ्याम्	भ्यस्	पचतः	पचद्भ्याम्	पचद्भ्यः
षष्ठी	अस्	ओस्	आम्	पचतः	पचतोः	पचताम्
सप्तमी	इ	ओस्	सु	पचति	पचतोः	पचत्सु

Table 15.10: सुप्-प्रत्ययs(without इत्) and when applied on प्रातिपदिक-पचत्

	एकवचन	द्विवचन	बहुवचन	एकवचन	द्विवचन	बहुवचन
प्रथमपुरुष	ति	तस्	झि	भवति	भवतः	भवन्ति
मध्यमपुरुष	सि	थस्	थ	भवसि	भवथः	भवथ
उत्तमपुरुष	मि	वस्	मस्	भवामि	भवावः	भवामः

Table 15.12: तिङ्-प्रत्ययs(without इत्) and having applied on धातु-भू

On application of ससजुषो रुँः(8-2-66), we get रुँ ending conversions such as:

(i) पचत्+अस् → पचतस् → पचतर्

(ii) पचत्+भिस् → पचद्भिस् → पचद्भिर्

(iii) भू + तस् → भवतस् → भवतर्

(2) र्-ending स्थानिन्.

Here, the set of प्रातिपदिकs that are naturally ending with र्. For example, प्रातर्, स्वर्, पुनर् etc.

Let's now discuss the three scenarios using the corresponding सूत्रs:

15.6.1 विसर्ग-सन्धि Type 1

This type of विसर्ग सन्धि, as mentioned earlier, deals with only रुँ-ending स्थानिन्s. There are two subtypes in it:

(1) ह्रस्व-अ as the preceding वर्ण AND ह्रस्व-अ or हश् as the following वर्ण. In this case the आदेश is either उत्व+गुण or उत्व+गुण+पूर्वरूप. This is dealt in सूत्रs 6-1-113 and 114.

(I) सूत्र 6-1-113 : अतो रोऽप्लुतादप्लुते

(i) अनुवृत्ति- अति (from 6-1-109), उत् (from 6-1-111)

(ii) Meaning : When रुँ-ending-स्थानिन्, is preceded by ह्रस्व-अ and followed by ह्रस्व-अ, रुँ is replaced by उ.

(iii) For example, रामस् + अत्र → रामर् + अत्र → राम+उ + अत्र. The final form is decided by appropriate rules discussed under अच्-सन्धि. Hence, राम+उ + अत्र → रामो + अत्र → रामोऽत्र (note गुण and पूर्वरूप आदेशs in this process).

Note: Even though this सूत्र is in सपादसप्ताध्यायी, it is aware of ससजुषोः रुः (8-2-66) which is in त्रिपादी. So, this is an exception for the default rule of असिद्ध. If this exception was not allowed, there would have been no role for this सूत्र since it can't be applied in the absence of knowledge of रुँ.

Similar exception is made for another सूत्र ढ्रलोपे पूर्वस्य दीर्घोऽणः (6-3-111) for the same reason (dealt under विसर्ग-सन्धि type 2).

(II) सूत्र 6-1-114 : हशि च

(i) अनुवृत्ति- अति (from 6-1-109), उत् (from 6-1-111), अतो रोः (from 6-1-113)

(ii) Meaning: When रुँ-ending-स्थानिन्, is preceded by ह्रस्व-अ and followed by हश् (i.e., मृदुव्यञ्जनs) रुँ is replaced by उ.

(iii) For example, रामस् + ददाति → रामर् + ददाति → राम+उ + ददाति. Here too, the final form is obtained after applying the अच्-सन्धि rules, i.e., गुण-सन्धि rule. Hence राम+उ + ददाति → रामो ददाति

(iv) अ as the preceding वर्ण AND अश् as the following वर्ण. Here, the आदेश is यत्व+लोप. This is dealt in सूत्र 8-3-17.

(2) Any variation of अ-वर्ण or one of these - भो, भगो, अघो as the preceding वर्ण and अश् is the following वर्ण. In this case the आदेश is य्

सूत्र (8-3-17) : भोभगोऽघोऽपूर्वस्य योऽशि

(i) अनुवृत्ति- रोः (from 8-3-16)

(ii) Meaning : When रुँ-ending-स्थानिन्, is preceded by भो, भगो, अघो or अ, and followed by अश् (i.e., स्वरs and मृदुव्यञ्जनs) रुँ is replaced by य्.

(iii) For example,
अर्जुनस् + उवाच → अर्जुनर् + उवाच → अर्जुनय् + उवाच. Now, the final form is decided by appropriate हल्-सन्धि-सूत्र : लोपः शाकल्यस्य. Since that is an optional prescription, we get, अर्जुनय् + उवाच → अर्जुनयुवाच or अर्जुन उवाच.
Note: Here one may wonder if this final form - अर्जुन उवाच - satisfies the condition for अच्-सन्धि (more specifically, गुण-सन्धि in this case). However, लोपः शाकल्यस्य (8-3-19) is in त्रिपादी, while the सूत्रs for अच्-सन्धिs are in सपाद-सप्ताध्यायी. Thus, the अच्-सन्धि सूत्रs are unaware of the result obtained by applying "लोपः शाकल्यस्य", and hence no अच्-सन्धि is possible on the final form.

(iv) छात्रास् + गच्छन्ति → छात्रार् + गच्छन्ति → छात्राय् + गच्छन्ति. The final form is after application of the सूत्र : हलि सर्वेषाम्. In this, the लोप is mandatory, and not optional. Hence we get छात्राय् + गच्छन्ति → छात्रा गच्छन्ति.

15.6.2 विसर्ग-सन्धि Type 2

Note that the सूत्रs discussed below apply to both र्s - रेफ and रुँ.

(1) सूत्र- रो रि (8-3-14)

(i) अनुवृत्ति- लोपः (from 8-3-13)

(ii) Meaning: र् is deleted if followed by another र्.

(iii) For example, गौस् + रक्षति → गौर् + रक्षति → गौ रक्षति

If we have a ह्रस्व-अ prior to रुँ, followed by र, such as रामर् + रक्षति or सम्पदर् + रक्षन्ति then हशि च takes precedence over रो रि because of the concept of असिद्ध. Hence, we get रामो रक्षति or सम्पदो रक्षन्ति.

(2) सूत्र- ढ्रलोपे पूर्वस्य दीर्घोऽणः (6-3-111)

(i) Meaning: अण् is transformed into दीर्घ-अण्, if followed by ढलोप or रलोप.

(ii) For example, हरिस् + रक्षति → हरिर् + रक्षति → हरि + (रलोप) + रक्षति → हरी रक्षति

(3) सूत्र- खरवसानयोर्विसर्जनीयः (8-3-15)

(i) अनुवृत्ति- रः (from 8-3-14)

(ii) Meaning: र् is transformed to विसर्ग, if followed by खर् (i.e., कर्कशव्यञ्जन) or if this र् is the last वर्ण with no other वर्ण after it.

(iii) For example,
रामस् + तारयति → रामर् + तारयति → रामः तारयति
रामस् at the end → रामर् → रामः

(4) सूत्र- विसर्जनीयस्य सः (8-3-34)

(i) अनुवृत्ति- खरि (from 8-3-15)

(ii) Meaning: विसर्ग is transformed into स्, when followed by खर्

(iii) For example, रामस् + तारयति → रामर् + तारयति → रामः + तारयति → रामस् + तारयति → रामस्तारयति

(5) सूत्र- शर्परे विसर्जनीयः (8-3-35)

(i) अनुवृत्ति- खरि (from 8-3-15)

(ii) Meaning: विसर्ग is retained as विसर्ग when followed by खर्, which in turn is followed by शर्

(iii) For example, रामस् + क्षान्तः → रामर् + क्षान्तः → रामः + क्षान्तः → रामः + क्षान्तः → रामः क्षान्तः

(6) सूत्र- वा शरि (8-3-36)

(i) अनुवृत्ति- विसर्जनीयस्य and सः (both from 8-3-34)

(ii) Meaning: विसर्ग is optionally transformed into स्, when followed by शर् (श्, ष् or स्)

(iii) For example, रामस् + शास्ति → रामर् + शास्ति → रामः + शास्ति → रामस् + शास्ति or रामः + शास्ति → रामश् + शास्ति or रामः + शास्ति → रामश्शास्ति or रामः शास्ति

(7) सूत्र- कुप्वोः कपौ च (8-3-37)

(i) अनुवृत्ति- विसर्जनीयस्य (from 8-3-34)

(ii) Meaning: विसर्ग is optionally transformed into जिह्वामूलीय when followed by क्/ख्, and उपध्मानीय when followed by प्/फ्.

(iii) For example,

रामस् + करोति → रामर् + करोति → रामः + करोति → राम + करोति or

रामः + करोति → रामकरोति or रामः करोति

रामस् + फलं ददाति → रामर् + फलं ददाति → रामः + फलं ददाति → राम + फलं ददाति or रामः + फलं ददाति → रामफलं ददाति or रामः फलं ददाति

(8) सूत्र- एतत्तदोः सुलोपोऽकोरनञ्समासे

(i) हलि (6-1-132)

(ii) Meaning: सुँ (i.e., the स्-प्रत्यय used in प्रथमाविभक्ति-एकवचन) following एतत् or तत् when followed by हल् is deleted.

(iii) For example,

एषस् + करोति → एष + करोति → एष करोति

सस् + ददाति → स + ददाति → स ददाति

(9) सूत्र- नश्छव्यप्रशान् (8-3-7)

(i) अनुवृत्ति- अम्परे (from 8-3-6), रुँ (from 8-3-1)

(ii) अधिकार- अत्रानुनासिकः पूर्वस्य तु वा (8-3-2) and अनुनासिकात् परोऽनुस्वारः (8-3-4)

(iii) Meaning: पदान्त न् is replaced by रुँ when followed by छव् (i.e., छ्, ठ्, थ्, च्, ट् or त्) which in turn is followed by अम् (i.e., अच्, अनुनासिक-व्यञ्जन and ह्, य्, व्, र् or ल्). And, based on the अधिकार-सूत्रs, preceding अच् of रुँ is replaced by its अनुनासिक or अनुस्वार.

(iv) For example, भवान् + चरति → भवारुँ + चरति → भवांरुँ + चरति or भवाँरुँ + चरति → भवांः + चरति or भवाँः + चरति → भवांस् + चरति or भवाँस् + चरति → भवांश्चरति or भवाँश्चरति

15.6.3 विसर्ग-सन्धि Type 3

In cases where रुँ is prescribed, but conditions for its further transformations mentioned in the first two types are unmet. In other words, when रुँ (prescribed by ससजुषोः रुः) is preceded by any वर्ण other than अ, AND followed by अश् (i.e., स्वर or मृदु व्यञ्जन) then र् remains as is. For example,

(i) हरिस् + ददाति → हरिर् + ददाति → हरिर् ददाति → हरिर्ददाति

(ii) गुरुस् + अपाठयत् → गुरुर् + अपाठयत् → गुरुर् अपाठयत् → गुरुरपाठयत्

This is summarized in Tables 15.14 and 15.15. The स्थानिन् and आदेश are highlighted in bold in the 'Conditions' and 'Result' columns respectively. Whatever precedes the स्थानिन् is पूर्वनिमित्त and whatever follows the स्थानिन् is परनिमित्त.

सूत्र	निमित्त	फल	Remarks	उदाहरण
ससजुषो रुँः (8-2-66)	पदान्त-स्	र् (रुँ)	The ष् of सजुष् is also replaced by र् (रुँ).	रामस् → रामर्
अतोरोरप्लुतादप्लुते (6-1-113)	*ह्रस्व-अ* रुँ *ह्रस्व-अ*	ह्रस्व-अ उ ह्रस्व-अ	गुण-सन्धि and पूर्वरूपसन्धि are applicable after this. This सन्धि is called उत्व-सन्धि.	रामर् अनन्त → राम उ अनन्त
हशि च (6-1-114)	*ह्रस्व-अ* रुँ *हश्*	ह्रस्व-अ उ हश्	गुण-सन्धि is applicable after this. हश् represents मृदु-व्यञ्जनs. This सन्धि is called उत्व-सन्धि.	रामर् वनम् → राम उ वनम्
भो-भगो-अघो-अपूर्वस्य योशि (8-3-17)	*अ* रुँ *अश्*	अ य् अश्	The रुँ in भोर्, भगोर्, अघोर् also gets य्. This सन्धि is called यत्व-सन्धि.	जनार् इच्छन्ति → जनाय् इच्छन्ति
खरवसानयोर्विसर्जनीयः (8-3-15)	र् *खर्/ अवसान*	विसर्ग खर्/अवसान	खर् represents कर्कश-व्यञ्जनs.	रामर् चलति → रामः चलति
विसर्जनीयस्य सः (8-3-34)	पदान्त-विसर्ग *खर्*	स् खर्	खर् represents कर्कश-व्यञ्जनs. This सन्धि is called सत्व-सन्धि.	रामः तनोति → रामस् तनोति
रो रि (8-3-14)	र् र्	र्		पुनर् रमते → पुन रमते

सूत्र	निमित्त	फल	Remarks	उदाहरण
ढ्रलोपे पूर्वस्य दीर्घोणः (6-3-111)	अण् र्-लोप	दीर्घ-अण् र्-लोप		पुन रमते → पुना रमते
नश्छव्यप्रशान् (8-3-7)	पदान्त-न् छव् अम्	अनुस्वार/अनुनासिक रुँ छव् अम्	अत्रानुनासिकः पूर्वस्य तु वा and अनुनासिकात् परोऽनुस्वारः are अधिकार-सूत्रs for this सूत्र.	तस्मिन् चित् → तस्मिं रुँ चित् or तस्मिँ रुँ चित्
वा शरि (8-3-36)	विसर्ग शर्	विसर्ग/स् शर्		रामः शूरः → रामः शूरः or रामस् शूरः
कुप्वोः कपौ च (8-3-37)	विसर्ग क्/ख् विसर्ग प्/फ्	जिह्वामूलीय/विसर्ग क्/ख् उपध्मानीय/विसर्ग प्/फ्		काककाकः/ काकः काकः पिकपिकः / पिकः पिकः

Table 15.14: विसर्ग-सन्धि

(1) ह्रस्व-अ <रुँ> ह्रस्व-अ → उत्व + गुण + पूर्वरूप

(2) ह्रस्व-अ <रुँ> हश् → उत्व + गुण

(3) आ <रुँ> अश् → यत्व + optional लोप

(4) अ <रुँ> आ/इच् → यत्व + optional लोप

(5) इच् <रुँ> अश् → No change

(6) Anything <रुँ/र्> खर् → विसर्ग → सत्व

(7) Anything <रुँ/र्> अवसान → विसर्ग

Table 15.15: Summary of विसर्ग-सन्धि

16 समास

16.1 Introduction

समास is one of the linguistic tools heavily employed in Saṃskṛta literature. One may even argue that it is impossible to understand Saṃskṛta texts without a basic understanding of different समासs. समास is the process of generating a new compound word (समस्तपद) by joining two or more semantically connected सुबन्त-पदs that finally refers to one entity.

Before discussing different types of समासs, let's briefly clarify some basic concepts and terms employed in all समासs. We use the example of a sentence with a compound word - " सीतापतिः रामः " (राम is the husband of सीता)- to explain these.

16.2 Essential Conditions for a समास

First of all, समास is only possible if a सूत्र prescribes it. As we see later, the सूत्रs prescribe समासs only between सुबन्तs. Hence, the component पदs in a समास must be सुबन्तs. In our example, सीतापतिः is the compound word. It has two पदs - सीतायाः and पतिः. Both are

सुबन्तs. This specific समास is prescribed by the सूत्र "षष्ठी" (2-2-8). The meaning of the सूत्र is detailed in a later section.

Second, the component पदs must have सामर्थ्य (potential). The सामर्थ्य refers to two features:

(1) एकार्थीभावरूपसामर्थ्य - Ability of the समस्तपद to refer to only one entity.

The component पदs have a meaning of their own. But when we use those पदs in the form of a sentence or a phrase (a part of a sentence), they provide "one" composite meaning. Now, the समास is possible only when the समस्तपद can refer to the same composite meaning. Therefore, the meaning of a समस्तपद is usually explained by वाक्यs (that typically have the same component पदs, used separately) called विग्रहवाक्यs. The विग्रहवाक्य and समपस्तपद refer to the same one entity as their primary meaning. In other words, the component पदार्थs have merged to provide one composite meaning. Thus the विग्रहवाक्यार्थ and the meaning of the समस्तपद are the same. This single composite meaning of समस्तपद is called प्रधानार्थ.

In our example of "सीतापतिः रामः" the समस्तपद i.e., सीतापतिः refers to रामः, since the two are समानाधिकरण-पदs. The विग्रहवाक्य of the समस्तपद is "सीतायाः पतिः". Here, the component words सीतायाः and पतिः may have individual and separate meanings, but the phrase

"सीतायाः पतिः" has one composite meaning, which refers to राम. Thus, the primary meaning of the विग्रहवाक्य and the meaning of the समस्तपद are the same. Therefore the component पदs are considered as समर्थ.

(2) व्यपेक्षारूपसामर्थ्य - The semantical connectedness between the two पदs.

The component पदs of the समास must be semantically connected. Consider our example of सीतापतिः रामः. The word सीतायाः means "of Sita", and the word "पतिः" refers to "husband". And, this "husband" (in this case, राम) is, in fact, "of सीता". Hence the two words are semantically connected.

Consider another sentence: "रामः पुत्रः दशरथस्य भ्रातरम् वालिनः सुग्रीवम् अपश्यत्" (= "राम, son of दशरथ, saw सुग्रीव, वालि's brother.") This can be rewritten after समास as "रामः दशरथपुत्रः वालिभ्रातरम् सुग्रीवम् अपश्यत्". Note that the समास is between (a) दशरथस्य and पुत्रः, and (b) वालिनः and भ्रातरम् since the two respective पदs within each set are semantically connected to each other. Here, दशरथस्य and भ्रातरम् are also two सुबन्त-पदs and are adjoining each other, but are not semantically connected, since सुग्रीव is, in fact, not the brother of दशरथ.

Note: Usually, the समस्तपद is complete in itself. In other words, the component पदs are dependent on each other to provide meaning. Still, they are generally not dependent on another पद which is not part of the समास, and vice versa; that is, the पद outside of the समास should not be dependent on component पदs. This rule is mentioned as "सापेक्षम् असमर्थं भवति".

Consider the example 'रामः दशरथस्य पुत्रः'. Here, दशरथस्य and पुत्रः are mutually related words. And they don't have any dependency on external words. Thus दशरथस्य and पुत्रः are समर्थ-पदs and a समास is permitted, leading to: "रामः दशरथपुत्रः". Consider a counter-example: "रामः शूरस्य दशरथस्य पुत्रः". In this case, a समास between दशरथस्य पुत्रः won't be permissible since the word दशरथस्य is connected/dependent on an external word शूरस्य.

However there is one exception. If a component पद is a सम्बन्धिपद denoting a 'related entity', such as पितृ, पुत्र, गुरु, शिष्य, ज्ञान etc., such पदs always expect (नित्यसापेक्ष) their correspondingly related entity, such as पुत्र, पितृ, शिष्य, गुरु, ज्ञेय etc. Such पदs can be part of समास even if the समास is not complete in itself.

Consider the example "देवदत्तस्य गुरुकुलम्". Here गुरु and कुल are component पदs. However, the word is not complete since the word गुरु begs the question 'whose गुरु'. Nevertheless, since गुरु is a सम्बन्धिपद and is नित्यसापेक्ष, we can connect the meaning of the word देवदत्तस्य with गुरु, even if गुरु is part of a समास and is not the primary meaning of the समास.

This is explained as : "नित्यसापेक्षत्वात् समासः" or "गमकत्वात् समासः" (The समास is allowed even between असमर्थ-पदs if the component पद is नित्यसापेक्ष or the reader can understand the meaning clearly).

16.3 पूर्वपद and उत्तरपद in a समास

समस्तपद has no restriction on the number of component पदs. Sometimes some of the component पदs can be समस्तपदs in their own right. However, mainly the basic समासs occur with two सुबन्तs taken at a time. Therefore, we can parse the समस्तपद into two पदs - an anterior पद (first पद) and a posterior पद (the second पद).[1] The anterior पद of the समस्तपद is called पूर्वपद, and the posterior one is called उत्तरपद.

16.4 Method to understand समास-सूत्रs

The first two पादs of the second अध्याय in अष्टाध्यायी deal with the समासs (i.e., 2-1-1 to 2-2-38).

16.4.1 Classification of समास-सूत्रs

There are two kinds of सूत्रs in the समास-प्रकरण:

[1] Since we are discussing only the समासs formed using two पदs, there cannot be a third पद after the second पद in the समस्तपद.

(1) अधिकारसूत्रs. There are two kinds of अधिकार-सूत्रs:

(i) Those that apply to all (or most) of the विधिसूत्रs. The first four सूत्रs are अधिकार-सूत्रs and belong to this first group. Hence all विधि-सूत्रs will have the following अनुवृत्तिs- समर्थः (2-1-1), सुप् (2-1-2), समासः (2-1-3), सुपा सह (2-1-4) and विभाषा (2-1-11). The last one applies to all those that come after 2-1-11.

(ii) Those applicable to some of the विधिसूत्रs. These are typically names of the समासs. Therefore, we see अनुवृत्ति of अव्ययीभावः (2-1-5) in all सूत्रs from 2-1-6 to 2-1-21, तत्पुरुषः (2-1-22) in all those from 2-1-23 to 2-2-22 and बहुव्रीहिः (2-2-23) from 2-2-24 to 2-2-27.

(2) विधिसूत्रs

There are two kinds of विधिसूत्रs -

(i) समास-विधायक-सूत्रs

These सूत्रs prescribe specific समासs. All of them will have two पदs. One in प्रथमा विभक्ति and the other in तृतीया विभक्ति. We will discuss these in detail below.

(ii) पौर्वापर्य-विधायक-सूत्रs

These are at the end of this section (2-2-29 to 2-2-38) and deal with the order of component पदs in समस्तपद.

Therefore, in summary, समास-विधायक-सूत्रs will have the अनुवृत्ति of

(1) समर्थः, सुप्, समासः, सुपा सह in all सूत्रs

(2) विभाषा in most of them

(3) a label (अव्ययीभावः, तत्पुरुषः or बहुव्रीहिः)

16.4.2 Structure and Meaning of समास-सूत्रs

Now, let us understand what these mean, how a समास-विधायक-सूत्र is structured, and how to interpret it using an example. We will then move on to discuss each सूत्र individually.

Consider this सूत्र that prescribes the समास (पञ्चमी-तत्पुरुष)- "पञ्चमी भयेन" (2-1-37)

With all the appropriate अनुवृत्तिs, this सूत्र will be expanded as: पञ्चमी सुप् भयेन सुपा सह तत्पुरुषः समर्थः समासः विभाषा

Here, note the following general principles:

(1) सुप् is in प्रथमा-विभक्ति and सुपा is in तृतीया. These refer to सुबन्त-पदs. And, they mean that a सुबन्त-पद joins with another सुबन्त-पद.

(2) समास-विधायक-सूत्रs specifically mention which सुबन्त-पदs are to be considered in a given type of समास. In this example, पञ्चमी is in प्रथमा and भयेन in तृतीया. Therefore, using the idea of समानाधिकरण,

we get पञ्चमी सुप् भयेन सुपा सह. In other words, a सुबन्त-पद that is in "पञ्चमी" joins with the सुबन्त-पद "भयेन".

(3) The word समर्थः applies to both सुप् and सुपा and prescribes that the समास is only between समर्थ-पदs as discussed in detail earlier. It thus expands as समर्थः सुप्, समर्थेन सुपा सह and means "a समर्थ-सुबन्त-पद joins with another समर्थ-सुबन्त-पद".

(4) The word विभाषा means that this process of joining is optional, barring a few exceptions of "नित्यसमास". In other words, one is free to use either the समस्तपद or the component पदs individually.

(5) The word समासः gives the label to this process of generating समस्तपद.

(6) The words such as अव्ययीभावः, तत्पुरुषः, बहुव्रीहिः provide an additional label to subset of those समासs.

Now, applying all these अनुवृत्तिs/अधिकारs in our example of "पञ्चमी भयेन" the complete meaning of the सूत्र will be: "पञ्चमीविभक्त्यन्तं समर्थं सुबन्तं पदं समर्थेन भयशब्दस्य सुबन्तेन पदेन सह विभाषया समस्यते। स च समासः तत्पुरुषः।" It translates as: "A समर्थ-सुबन्त-पद in पञ्चमी-विभक्ति may optionally join with a समर्थ-सुबन्त-पद of भय. This समास is called तत्पुरुष". For example,

(1) व्याघ्रात् भयम् $\rightarrow$ व्याघ्रभयम्

(2) शत्रोः भये $\rightarrow$ शत्रुभये

16.4.3 Order of the component पदs

In Saṃskṛta, the order of words in a sentence is typically not fixed since the words are inflected. However, this flexibility cannot be applied in समास since the inflections (विभक्तिs) are deleted while forming a समस्तपद, as described later. Hence, a specific order is prescribed for two component पदs in a समस्तपद. This order is explained by two सूत्रs; the first gives the label उपसर्जन and the second says that the word that is given this label comes first in a समस्तपद -

(1) प्रथमानिर्दिष्टं समास उपसर्जनम् (1-2-43): A पद that is denoted by the प्रथमा-विभक्ति in a समास-विधायक-सूत्र is labelled उपसर्जन. For example, in the case of "व्याघ्रात् भयम्" described above, the word व्याघ्रात् is denoted by the word "पञ्चमी" in the सूत्र "पञ्चमी भयेन". And, the word पञ्चमी is in प्रथमा-विभक्ति. Therefore, "व्याघ्रात्" is labelled उपसर्जन.

(2) उपसर्जनं पूर्वम् (2-2-30) : In a समास, the word with the label उपसर्जन should come first. Therefore in our example, "व्याघ्र" appears before "भय" to result in "व्याघ्रभयम्".

16.4.4 Steps in a समास

Till now, we have seen that समास is possible only when there is a समास-विधायक-सूत्र and the two-component पदs have सामर्थ्य. We also saw that there is a specific order for the joining पदs, thus making one of them पूर्वपद and उत्तरपद.

Additionally, पूर्वपद and उत्तरपद undergo a few modifications while joining.

First, both पूर्वपद and उत्तरपद drop their विभक्तिs and take their प्रातिपदिक forms. Therefore in a sense, the physical joining is between two प्रातिपदिकs. Second, if any सन्धि-rule is applicable between them, then such a सन्धि is to be done mandatorily. Thus we now have a new प्रातिपदिक created. This प्रातिपदिक behaves like any other प्रातिपदिक, lending itself to suitable modifications such as the addition of स्त्री-प्रत्ययs, सुप्-प्रत्ययs etc.

Some additional changes may happen to पूर्वपद and/or उत्तरपद. For example, sometimes, the पूर्वपदs may drop their स्त्रीप्रत्ययs. A few additional प्रत्ययs called समासान्त-प्रत्ययs get added to the समस्तपद. We discuss these later while describing individual समासs.

With this background, let's now look at individual समासs, their subtypes, सूत्रs and a few examples.

16.5 Classification of समासs

16.5.1 तत्पुरुष-समास

तत्पुरुष-समासs are prescribed in सूत्रs 2.1.22 to 2.2.22. Of these the first सूत्र तत्पुरुषः (2.1.22) gives the label "तत्पुरुष" to all those prescribed till 2.2.22.

In all तत्पुरुष-समासs the primary meaning of the समास is same as the meaning of the उत्तरपद, and hence this समास is known as उत्तर-पदार्थ-प्रधान समास.

For contrast, it may be helpful to note that बहुव्रीहि is अन्य-पदार्थ-प्रधान; द्वन्द्व is उभय-पदार्थ-प्रधान, and अव्ययीभाव is पूर्व-पदार्थ-प्रधान. We will discuss these under those heads.

तत्पुरुष-समासs are broadly categorized based on the nature of the पूर्वपद.

(1) It may have one of the विभक्तिs from द्वितीया to सप्तमी, which are then called द्वितीया-तत्पुरुष, तृतीया-तत्पुरुष etc.

(2) If पूर्वपद is in सामानाधिकरण्य with उत्तरपद, then it is called कर्मधारय-समास.

(3) If पूर्वपद is denoting a सङ्ख्या then it is called द्विगु-समास.

(4) If पूर्वपद is नञ्, then it is called नञ्-समास.

Tables 16.2 and 16.4 summarize some of the important सूत्रs, their meanings, and a few examples. Some सूत्रs that need explanations are marked with an asterisk and are explained subsequently. The सूत्रs marked with '#' at the beginning are कर्मधारय-समासs.[2]

सूत्र	Meaning	Examples
द्वितीया श्रितातीतपतितगतात्यस्तप्राप्तापन्नैः (2-1-24)	Any समर्थ-सुबन्त in द्वितीया-विभक्ति can form a समास with सुबन्त forms of- श्रित, अतीत, पतित, गत, अत्यस्त, प्राप्त and आपन्न.	कृष्णं श्रितः - कृष्णश्रितः, आपदम् आपन्नः - आपदापन्नः
अत्यन्तसंयोगे च (2-1-29)	काल-वाचक-द्वितीया-विभक्त्यन्त-सुबन्तs can form समास with any समर्थ-सुबन्त if अत्यन्तसंयोग is to be indicated.	मुहूर्तं सुखम् - मुहूर्तसुखम्, सर्वरात्रं कल्याणी - सर्वरात्रकल्याणी
पूर्वसदृशसमोनार्थकलहनिपुणमिश्रश्लक्ष्णैः (2-1-31)	Any समर्थ-सुबन्त in तृतीया-विभक्ति can form समास with सुबन्त forms of - पूर्व, सदृश, सम, ऊनार्थ, कलह, निपुण, मिश्र and श्लक्ष्ण.	मासेन पूर्वः - मासपूर्वः, मात्रा सदृशः - मातृसदृशः

[2]Refer to the resources online using the link mentioned on the last page of the book for a complete list of प्रातिपदिकs in the गणs referred by some सूत्रs.

सूत्र	Meaning	Examples
कर्तृकरणे कृता बहुलम् (2-1-32)	A तृतीया-विभक्त्यन्त-सुबन्त in the meaning of कर्तृ or करण can form समास with any समर्थ-सुबन्त which is a कृदन्त.	अहिना हतः - अहिहतः, नखैः निर्भिन्नः - नखनिर्भिन्नः
चतुर्थी तदर्थार्थबलिहितसुख-रक्षितैः (2-1-36)*	Any समर्थ-सुबन्त in चतुर्थी-विभक्ति can form समास with the सुबन्त forms of - तदर्थ, अर्थ, बलि, हित, सुख and रक्षित.	यूपाय दारु यूपदारु, बालकाय पयः - बालकार्थं पयः (नित्यसमास)
पञ्चमी भयेन (2-1-37)	Any समर्थ-सुबन्त in पञ्चमी-विभक्ति can form समास with the सुबन्त forms of - भय,भीति,भीत and भी.	वृकेभ्यः भयं - वृकभयम्, वृकेभ्यः भीतः - वृकभीतः
अपेतापोढमुक्तपतितापत्रस्तै-रल्पशः (2-1-38)	Any समर्थ-सुबन्त in पञ्चमी-विभक्ति can form समास with the सुबन्त forms of - अपेत, अपोढ, मुक्त, पतित and अपत्रस्त.	प्रासादात् पतितः - प्रासादपतितः, सुखात् अपेतः - सुखापेतः

सूत्र	Meaning	Examples
सप्तमी शौण्डैः (2-1-40)	Any समर्थ-सुबन्त in सप्तमी-विभक्ति can form समास with the सुबन्त forms of प्रातिपदिकs in the गण starting from शौण्ड.	अक्षेषु शौण्डः - अक्षशौण्डः, शास्त्रेषु निपुणः - शास्त्रनिपुणः
सिद्धशुष्कपक्वबन्धैश्च (2-1-41)	Any समर्थ-सुबन्त in सप्तमी-विभक्ति can form समास with the सुबन्त forms of सिद्ध, शुष्क, पक्व and बन्ध.	काश्यां सिद्धः - काशीसिद्धः, स्थाल्यां पक्वः - स्थालीपक्वः
षष्ठी (2-2-8)*	The सुबन्तs in षष्ठी-विभक्ति can form समास with any समर्थ-सुबन्त.	राज्ञः पुरुषः - राजपुरुषः, छात्रस्य पुस्तकम् - छात्रपुस्तकम्
याजकादिभिश्च (2-2-9)	A षष्ठी-विभक्ति-सुबन्त will form समास with समर्थ-सुबन्तs in the गण starting with याजक.	देवस्य पूजकः - देवपूजकः
# पूर्वकाल-एक-सर्व-जरत्-पुराण-नव-केवलाः समानाधिकरणेन (2-1-49)	पूर्वकाल, एक, सर्व, जरत्, पुराण, नव, and केवल - these सुबन्तs form समास with सुबन्तs that are समानाधिकरण to them.	एका शाटी - एकशाटी, सर्वे देवाः - सर्वदेवाः

सूत्र	Meaning	Examples
# उपमानानि सामान्यवचनैः (2-1-55)	उपमान-वाचक-सुबन्तs will form समास with सामान्य-वचन-सुबन्तs that are समानाधिकरण to them. In a simile, the object of comparison is उपमान, the common attribute between the subject and object of comparison is the सामान्य. The subject of comparison is called उपमेय or उपमित.	मेघः इव श्यामः - मेघश्यामः, शैलः इव उन्नतः - शैलोन्नतः
# उपमितं व्याघ्रादिभिः सामान्याप्रयोगे (2-1-56)	उपमित(उपमेय)-वाचक-सुबन्तs will form समास with सुबन्तs in गण starting with व्याघ्र and when सामान्य is not explicitly mentioned	पुरुषः व्याघ्र इव - पुरुषव्याघ्रः, राजा ऋषभः इव - राजर्षभः
# विशेषणं विशेष्येण बहुलम् (2-1-57)*	विशेषण-वाचक-सुबन्तs will form समास with विशेष्य-वाचक-सुबन्तs.	नीलम् उत्पलम् - नीलोत्पलम् तपः एव धनम् - तपोधनम् आम्र इति फलम् - आम्रफलम्

सूत्र	Meaning	Examples
मयूरव्यंसकादयश्च (2-1-72)	The words in the list starting from मयूरव्यंसक are समासs, to be taken as they are.	व्यंसकः मयूरः - मयूरव्यंसकः अन्यः राजा - राजान्तरम् चिद् एव - चिन्मात्रम्
सङ्ख्यापूर्वो द्विगुः (2-1-52)*	A certain type of समास, in which the पूर्वपद is a numeral, is called द्विगु.	पञ्चसु कपालेशु संस्कृतः पञ्चकपालः
नञ् (2-2-6)*	नञ् (an अव्यय used in the meaning of negation), forms समास with a समर्थ-सुबन्त.	न पशुः अपशुः, न ईश्वरः अनीश्वरः
कुगतिप्रादयः (2-2-18)*	The अव्यय- कु, प्रातिपदिकs with गति-संज्ञा (सूत्रs 1-4-60 to 1-4-79 define गति-संज्ञा) and अव्ययs in प्रादि-गण- these will form समास with a समर्थ-सुबन्त (नित्य-समास).	प्रगतः आचार्यः प्राचार्यः, कुत्सितः पुरुषः कुपुरुषः, अशुचिः शुचिः सम्पद्यमानः भूतः शुचीभूतः

सूत्र	Meaning	Examples
उपपदमतिङ् (2-2-19)*	The सुबन्तs having उपपद-संज्ञा will form समास[3] with any समर्थ-सुबन्त (नित्य-समास).	कुम्भं करोति इति कुम्भकारः, सोमेन यजते इति सोमयाजी

Table 16.2: समास

सूत्र	Meaning	Examples
न निर्धारणे (2-2-10)	In the case where षष्ठी-विभक्ति is used in the meaning of निर्धारण, समास is prohibited.	मनुष्याणां क्षत्रियः शूरतमः (here, समास between मनुष्याणां and क्षत्रिय is prohibited.)

[3]Refer to the Section-10.3 that deals with the प्रत्ययs - अण्, क, णिनिँ that are prescribed only in the presence of उपपदs.

सूत्र	Meaning	Examples
पूरण-गुण-सुहितार्थ-सत्-अव्यय-तव्य-समानाधिकरणेन (2.2.11)	षष्ठी-समास is prohibited with सुबन्तs (a) having meanings of पूरण (ordinal number), गुण (quality) and सुहित (content) (b) having these प्रत्ययs - सद्(शतृ/शानच्) (c) that are अव्ययs (d) having the प्रत्यय तव्य and (e) which are in समानाधिकरण with the सुबन्त षष्ठी-विभक्ति.	(पूरण) - छात्राणां पञ्चमः, (गुण) काकस्य कार्ष्ण्यम्, (सुहित) फलानां सुहितः, (सत्) ब्राह्मणस्य कुर्वाणः, (अव्यय) ब्राह्मणस्य कृत्वा, (तव्य) ब्राह्मणस्य कर्तव्यम्, (समानाधिकरण) शुकस्य माराविदस्य
क्तेन च पूजायाम् (2-2-12)	षष्ठी-समास is prohibited with a सुबन्त having a क्त-प्रत्यय and in the meaning of पूजा, मति and बुद्धि.	राज्ञां पूजितः, राज्ञां बुद्धः
कर्मणि च (2-2-14)	A षष्ठी-विभक्ति-सुबन्त which is in the meaning of कर्मकारक, cannot form समास.	आश्चर्यः गवां दोहः अगोपालकेन

Table 16.4: षष्ठी-तत्पुरुष-समास-निषेध-सूत्रs*

Explanations:

(1) चतुर्थी तदर्थ-अर्थ-बलि-हित-सुख-रक्षितैः (2-1-36)

This सूत्र prescribes that सुबन्त-पद in चतुर्थी-विभक्ति can form समास with the सुबन्त forms of the following words: तदर्थ, अर्थ, बलि, हित, सुख and रक्षित. Here, the four words बलि, हित, सुख, and रक्षित are to be seen as words per se, but there are some special rules for first two words - तदर्थ and अर्थ.

तदर्थ refers to an idea or a set of words. It means "for this purpose" and denotes a raw material that can be converted to the entity referred to by चतुर्थी-विभक्त्यन्त-पद. For example, consider that we have raw gold (हिरण्य) that is made into an earring (कुण्डल). We say, "कुण्डलाय हिरण्यम्". Here हिरण्य is the raw material that has transformed into कुण्डल. Hence these two can form a समास and result in the समस्तपद - कुण्डलहिरण्यम्. Similarly, दध्ने पयः → दधिपयः, पटाय तन्तवः → पटतन्तवः etc.

The second word, अर्थ in the सूत्र is prescribed for a नित्यसमास. In other words, we cannot show a विग्रहवाक्य using the exact words since those two words will always be in समास. The विग्रहवाक्य needs to be explained using a different word(s) than those used in the समास itself. This is called अ-स्वपद-विग्रह. The word "चतुर्थी" in the

सूत्र only denotes how you explain the विग्रहवाक्य using different words.

For example, बालकाय इदम् → बालकार्थम्. Here, बालक and अर्थ have resulted in the समास. And, when we explain the विग्रहवाक्य we use a different word (other than अर्थ) but use बालक in चतुर्थी-विभक्ति.

Secondly, this समस्त-पद is विशेष्यनिघ्न. Therefore we get all three forms depending on the विशेष्य. For example, (1) बालकेभ्यः अयं मार्गः → बालकार्थः मार्गः (2) बालकाय इयं लेखनी → बालकार्था लेखनी and (3) बालकाय इदं पयः → बालकार्थं पयः

(2) षष्ठी (2-2-8) : This सूत्र prescribes that a षष्ठी-विभक्त्यन्त-पद would join with any समर्थ-सुबन्त to result in a समस्तपद. However, some exceptions are mentioned in the subsequent सूत्रs. A few important ones are:

(i) न निर्धारणे (2-2-10) : We may recall that षष्ठी-विभक्ति is prescribed in the sense of निर्धारण too. For example, when we distinguish one entity from a group, we use षष्ठी. For example, 'मनुष्याणां क्षत्रियः शूरतमः'. Here, क्षत्रिय is distinguished among the मनुष्यs because of his distinctive quality शूरतमत्व. Therefore, मनुष्याणां is निर्धारण-षष्ठी. And, if षष्ठी is in the meaning of निर्धारण, then समास between those two words (here, मनुष्य and क्षत्रिय) is prohibited.

(ii) पूरण-गुण-सुहितार्थ-सत्-अव्यय-तव्य-समानाधिकरणेन (2-2-11) : षष्ठी-समास is prohibited with the following:

(a) पूरण- In an earlier section on तद्धित-प्रत्ययs, the concept of पूरण was explained as ordinality, such as प्रथम, षष्ठ, etc. In such cases, षष्ठी-समास is prohibited. For example, छात्राणां तृतीयः, वेदानां पञ्चमः, रसानां सप्तमः etc.

(b) गुण- Here, गुण refers to quality or attribute. For example, गोः कार्ष्ण्यम्, दन्तानां शौक्ल्यम्, पुरुषस्य सुखम् etc.

(c) समानाधिकरण- As we see later, कर्मधारय-समास is prescribed for समानाधिकरण-पदs. However, this सूत्र prohibits such समास if the विशेषण is the उत्तरपद. For example, राज्ञः पाटलिपुत्रकस्य, पाणिनेः सूत्रकारस्य etc. However, if the order is reversed, then समास is permitted. For example, सूत्रकारपाणिनेः.

Some less-used cases are:

(d) सुहितार्थ- This refers to words denoting the meaning तृप्ति (satisfaction/contentment). For example, फलानां तृप्तः.

(e) सत्-This is a label to शतृ and शानच्-प्रत्ययs (given in सूत्र 3.2.127). For example, रामस्य कुर्वन्.

(f) अव्यय- This refers to only कृत्-अव्ययs such as क्त्वा, ल्यप्, and तुमुन्. For example, गुरोः कृत्वा.

(g) तव्य- There are two similar प्रत्ययs, तव्य and तव्यत्, which only differ in स्वर. Here, the prohibition applies only to तव्य. For example, मनुष्यस्य कर्तव्यम्.

(3) तत्पुरुषः समानाधिकरणः कर्मधारयः (1-2-42) : This सूत्र gives a new label कर्मधारय to a subset of तत्पुरुष-समासs, in which both पूर्वपद and उत्तरपद are समानाधिकरण to each other. We deal with examples of कर्मधारय in some of the below सूत्रs:

(i) विशेषणं विशेष्येण बहुलम् (2-1-57):[4] This सूत्र by default prescribes a विशेषण-पूर्वपद-समास. For example, नीलम् उत्पलम् $\rightarrow$ नीलोत्पलम्.

(ii) Another related type of कर्मधारय-समास is मध्यमपदलोपि-समास. This comes from the वार्तिक "समानाधिकरणाधिकारे शाकपार्थिवादीनामुपसङ्ख्यानम्, उत्तरपदलोपश्च". Here, the वार्तिक is accounting for the existence of समस्तपदs such as शाकपार्थिव. विग्रहवाक्य for these समस्तपदs would have an additional word. For example, शाकपार्थिव is explained as शाकप्रियः पार्थिवः. However, the उत्तरपद of पूर्वपद (which is effectively the मध्यमपद), which is the word "प्रिय", is dropped and is not part of the समस्तपद. Similarly, we can see examples such as 'देवपूजको ब्राह्मणः देवब्राह्मणः'.

[4]The word बहुलम् implies that this prescription is variedly applicable - sometimes mandatorily, sometimes optionally, sometimes not applicable at all, and sometimes in an unusual way. The main idea is that it should allow for variations found in classical usage. This concept of बहुलम् is explained in this verse : "क्वचित् प्रवृत्तिः क्वचिदप्रवृत्तिः क्वचिद् विभाषा क्वचिदन्यदेव । विधेर्विधानं बहुधा समीक्ष्य चतुर्विधं बाहुलकं वदन्ति ॥"

These ideas suggest a few other types of समासs also:

(iii) अवधारणापूर्वपद- Here, अवधारणा suggests "the same as" or "is in the form of". To indicate this अवधारणा, the word एव is used in विग्रहवाक्य. For example, विद्या एव धनम् → विद्याधनम्, गुरुः एव देवः → गुरुदेवः.

(iv) सम्भावनापूर्वपद- Here, सम्भावना usually refers to popularly known name. The word इति is used in the विग्रहवाक्य to indicate this सम्भावना. For example, हिमालयः इति पर्वतः → हिमालयपर्वतः.

Note: A special rule is applicable in कर्मधारय-समास dealing with स्त्रीलिङ्ग-पदs. If the समानाधिकरण-पदs are स्त्रीलिङ्ग-पदs and the पूर्वपद is विशेष्यनिघ्न then, the स्त्री-प्रत्यय of पूर्वपद is dropped in समास. For example, दृढा भक्तिः → दृढभक्तिः, सुन्दरी स्त्री → सुन्दरस्त्री,दीर्घा रज्जुः → दीर्घरज्जुः.

(4) नञ् (2-2-6) : This सूत्र prescribes that नञ् forms a समास with a समर्थ-सुबन्त. For example, न क्षरः → अक्षरः, न तृप्तः → अतृप्तः, न अनुकूलम् → अननुकूलम्, न अश्वः → अनश्वः. Here note that some of the forms have a simple addition of "अ" while others have "अन्". The rules for these transformations are prescribed in the below explained सूत्रs:

(i) नलोपो नञः (6-3-76) : In नञ्-समास, that is in a situation where नञ् is a पूर्वपद and is followed by an उत्तरपद, "न्" of "नञ्" is deleted in the समस्तपद. For example, नञ् + क्षरः → न + क्षरः

(since ञ् is इत्) → अ + क्षरः (since न् is deleted as prescribed in this सूत्र) → अक्षरः

(ii) तस्मान्नुडचि (6-3-77) : If the उत्तरपद is starting with an अच्, then नुट् is inserted before this अच्. In नुट्, the content is "न्". For example, नञ् + अश्वः → न + अश्वः (since ञ् is इत्) → अ + अश्वः (from the previous सूत्र) → अ + न् + अश्वः (since नुट् is added based on this सूत्र) → अनश्वः

(5) The सूत्र "सङ्ख्यापूर्वो द्विगुः" provides the label द्विगु for the तत्पुरुष-समास that has सङ्ख्या as पूर्वपद. This समास mostly occurs when the समस्तपद is denoting the meaning of समाहार (a group).

For example, पञ्चानां कुमारीणां समाहारः → पञ्चकुमारि त्रयाणां लोकानां समाहारः → त्रिलोकी.

Note the following features of द्विगु-समास -

(a) The resultant समस्तपद is in singular (as prescribed in the सूत्र 2-4-1, "द्विगुरेकवचनम्")

(b) The resultant समस्तपद is in नपुंसक-लिङ्ग by default (as prescribed in the सूत्र 2-4-17, "स नपुंसकम्").

(c) If the उत्तरपद is ending with अत, then the समस्तपद gets a स्त्रीप्रत्यय (ङीप्) (as mentioned in सूत्र 4-1-21 "द्विगोः") Example: अष्टानाम् अध्यायानां समाहारः= अष्टाध्यायी.

(d) The above rule is exempted for a set of words that still take नपुंसक form even though they have an अत्-ending. For example, पञ्चानां पात्राणां समाहारः → पञ्चपात्रम्, त्रयाणां भुवनानां समाहारः → त्रिभुवनम्, चतुर्णां युगानां समाहारः → चतुर्युगम्

(6) There are two other subtypes in तत्पुरुष-समास:

(i) कु-गति-प्रादि-समास - कुगतिप्रादयः (2-2-18) : This सूत्र prescribes a mandatory समास with कु which is an अव्यय, the निपातs called गति and the गण starting from प्र with a समर्थ-सुबन्त.

Here, कु is an अव्यय usually used in the meaning of bad or wicked. गति is a label prescribed in सूत्रs 1-4-60 to 79. प्रादिगण is a set mentioned in गणपाठ.

Examples for कु-गति-प्रादि-समास include:

(a) कुत्सितः पुरुषः → कुपुरुषः
(b) अङ्गीकारं कृत्वा → ऊरीकृत्य
(c) शोभनाः प्रजाः → सुप्रजाः

Generally, the कृदन्तs with उपसर्गs also fall in the third category mentioned above.

For example, प्रकर्षेण नत्वा → प्रणम्य, विशेषतः ज्ञातः → विज्ञातः.

It is useful to recollect that the विग्रहवाक्यs do not contain the exact component words but those that give a similar meaning, since these are नित्य-समासs. Such विग्रहवाक्यs are therefore called "अ-स्वपद-विग्रह"s as mentioned earlier.

(ii) उपपद-समास - उपपदमतिङ् (2-2-19) : शब्दs that are labelled as उपपदs, mandatorily form a समास with another समर्थ-शब्द. This is also a नित्य-समास and hence will have अ-स्वपद-विग्रह. Here, the label उपपद is prescribed in 3-1-92(तत्रोपपदं सप्तमीस्थम्). For example,

(a) कुम्भं करोति इति $\longrightarrow$ कुम्भकारः

(b) सर्वं जानाति इति $\longrightarrow$ सर्वज्ञः

(c) सोमेन यष्टुम् शीलम् अस्य अस्ति इति $\longrightarrow$ सोमयाजी

Here, in example (a), कुम्भ is given the label उपपद. In the presence of such उपपद, the कृ-धातु gets अण्-प्रत्यय resulting in the word "कार", which is a कृदन्त. Note that this word cannot be used independently, but only with उपपद. And, since the उपपद mandates समास, we have usable words such as कुम्भकार, कृतिकार etc and never "कारः" alone. In other words, the समास occurs before the formation of an independently functional सुबन्त form.

16.5.2 बहुव्रीहि-समास

As mentioned briefly in the previous section, बहुव्रीहि is a label given to a type of समास, in which the समस्तपद refers to an entity that is different from those referred individually by the component पदs. For this reason it is called "अन्य-पदार्थ-प्रधान-समास".

These समासs are prescribed in सूत्रs 2-2-24 to 2-2-28 and they get the label बहुव्रीहि from the सूत्र 2-2-23 (शेषो बहुव्रीहिः).

Let's take a few popular examples to understand how बहुव्रीहि-समास operates.

(1) पीतम् अम्बरं यस्य (=विष्णोः) सः (=विष्णुः) → पीताम्बरः.

Here there are two-component पदs - पीतम् and अम्बरम्, and they both refer to the same entity (समानाधिकरण), which is the yellow robe. However, the term पीताम्बरः refers to a different entity (अन्यपदार्थ), विष्णु, who wears that robe. This अन्यपदार्थ is usually indicated by the यद् and तद् words in विग्रहवाक्य. The exact relationship between the entities directly referred to by component पदs and the entity (अन्यपदार्थ) referred by the समस्तपद is indicated by the विभक्ति attached to यद्. And, therefore these समस्तपदs also carry the विभक्त्यर्थ (which can also be कारकार्थ). In this case, the षष्ठी used in यस्य is in the form of a simple सम्बन्ध. The yellow robes are worn by Vishnu and hence are related to Him.

(2) हतः रावणः येन (=रामेण) सः (=रामः) → हतरावणः

In this case, too, we have two समानाधिकरण-पदs, referring to one entity, forming a समास resulting in a समस्तपद that refers to a different entity. हत and रावण refer to रावण, while हतरावण refers to राम. रावण (the entity referred to by the component पदs) and राम (the entity referred to by the समस्तपद) are connected in the form of a कर्म-कर्तृ relationship. In other words, हतरावण refers to someone (राम in this case) as the कर्तृ of हननक्रिया. रावण is कर्म in the same क्रिया. In other words, the कर्तृ is अभिहित by this समस्तपद. Hence, the तृतीया-विभक्ति is not applicable, and the समस्तपद will be in समानाधिकरण with the कर्तृ, which is राम in this case. However, in the विग्रहवाक्य, the कर्म that is रावण is अभिहित by the word हतः, but not कर्तृ, and hence कर्तृ gets तृतीया as "येन".

(3) बहुव्रीहि, the very name of this समास, is also an example for बहुव्रीहि-समास. बहुव्रीहि is not only a technical term in a sense described as a type of समास, but is also used to mean "a person (or an entity) who (or that) has a lot of grains". This second meaning is a resultant of बहुव्रीहि-समास.

Its विग्रहवाक्य is as follows: बहवः व्रीहयः यस्य पुरुषस्य सः पुरुषः → बहुव्रीहिः or बहवः व्रीहयः यस्मिन् पदार्थे सः पदार्थः → बहुव्रीहिः

In the above examples we saw that the relationship between the meaning of the component पदs and the meaning of the

समस्तपद are mentioned by the विभक्तिs in the विग्रहवाक्य. And, that विभक्ति can be any of the six from द्वितीया to सप्तमी. Here is a glance at examples for each.

(i) द्वितीया

प्राप्तम् उदकं यं (=ग्रामं) सः (=ग्रामः) → प्राप्तोदकः (=ग्रामः)

Here समस्तपद is referring to ग्राम and is in fact mentioning that ग्राम is कर्म in प्रापण-क्रिया. This कर्मत्व is indicated by यम् in विग्रहवाक्य.

(ii) तृतीया

(a) हतः रावणः येन (=रामेण) सः (=रामः) → हतरावणः (=रामः).
Here समस्तपद is referring to राम as the कर्तृ in हनन-क्रिया. This कर्तृत्व is indicated by येन in विग्रहवाक्य.

(b) पीतं पयः येन (=पात्रेण) तत् (=पात्रम्) → पीतपयस्कम् (=पात्रम्).
Here पात्र is करण in पान-क्रिया. The तृतीया-विभक्ति, i.e., "येन" in विग्रहवाक्य indicates this करणत्व.

(iii) चतुर्थी

दत्ता कन्या यस्मै (=पुरुषाय) सः (=पुरुषः) → दत्तकन्यः (=पुरुषः).
यस्मै indicates सम्प्रदान-कारक.

(iv) पञ्चमी

पतितानि फलानि यस्मात् (=वृक्षात्) सः (=वृक्षः) → पतितफलः (=वृक्षः).

This is an example for अपादान-कारक.

(v) षष्ठी

Most cases of बहुव्रीहि are in षष्ठी.

(a) पीतम् अम्बरं यस्य (=विष्णोः) सः (=विष्णुः) → पीताम्बरः (=विष्णुः)
(b) बहवः व्रीहयः यस्य (=पुरुषस्य) सः (=पुरुषः) → बहुव्रीहिः (=पुरुषः).
The above are examples of सम्बन्ध.
(c) पुण्ये श्रवणकीर्तने यस्य (=विष्णोः) सः (=विष्णुः) → पुण्यश्रवणकीर्तनः (=विष्णुः).
Here षष्ठी indicates कर्म.
(d) सूक्ष्मं दर्शनं यस्य (=ऋषेः) सः (=ऋषिः) → सूक्ष्मदर्शनः (=ऋषिः).
In this case, षष्ठी indicates कर्तृ.

(vi) सप्तमी

वीराः पुरुषाः यस्मिन् (=देशे) सः (=देशः) → वीरपुरुषः (=देशः).

Here, अधिकरण is indicated by सप्तमी.

In these examples, we have mainly dealt with कारकs, but the विभक्तिs can be in non-कारक meanings also.

(4) We have seen समानाधिकरण-बहुव्रीहि till now, since the component पदs were समानाधिकरण to each other as indicated by same विभक्ति in विग्रहवाक्य. And this covers most cases. Exceptionally, we may

have व्यधिकरण-बहुव्रीहि also, in which the component पदs are not समानाधिकरण to each other. For example,

(i) चक्रं पाणौ यस्य (=नारायणस्य) सः (=नारायणः) → चक्रपाणिः (=नारायणः)
(ii) दाम उदरे यस्य (=कृष्णस्य) सः (=कृष्णः) → दामोदरः (=कृष्णः)
(iii) विषः कण्ठे यस्य (=शिवस्य) सः (=शिवः) → विषकण्ठः (=शिवः)

Sometimes, बहुव्रीहि is categorised into two: तद्गुणसंविज्ञान and अतद्गुणसंविज्ञान. Here, गुण refers to the meaning of component पदs. संविज्ञान refers to knowledge about them. Hence, if the meaning of the component पदs is an attribute (or part) of the अन्यपदार्थ, then it is तद्गुणसंविज्ञान.[5]

For example, consider the word लम्बकर्ण. This refers to a person who has long ears - लम्बौ कर्णौ यस्य (=पुरुषस्य) सः (=पुरुषः) → लम्बकर्णः (=पुरुषः). However, long ears are also an attribute of that person (अन्यपदार्थ). Hence, लम्बकर्ण is an example of तद्गुणसंविज्ञान-बहुव्रीहि.

On the other hand, the word गोधन refers to a person for whom cows are his assets, गावः धनं यस्य (=पुरुषस्य) सः (=पुरुषः) → गोधनः. Here, cows are not an attribute of the person (अन्यपदार्थ) but merely his belongings. Hence, गोधन is a case of अतद्गुणसंविज्ञान-बहुव्रीहि. Some

[5]"तस्य गुणस्य उपसर्जनीभूतस्यान्यपदार्थे सम्यग्विज्ञानं विशेषणत्वेनोपादानं यस्मिन् बहुव्रीहौ स तद्गुणसंविज्ञानः" इति राघवेन्द्रतीर्थाः। "तेषां गुणानामवयवपदार्थानां संविज्ञानं विशेषान्वयित्वमिति तदर्थः। यत्र समवायसम्बन्धेन सम्बन्ध्यन्यपदार्थः, तत्र प्रायस्तद्गुणसंविज्ञानम्। अन्यत्र प्रायोऽन्यत्। 'लम्बकर्णचित्रगू' उदाहरणे। 'सर्वादीनि, जक्षत्यादयः' इति चोदाहरणे" - इति नागोजिभट्टाः परिभाषेन्दुशेखरे।

of the examples that we saw, such as हतरावणः, बहुव्रीहिः, etc., also belong to this group.

(5) In the previous discussion we saw that तत्पुरुष is उत्तरपदार्थप्रधान. Hence, the entity referred by उत्तरपद is also the meaning of the समस्तपद. Therefore, in तत्पुरुष-समासs, the लिङ्ग of उत्तरपद is generally the लिङ्ग of समस्तपद too. However, since बहुव्रीहि refers to अन्यपदार्थ, the समस्तपद takes the लिङ्ग of अन्यपद. Therefore, the लिङ्ग of उत्तरपद has no bearing on the final लिङ्ग of the समस्तपद. For example,

(i) अधीता विद्या येन (=बालकेन) सः (=बालकः) $\rightarrow$ अधीतविद्यः (=बालकः)

(ii) अधीता विद्या यया (=बालिकया) सा (=बालिका) $\rightarrow$ अधीतविद्या (=बालिका)

(iii) अधीता विद्या येन (=मित्रेण) तत् (=मित्रम्) $\rightarrow$ अधीतविद्यम् (=मित्रम्)

Here, even though विद्या is a स्त्रीलिङ्ग-पद, the लिङ्ग of समस्तपद is determined by the विशेष्य. Hence, it can take any appropriate gender, -विद्यः, -विद्या, -विद्यम्. Similarly, words like गोधनः, गोधना, गोधनम्, सूक्ष्मदर्शनः, सूक्ष्मदर्शना, सूक्ष्मदर्शनम् or तीक्ष्णकोपः, तीक्ष्णकोपा, तीक्ष्णकोपम् serve as examples for the same, wherein the समस्तपदलिङ्ग varies in accordance with the विशेष्य-लिङ्ग.

In the case of अधीतविद्या/अधीतविद्यः/अधीतविद्यम्, we can observe an additional change - that the स्त्री-प्रत्यय of the पूर्वपद is dropped. This generally happen if पूर्वपद is विशेष्यनिघ्न. Other examples include दीर्घजङ्घः, ऊढकन्यः, श्लक्ष्णचूडः etc.

(6) One special type of बहुव्रीहि-समास is prescribed in 2-2-28 : "तेन सहेति तुल्ययोगे". Here, the word सह forms समास with समर्थ-तृतीयान्त-प्रातिपदिक when the meanings of intended समस्तपद and the component प्रातिपदिक are related in a similar way.

For example, if राम and लक्ष्मण have come together, we say "सहलक्ष्मणः रामः आगतः". It means "राम, along with लक्ष्मण, came". Here, both राम and लक्ष्मण are connecting similarly to the action of आगमन. Hence there is तुल्ययोग. Thus we get the समास - लक्ष्मणेन सह आगतः $\rightarrow$ सहलक्ष्मणः आगतः. It can also be used as सलक्ष्मणः आगतः. The word सह optionally is changed to स based on सूत्र "वोपसर्जनस्य" (6.3.82).

16.5.3 द्वन्द्व-समास

This is a समास in the meaning of "AND", in which both पूर्वपदार्थ and उत्तरपदार्थ are involved in the same way with regard to a क्रिया. It is therefore called उभयपदार्थप्रधान. This is prescribed in the सूत्र चार्थे द्वन्द्वः (2-2-29).

The द्वन्द्व-समास is prescribed in two meanings of च :

(1) इतरेतरयोगः: in which two (or more) entities depend on each other to perform a क्रिया.

For example, देवदत्तेन च यज्ञदत्तेन च इदं कार्यम् → देवदत्तयज्ञदत्तभ्याम् इदं कार्यम्. Here, both देवदत्त and यज्ञदत्त are required to accomplish a given task. However, these components are still seen as two individuals collaborating to perform this work.

(2) समाहार: in which two (or more) entities are seen as one unit. Their identity is not considered. In a sense, the components have merged to form a new group identity.

For example, सञ्ज्ञाः च परिभाषाः च अध्येतव्याः → सञ्ज्ञापरिभाषम् अध्येतव्यम्[6]

Note that इतरेतर-द्वन्द्व is in द्विवचन (or बहुवचन if the components are more than two) since components aren't seen as one unit. However, in समाहार-द्वन्द्व, they get एकवचन because all of them are

[6] च, the अव्यय, is used in four meanings. Of these, समास is possible when used in one of the two meanings - इतरेतरयोग or समाहार. In the other two - समुच्चय and अन्वाचय, समास is not possible since there is no सामर्थ्य.

समुच्चय refers to connecting two independent entities that are participating in a similar (but two independents) क्रियाs. For example, हरिं च गुरुं च भजस्व। Here since both हरि and गुरु are कर्म in भजन-क्रिया, we connect the two using च. However, when viewed closely, the two भजन-क्रियाs are different - one in which हरि is कर्म and the other in which गुरु is कर्म. In other words, the two are not semantically connected, and hence समास is not possible.

अन्वाचय is similar to above, except that one of the क्रियाs is primary, and the other is secondary. अन्वाचय refers to joining that secondary क्रिया. For example, भिक्षाम् अट, गां च आनय। Here, भिक्षाटन is primary क्रिया. Bringing cows is incidentally done at that time. च is used for the अन्वाचन of that second क्रिया. In this case, also, there is no semantic connectedness, and hence समास is not possible.

seen as one unit. When एकवचन is used for a unit, then it should also get नपुंसकलिङ्ग as per सूत्र "स नपुंसकम्" (2-4-17).

16.5.3.1 In द्वन्द्व-समास the पूर्व-उत्तर-योजना

We noted that two or more words with equal importance are joined in द्वन्द्व-समास. Hence, it may appear that the order of पदs may not be significant. However, there are a few rules that define the order. Among these, the latter rules supersede the former rules:

(1) द्वन्द्वे घि (2-2-32): This सूत्र prescribes that the words that are labelled घि should come first (i.e., as पूर्वपद) in द्वन्द्व-समास. सूत्र 1-4-7(शेषो घ्यसखि) defines the label घि. ह्रस्व-इकारान्त-शब्दs and ह्रस्व-उकारान्त-शब्दs, except सखि-शब्द get the label घि. For example, हरि, गुरु, शम्भु are घि. Therefore these words come first in द्वन्द्व-समास. For example, हरिहरौ, गुरुशिष्यौ, वायुजले etc.

(2) अजाद्यदन्तम् (2-2-33): The words that have अच् at the beginning and अत् (that is, ह्रस्व-अ) at the end, should be पूर्वपद. For example, (a) ईशश्च कृष्णश्च → ईशकृष्णौ, (b) इन्द्रश्च अग्निश्च → इन्द्राग्नी. Note that in the second example, अग्नि is घि. Based on 2-2-32, it should come first. However, since later rules overrule the earlier rules, 2-2-33 takes precedence, and इन्द्र, which is an अजादि-अदन्त word, comes first.

(3) अल्पाच्तरम् (2-2-34): Those that have less number of अच्-वर्णs should come first. For example, कृष्णश्च अर्जुनश्च → कृष्णार्जुनौ. The word कृष्ण has two अच्-वर्णs, while अर्जुन has three. Hence, कृष्ण comes first.[7]

16.5.4 अव्ययीभाव-समास

अव्ययीभाव is a label prescribed in 2-1-5(अव्ययीभावः). As the name indicates, this समास "creates" अव्ययs. In fact, सूत्र 1-1-41(अव्ययीभावश्च) explicitly states that the समस्त-पदs resulting from अव्ययीभाव-समास get the label अव्यय. Hence, these resultant words behave as अव्ययs.

सूत्रs from 2-1-6 to 2-1-21 prescribe this समास. The first in these is the most commonly used one: "अव्ययं विभक्ति-समीप-समृद्धि-व्यृद्धि-अर्थाभाव-अत्यय-असम्प्रति-शब्दप्रादुर्भाव-पश्चाद्-यथा-आनुपूर्व्य-यौगपद्य-सादृश्य-सम्पत्ति-साकल्य-अन्तवचनेषु". This सूत्र prescribes that an अव्यय in the meaning of विभक्ति, समीप etc., forms समास with a समर्थ-सुबन्त. Since the meaning of the समस्तपद is primarily that of the अव्यय, (which is always a पूर्वपद in अव्ययीभाव), this समास is known as पूर्वपदार्थ-प्रधान-समास. For examples,

(1) In the meaning of विभक्ति- देशे → अधिदेशम्
Here the अव्यय "अधि" is in the meaning of सप्तमी-विभक्ति.

[7] This सूत्र has many वार्तिकs that deal with cases such as two नक्षत्रs, two brothers or two entities with superiority-inferiority relations, etc. Interested may refer to the original.

(2) In the meaning of समीप - वनस्य समीपम् → उपवनम्
Here, "उप" means "समीप".

(3) Similarly, जलस्य अभावः → निर्जलम्; शक्तिम् अनतिक्रम्य → यथाशक्ति; रूपस्य योग्यम् → अनुरूपम् etc.

16.6 Conventions on writing विग्रहवाक्यs

There are a few conventions about विग्रहवाक्य that traditional scholars follow:

(1) In नित्यसमास, we cannot show a विग्रहवाक्य using the exact words since those two words will always be in समास. The विग्रहवाक्य needs to be explained using a different word(s) than those used in the समास itself. This is called अ-स्वपद-विग्रह. For example, consider a case of उपपद-नित्यसमास. Here the समस्तपद "सर्वज्ञः" is explained in विग्रहवाक्य as "सर्वं जानाति इति सर्वज्ञः".

(2) In usage, the समस्तपद can be in any विभक्ति. However, as a convention, we usually show the विग्रहवाक्य as if the समस्तपद is in प्रथमाविभक्ति. As a next step, we add the corresponding विभक्ति to indicate the specific form of the समस्तपद that is used in the given context. It isn't incorrect to merge the two steps; however, the traditional commentaries usually follow this two-step approach to

help students understand. For example, consider the समस्तपद, "दशरथपुत्रेण". Its विग्रहवाक्य is usually written as "दशरथस्य पुत्रः दशरथपुत्रः, तेन दशरथपुत्रेण", although simply saying "दशरथस्य पुत्रेण" isn't incorrect either.

16.7 समासान्त-प्रत्ययS

Till now, we have discussed the meaning of different समासs. We have seen that by default, the समास is between two सुबन्त-पदs. We have also noted that in the process of forming समासs with सुबन्तs, a few changes occur such as the dropping of विभक्तिs, स्त्रीप्रत्ययs, and also the final प्रातिपदिक changing its लिङ्ग if need be. There is another set of such changes that happen in the process of समास, due to the addition of some प्रत्ययs at the end of समस्तपदs in the making. These प्रत्ययs are called समासान्त-प्रत्ययs. These प्रत्ययs do not convey any new meaning but only impact the final form of समस्तपद.

These प्रत्ययs are labelled समासान्त in सूत्र 5.4.68(समासान्ताः). This सूत्र is within the तद्धित-अधिकार. समासान्त-प्रत्ययs are rightly categorised under तद्धित, since they are applicable to प्रातिपदिकs. They are prescribed from 5.4.69 to 5.4.168.

We discuss some of the common समासान्त-प्रत्ययs with some examples below:

(1) ऋक्-पूर्-अप्-धूर्-पथाम् अ अनक्षे (5.4.74) : अ is added to the words ऋक्, पूर्, अप्, धूर्, and पथिन्, except when धूर् refers to अक्ष (axis of a wheel). For example,

(i) अर्धम् ऋचः → अर्ध + ऋच् + अ → अर्धर्चम्

(ii) विष्णोः पूः → विष्णु + पुर् + अ → विष्णुपुरम्

(iii) विमलाः आपः यस्मिन् → विमल + अप् + अ → विमलापः

(iv) राज्ञः धूः → राज + धुर् + अ + टाप् → राजधुरा

(v) जलस्य पन्थाः → जल + पथिन् + अ → जलपथ् + अ → जलपथः

Here the last two examples need some explanation. The fourth example has two more changes in addition to समासान्त-प्रत्यय: (a) the पूर्वपद has changed from राजन् to राज; and (b) "टाप्", an additional प्रत्यय, has been added. The first change is due to पूर्वपद related rule that we discuss in the next section. The second change is due to a सूत्र that prescribes the लिङ्ग of उत्तरपद to the समस्तपद in द्वन्द्व and तत्पुरुष-समासs - "परवल्लिङ्गं द्वन्द्वतत्पुरुषयोः (2.4.26)". Since धुर् is a स्त्रीलिङ्गपद, an additional स्त्रीप्रत्यय is added after the समासान्त-अ-प्रत्यय[8]

[8]One may wonder why the same is not applied in the case of the second example विष्णुपुर, since पुर् is also स्त्रीलिङ्ग. However, this rule is overruled by usage. At a fundamental level, व्याकरण is a method to make sense of what is in use and not overrule the usage itself. Since, विष्णुपुर is in use as a नपुंसकलिङ्गशब्द, no स्त्रीप्रत्यय is added.

In the fifth example, पथिन् is changed to पथ् due to a सूत्र: नस्तद्धिते (6-4-144)[9]

(2) राजाहःसखिभ्यष्टच् (5.4.91) टच् is added to the words राजन्, अहन् and सखि in तत्पुरुष-समास. Here, ट् and च् are इत्-वर्णs and hence the प्रत्यय is effectively अ. For example,

(i) यदूनां राजा → यदु + राजन् + टच् → यदु + राज् + टच् → यदुराजः

(ii) उत्तमं अहन् → उत्तम + अहन् + टच् → उत्तम + अह् + टच् → उत्तमाहः

(iii) पार्थस्य सखा → पार्थ + सखि + टच् → पार्थ + सख् + टच् → पार्थसखः

(3) उरःप्रभृतिभ्यः कप् (5.4.151) : In बहुव्रीहि-समास, कप् is mandatorily added to words in the following list : उरस् सर्पिस् उपानः पुमान् अनड्वान् नौः पयः लक्ष्मीः दधि मधु शालि अर्थान्नञः. For example,

(i) दृढं उरः यस्य सः → दृढ + उरस् + कप् → दृढोरस्कः

(ii) पयसा सह → सह + पयस् + कप् → सहपयस्कः

(iii) प्राप्ता लक्ष्मीः यस्य सः → प्राप्त + लक्ष्मी + कप् → प्राप्तलक्ष्मीकः

The last mention in this list is akin to a सूत्र - It means the word अर्थ also mandatorily gets कप् only when the बहुव्रीहि is with नञ्. न विद्यते अर्थः यस्मिन् सः → अनर्थकः.

[9]The discussion of this सूत्र is beyond the scope of this book. Interested readers can refer to the original.

(4) शेषाद् विभाषा (5.4.154) : In बहुव्रीहि-समास, कप् is optionally added as a समासान्त-प्रत्यय in cases where any other समासान्त-प्रत्यय is not prescribed. For example,

(i) वीराः पुरुषाः यस्मिन् देशे स देशः → वीरपुरुषः or वीरपुरुषकः
(ii) बहूनि रूपाणि यस्य सः देवः → बहुरूपः or बहुरूपकः

16.8 पूर्वपदान्त-प्रक्रिया

In the examples discussed above, we have focussed on changes that occur at the end of समास. There are some cases where minor variations are seen at the end of पूर्वपद too.

We discuss some prominent such cases below.

(1) न् at the end of पूर्वपद is dropped. [नलोपः प्रातिपदिकान्तस्य (8.2.7)]. For example,

(i) राज्ञः पुरुषः → राजन् + पुरुष → राज + पुरुष → राजपुरुषः
(ii) ब्रह्मणः ज्ञानम् → ब्रह्मन् + ज्ञानम् → ब्रह्म + ज्ञानम् → ब्रह्मज्ञानम्
(iii) कर्म बन्धनं यस्य सः → कर्मन् + बन्धन → कर्म + बन्धन → कर्मबन्धनः

(2) महत् is changed as महा- [आन्महतः समानाधिकरणजातीययोः (6.3.46)]. For example,

(i) महान् गुणः → महत् + गुण → महा + गुण → महागुणः

(ii) महती बुद्धिः यस्य सः → महती + बुद्धि → महत् + बुद्धि → महा + बुद्धि → महाबुद्धिः

(3) ऋ at the end of some words is changed to आ [आनङ् ऋतो द्वन्द्वे (6.3.25)]. For example,

(i) माता च पिता च → मातृ + पितृ → माता +पितृ → मातापितरौ
(ii) पिता च पुत्रः च → पितृ + पुत्र → पिता + पुत्र → पितापुत्रौ
(iii) होता च पोता च → होतृ + पोतृ → होता + पोतृ → होतापोतारौ

(4) अलुक्

We have seen earlier that in the process of समास, both पूर्वपद and उत्तरपद drop their विभक्तिs. However, there are certain instances in which the विभक्ति of पूर्वपद is retained (अलुक् = non-deletion). Most such instances are in सप्तमी, but some are seen in other विभक्तिs also: For example,

(i) आत्मने + पदम् → आत्मनेपदम् [वैय्याकरणाख्यायां चतुर्थ्याः (6.3.7)]
(ii) युधि + स्थिरः → युधिष्ठिरः [हलदन्तात् सप्तम्याः सञ्ज्ञायाम् (6.3.9)]

These are popularly referred to as "अलुक्-समास".

17 कारकद्वारा वाक्यार्थविमर्शः

17.1 Introduction

In the previous Chapters, we have discussed different elements of संस्कृत-व्याकरण. It is time to bring them all together for an actual application.

We can look at language in two stages. In stage one, we associate words with their meanings. The meanings are mainly in the domain of vocabulary and dictionaries. In the second, we communicate the relationship between those meanings in a sentence. This is achieved by the grammar of the language.

In other words, equipping oneself with the ability to understand a sentence by relating all its component words meaningfully is the primary objective of learning a language. And grammar helps us precisely in doing that.

Thus we need to focus on our ability to decipher वाक्यार्थ (the meaning of a sentence) as a benchmark to know our skills in grammar. Thankfully, संस्कृत-व्याकरण has provided us with systematic tools to decipher the वाक्यार्थ. All concepts that we have learnt till now - विभक्तिs, कारकs, कृदन्त, तद्धित, तिङन्त, सामानाधिकरण्य, समास etc., are nothing but those tools. कारकs are the most critical of these.

In this section, we take some sentences/verses as examples to apply these concepts and attempt a systematic derivation of the meaning of those sentences/verses using the व्याकरण concepts.

17.2 First Example

आपदामपहर्तारं दातारं सर्वसम्पदाम् ।
लोकाभिरामं श्रीरामं भूयो भूयो नमाम्यहम् ॥

Analysis of any verse (or any prose, too) can be undertaken in two steps: पदज्ञान and अन्वयज्ञान.

17.2.1 पदज्ञान

पदज्ञान requires identification of पदs and their forms.

(1) पदच्छेद (Parsing the sentence to identify पदs)
The above verse is how we see this in modern books. However, in earlier times, this verse used to be written without any space in between the words. Thus the verse would read as : आपदामपहर्तारंदातारंसर्वसम्पदाम् । लोकाभिरामंश्रीरामंभूयोभूयोनमाम्यहम् ॥

As a first step, we need to identify individual पद्s in this verse. The modern spacing notation helps identify most points where one can parse the sentence. However, there are two caveats. One, this doesn't mean that the parsing should happen only where we find a "space". Two, the words which end with a space are not necessarily the parsed forms. Therefore, while one may crudely use the "spaces" for a gross identification, we should check for two grammatical principles while parsing the sentence: the notion of पद् and the idea of सन्धि.

A पद्, as we have seen is that which ends with सुप् or तिङ्. Therefore, one should actively look for a सुप् or a तिङ् as पद्-delimiters. In doing so, one needs to keep the principles of सन्धि in mind so that we look for the word's original form that is unaffected by its following वर्ण. (i.e., to think about the form before it is transformed because of सन्धि). We can see that in the example of नमाम्यहम्= नमामि+अहम् in verse.

Thus the above verse can be parsed as: आपदाम्, अपहर्तारम्, दातारम्, सर्वसम्पदाम्, लोकाभिरामम्, श्रीरामम्, भूयः, भूयः, नमामि, अहम्

This concept of पदच्छेद् is one of the unique features in संस्कृत (as compared to any other modern language). It requires familiarity with संस्कृत vocabulary (both प्रातिपदिक and धातु), सुबन्त and तिङन्त forms, and an ability to look at सन्धि operations in the reverse direction.

(2) पद-स्वरूप-चिन्तनम् (Analysing the grammatical form of each word): This activity is straightforward and clearly explains why and how we identified these पदs. In other words, we record all details of the पद encoded in their सुबन्त or तिङन्त form.

Here on, we can follow these simple steps.

(i) Classify each पद into सुबन्त/तिङन्त/अव्यय[1]

(ii) For अव्ययs, identify their अर्थ.

(iii) For सुबन्तs, identify प्रातिपदिक, लिङ्ग (नियत/विशेष्यनिघ्न and current लिङ्ग) विभक्ति, वचन, प्रातिपदिक-अर्थ. (and कृत्/तद्धित-प्रत्यय or समास if applicable)

(iv) For तिङन्तs, identify धातु, लकार, पुरुष, वचन, आत्मने/परस्मै/उभय (its nature and current form), सकर्मक/अकर्मक, कर्तरि/कर्मणि/भावे, if applicable णिच्/सन्/etc.

In our given example, we can do this activity as shown below:

(i) आपदाम् - सुबन्त - आपद्, स्त्री (नियत), 6/3, distress,

(ii) अपहर्तारम् - सुबन्त - अपहर्तृ, पु (विशेष्यनिघ्न),2/1, destroyer, कृत् - तृच्, कर्तरि

(iii) दातारम् - सुबन्त - दातृ, पुं (विशेष्यनिघ्न),2/1, provider, कृत् - तृच्, कर्तरि

(iv) सर्वसम्पदाम् - सुबन्त - सर्वसम्पद्, स्त्री (नियत),6/3, all weath, समास

(v) लोकाभिरामम् - सुबन्त - लोकाभिराम, पुं (विशेष्यनिध्न), 2/1, pleasing to the people, समास

[1]Even though in a strictly grammatical sense, अव्यय is also a सुबन्त, we treat it separately in this section since many details of a regular सुबन्त do not apply to अव्यय.

(vi) श्रीरामम्- सुबन्त - श्रीराम, पुं (नियत), 2/1, Sri Rama, समास,

(vii) भूयः - अव्यय - again

(viii) भूयः - same as above

(ix) नमामि - तिङन्त - णमँ प्रह्वत्वे शब्दे च, लट्, उत्तमपुरुष, एकवचन, परस्मै, सकर्मक, कर्तरि, to pray/bow down

(x) अहम् - सुबन्त - अस्मद्, त्रि,1/1, I

17.2.2 अन्वयज्ञान

We now know all the words and the details of their grammatical forms. We can move to the second step of analysing their meanings and understanding the relationship between the meanings of different पद्s. This relationship is technically called अन्वय. In practice, अन्वय refers to an orderly construction of a sentence that starts with a कर्तृपद and ends with a क्रियापद. We arrange other कारकs in the middle, ensuring that विशेषणs and विशेष्य are positioned adjacent to each other. For the sake of simplicity, it helps to divide a verse/sentence into multiple parts, one for each क्रियापद. अन्वय related to each क्रियापद can be further divided into two parts: (a) a basic अन्वय that has only कारकs and क्रियाs and (b) a complete अन्वय that includes all विशेषणs and other सम्बन्धs.

The process of making sense of अन्वय involves two concepts - क्रिया-कारक-सम्बन्ध and समास.

17.2.2.1 Analysis of क्रिया-कारक-सम्बन्ध

This analysis includes the following steps:

(1) Identification of all क्रियापदs (both तिङन्त and कृदन्त) and the कारकs associated with each of those क्रियाs, applying the idea of अभिहित/अनभिहित.
(2) Identification of all विशेषण-विशेष्य-सम्बन्धs applying the idea of सामानाधिकरण्य.
(3) Identification of other सम्बन्धs indicated by non-कारक-विभक्तिs.

Therefore, in our example, we can analyze as below:

(1) There are three क्रियापदs: two कृदन्तs - अपहर्तारम् and दातारम्, and one तिङन्त - नमामि. Usually, there will be at least one तिङन्त-क्रियापद. Even in the absence of it, the default forms such as अस्ति or भवति are assumed to be present. For this reason, some call तिङन्त-क्रियापदs as primary or प्रधान and कृदन्तs as secondary or अप्रधान.
(2) Let's start with the तिङन्त.
    (i) As discussed under पदस्वरूप, नमामि is कर्तरि form of a सकर्मक-धातु and is in एकवचन. In other words, कर्तृ is अभिहित. Therefore, we should look for कर्तृकारक which will be in प्रथमा-विभक्ति and एकवचन. Here, we have only one such word - अहम्.[2]

[2]Even if 'अहम्' were not mentioned, it is to be understood as such since नमामि is an उत्तम-पुरुष-एकवचन form, which can take only 'अहम्'.

(ii) Since the धातु is सकर्मक, and since कर्म for this क्रिया is अनभिहित, we should have the कर्म mentioned in द्वितीया. There are four such words - अपहर्तारम्, दातारम्, लोकाभिरामम् and श्रीरामम्. Since all four of them are in same विभक्ति, वचन and लिङ्ग and refer to the same entity (i.e., श्रीराम), they are समानाधिकरण to each other. Of these, the प्रातिपदिक श्रीराम is referring to the specific entity (i.e., the person श्रीराम) directly, while the three others are general प्रातिपदिकs, that in the current case, are used to describe श्रीराम. Therefore, श्रीराम is विशेष्य while others are विशेषणs.

(iii) There are no other कारकs mentioned in relation to नमामि.

(iv) Therefore, the basic अन्वय is: अहं श्रीरामं नमामि.

(v) Moving forward, we have an अव्यय - भूयः - which is a क्रियाविशेषण and applies to नमामि. It describes an action as being done again and again. Therefore, here, it refers to नमन being done again and again.

(vi) At this stage, we can come to a partial अन्वय - अहं श्रीरामं भूयः भूयः नमामि।

(3) We now move to the other क्रियापदs. As mentioned earlier, this example has two कृदन्त-क्रियापदs : अपहर्तारम् and दातारम्.

(i) The प्रातिपदिक of अपहर्तारम् is अपहर्तृ, which in turn has तृच्-प्रत्यय in the meaning of कर्तृ. Thus कर्तृ is अभिहित. And, therefore we should look for a word that is in समानाधिकरण with the current word so that we will be able to identify the कर्तृ. In other words, since अपहर्तारम् is in पुंलिङ्ग-द्वितीया-एकवचन, another विशेष्य-वाचक-पद that is also in पुंलिङ्ग-द्वितीया-एकवचन will inform us who that कर्तृ is. And, such word is श्रीरामम्. Hence कर्तृ in the क्रिया of अपहरण is श्रीराम.

(ii) Now, similar to the above तिङन्त analysis process, we should look for कारकs. Since कर्तृ is अभिहित, अपहरण is सकर्मक, and कर्म is अनभिहित, we should search for a word that has the कर्म-कारक-बोधक-विभक्ति. अनभिहित-कर्म is generally mentioned in द्वितीया. But in the case of कृदन्तs, it will be in षष्ठी.[3] Here, आपदाम् is in षष्ठी. Hence, आपद् (difficulty) is the कर्म in अपहरण-क्रिया.[4]

(iii) There is no other कारक associated with this क्रिया mentioned in this verse.

(iv) The final क्रियापद is दातारम्. It can be analysed in the exact way as with the word अपहर्तारम्. It too is कर्तृ-अभिधायक, has श्रीरामं as विशेष्य, needs a कर्म-बोधक-पद, which is mentioned in षष्ठी - सर्वसम्पदाम्.

(v) Here one may wonder if सर्वसम्पदाम् can have अन्वय with अपहर्तारम् or if आपदाम् can have अन्वय with दातारम् since Saṃskṛta has a free word order. However, by default, we usually consider those that are close to each other as अन्वित with each other. Since आपदाम् and अपहर्तारं are closer to each other,

[3]Except in some cases mentioned in the सूत्र न लोकाव्यय.... (2-3-69), discussed in the Chapter on विभक्ति

[4]The plural form indicates that the difficulties are many.

compared to अपहर्तारम् and सर्वसम्पदाम्, we choose the former as अन्वित to each other. More importantly, the semantically meaningful अन्वय is to be selected. In a verse that praises Lord Rama, it would be absurd to state that he gives difficulties or removes all wealth!

17.2.2.2 Analysis of समासs

The second important part of अन्वयज्ञान is to understand the समासs.

As we have seen earlier, many words in Saṃskṛta are more than just words, as they contain contextual information too. We have seen this with विभक्तिs, तद्धितs, कृदन्तs etc. Therefore, the meaning of those words should be understood in relation to other words so that we get a semantically sensible meaning. This understanding is even more critical while analysing समासs since समासs have many visible प्रातिपदिकs and invisible विभक्तिs and other words embedded in them. Deciphering them necessarily requires one to look for other words in relation to the समस्त-पद so that we can understand their semantic connectedness. Since most समस्त-पदs are in the form of विशेषणs, looking for the विशेष्य becomes crucial in this process. Some समासs may themselves be in the form of विशेष्यs, in which case this analysis may be more straightforward than others.

Let us illustrate this with examples in this verse. Here, we have two समस्तपदs : (a) लोकाभिरामम् and (b) सर्वसम्पदाम्.

लोकाभिरामम् is in समानाधिकरण with श्रीराम, and is therefore a विशेषण to श्रीराम. It has two प्रातिपदिकs - लोक and अभिराम. Therefore, we need to analyse the semantic connectedness of लोक (=people), अभिराम (=pleasing entity) and श्रीराम. Evidently, the most meaningful construction is - "Rama is pleasing to people". Technically, it means that people (लोकs) are कर्तृ, the pleasing entity (अभिराम) is अधिकरण in रमणक्रिया, and श्रीराम is that pleasing entity. Therefore, the विग्रह is लोकानां अभिरामः = लोकाभिरामः.

सर्वसम्पदाम् is not a विशेषण to anything else. Its immediate अन्वय is with दातारम्. We know that it refers to कर्म in दान. The समस्त-पद has two प्रातिपदिकs- सर्व (=all) and सम्पद् (=wealth). It is easy to notice that सर्व is विशेषण to सम्पद् - meaning "all the wealth". Hence this is कर्मधारय समास.

This verse can therefore be translated as:

"I bow down again and again to Sri Rama, [who is] the destroyer of distress, the provider of all the wealth and pleasing to the people."

17.3 Second Example

तपःस्वाध्यायनिरतं तपस्वी वाग्विदां वरम् ।

नारदं परिपप्रच्छ वाल्मीकिर्मुनिपुङ्गवम् ॥

17.3.1 पदज्ञान

(1) पदच्छेद (Parsing the sentence to identify पदs)

तपःस्वाध्यायनिरतम्, तपस्वी, वाग्विदाम्, वरम्, नारदम्, परिपप्रच्छ, वाल्मीकिः, मुनिपुङ्गवम् ।

(2) पद-स्वरूप-चिन्तनम्

(i) तपःस्वाध्यायनिरतम् - सुबन्त, तपःस्वाध्यायनिरत, नपुं/पुं(विशेष्यनिघ्न), 1/1 or 2/1, 2/1 engaged in penance and the study of vedas, कृदन्त - क्त, कर्तरि, समास - द्वन्द्व + सप्तमी-तत्पुरुष

(ii) तपस्वी - सुबन्त, तपस्विन्, पुं (विशेष्यनिघ्न), 1/1, ascetic, तद्धित - विनिँ-प्रत्यय in the meaning of मतुप् (possessor)

(iii) वाग्विदाम् - सुबन्त, वाग्विद्, पुं (विशेष्यनिघ्न), 6/1, eloquent, कृदन्त - क्विप्, कर्तरि, समास

(iv) वरम्- सुबन्त, वर, (विशेष्यनिघ्न), नपुं 1/1 or 2/1/ पुं 2/1, best

(v) नारदम् - सुबन्त, नारद, पुं (नियत) 2/1, Narada

(vi) परिपप्रच्छ- तिङन्त, परि (उपसर्ग) + प्रच्छँ ज्ञीप्सायाम्, लिट्, 1/1, सकर्मक, परस्मैपदि-धातु, कर्तरि, to ask

(vii) वाल्मीकिः- सुबन्त, वाल्मीकि, पुं (नियत) 1/1, Valmiki

(viii) मुनिपुङ्गवम् - सुबन्त, मुनिपुङ्गव, (विशेष्यनिघ्न) नपुं 1/1 or 2/1 / पुं 2/1, great sage, समास

17.3.2 अन्वयज्ञान

17.3.2.1 Analysis of क्रिया-कारक-सम्बन्ध

There are three क्रियापद्s: one तिङन्त - परिप्रपच्छ; and two कृदन्तs - निरत and वाग्विद्.

(1) परिपप्रच्छ is तिङन्त - कर्तरि and सकर्मक.

   (i) Here, the क्रिया is that of asking.
   (ii) वाल्मीकिः mentions कर्तृ.
   (iii) नारदम् indicates कर्म.
   (iv) Basic अन्वय at this stage: वाल्मीकिः नारदं परिपप्रच्छ।
   (v) तपस्वी is in समानाधिकरण to वाल्मीकिः and is therefore its विशेषण.
   (vi) तपःस्वाध्यायनिरतम्, मुनिपुङ्गवम् and वरम् are विशेषणs to नारदम्
   (vii) वरम् (=best) requires a referent. वाग्विदां provides that referent. "Best among वाग्विद्s". Note that the षष्ठी is in निर्धारण.

(2) वाग्विद् is कृदन्त - कर्तरि (वाच् + विद् + क्विप्)

   (i) The क्रिया in this प्रातिपदिक refers to वेदन - knowing, and the प्रातिपदिक refers to the कर्तृ of that क्रिया, that is the knower.
   (ii) Here this is a विशेषण and कर्तृ is अभिहित by it. And, therefore we should look for a विशेष्य that is in समानाधिकरण with the current word so that we will be able to identify the कर्तृ. However, विशेष्य is not mentioned. Hence, we assume it to refer to the most suitable possibility - जन.

(iii) वाच् is the कर्म in this क्रिया. Therefore, the विग्रह-वाक्य will be वाचं वेत्ति इति वाग्वित्.

(3) निरत is कृदन्त - कर्तरि

(i) Here, निरत is a part of the समस्तपद. However, in क्रिया-कारक-सम्बन्ध-विचार it is useful to look at कृदन्तs wherever they are, even if they are प्रातिपदिकs embedded in a समस्तपद.[5]

(ii) The क्रिया here is नि+रम् which refers to अभिनिवेश (to engage). It has क्तप्रत्यय. Since, रम् is अकर्मक-धातु, the क्तप्रत्यय here refers to the कर्तृ.

(iii) निरत is in समानाधिकरण with नारद and hence नारद is the कर्तृ of this अभिनिवेश.

(iv) We had seen earlier that mental faculties such as अभिनिवेश need अधिकरण-कारक. Here, तपस् and स्वाध्याय are those अधिकरणs.

17.3.2.2 Analysis of समासs

(1) तपःस्वाध्यायनिरतम् - is a विशेषण to नारदम्.

(i) It has three प्रातिपदिकs - तपस्, स्वाध्याय and निरत.

(ii) The meaningful association between these and नारद as explained above is to consider तपस् and स्वाध्याय as अधिकरण for the अभिनिवेश-क्रिया of नारद.

[5]Ideally, we should have looked at विद् in the case of वाग्विद्, also. However, this is an उपपदसमास which is a नित्यसमास. In other words, विद् can not be used as an independent प्रातिपदिक, and we, therefore, used the समस्तपद.

(iii) Therefore, तपस् and स्वाध्याय are at the same pedestal and we join them in the form of a द्वन्द्व-समास as तपः च स्वाध्यायः च = तपःस्वाध्याये.

(iv) Then we mention it in सप्तमी to indicate अधिकरण - तपःस्वाध्याययोः निरतः = तपःस्वाध्यायनिरतः (सप्तमी-तत्पुरुषः).

(2) वाग्विदाम् - As discussed above - वाचं वेत्तीति वाग्वित् (उपपदसमासः) तेषाम्

(3) मुनिपुङ्गवम् - is also a विशेषण to नारदम्.

(i) It has two प्रातिपदिकs - मुनि (sage) and पुङ्गव (ox).

(ii) A meaningful construction between these and नारद is to say that the मुनि (sage) नारद (Narada) is [great] like a पुङ्गव (ox): मुनिः पुङ्गव इव = मुनिपुङ्गवः (कर्मधारय-समासः).

The verse, therefore, can be translated as:

"Ascetic Valmiki inquired Narada, a great sage, engaged in penance and study of the Vedas, the best among eloquent [people]."

Online Resources

This book is mainly comprehensive in its subject matter. To supplement your learning, we have compiled a few additional resources online. Please scan the QR code provided or visit the website indicated to access online resources, such as शब्द-रूपs, गण-पाठ, mindmaps and more. These resources can help you deepen your understanding of the material and apply what you've learned in practical ways. We strongly encourage you to use these resources from time to time.

https://www.vidyasvam.in/karavalambanam

About the Authors

Dr Sridhar Subbanna holds a BE in computer science and a PhD in Saṃskṛta. He has worked with leading technology companies while learning Saṃskṛta and Śāstra from renowned traditional scholars. In his doctoral thesis, Dr Sridhar has explored the similarities between Pāṇini's Aṣṭādhyāyī and computational sciences. He later developed a novel method to teach Saṃskṛta based on the Pāṇinian approach and has trained hundreds of students in this method.

He has established Vidyāsvam, a platform for learning traditional knowledge systems. Vidyāsvam is currently offering courses on foundational Saṃskṛta for modern-educated professionals and students in higher education. He is also a member of the founding team of Pūrṇapramati, an alternative school in Bengaluru that attempts to integrate Indic knowledge systems with mainstream learning.

* * * * *

Dr V. Srinidhi is an MBBS from Bangalore Medical College and a PhD in Public Policy from IIM Bangalore. His primary interests are integrative medicine, health policy and systems research. He has also worked in medical education, knowledge translation, respectful maternity care and digital health.

Dr Srinidhi has been a student of Saṃskṛta literature and the Dvaita School of Vedānta for over two decades under various traditional scholars and Svāmījis. Passionate in manuscriptology, he has collected and edited over ten unpublished manuscripts from the Dvaita tradition and published them from many research institutes and Mathas. Dr Srinidhi is also a member of the founding team of Pūrṇapramati. He is also active in the research activities of Udupi Sri Bhandarakeri Matha.

www.ingramcontent.com/pod-product-compliance
Lightning Source LLC
Chambersburg PA
CBHW062134160726
48282CB00027B/816
9789357865678